# THE BALLAD BOOK

## OF

# JOHN JACOB NILES

# THE BALLAD BOOK

OF

# JOHN JACOB NILES

DECORATIONS BY WILLIAM BARSS

DOVER PUBLICATIONS, INC.

NEW YORK

Copyright © 1960, 1961 by John Jacob Niles.
All rights reserved under Pan American and Internatonal Copyright Conventions.

Published in Canada by General Publishing Company, Ltd., 30 Lesmill Road, Don Mills, Toronto, Ontario.

This Dover edition, first published in 1970, is an unabridged and unaltered republication of the work originally published in 1961. The work is reprinted by special arrangement with Houghton Mifflin Company, publisher of the original edition.

*International Standard Book Number: 0-486-22716-2*
*Library of Congress Catalog Card Number: 71-139205*

Manufactured in the United States of America
Dover Publications, Inc.
180 Varick Street
New York, N.Y. 10014

For Lula Sarah Niles
and Rena Niles

# Acknowledgments

THE WRITING of this book started a few more than fifty years ago. In that half-century many fine people gave me the kind of encouragement, advice, and assistance such a book naturally requires. Space will not permit me to list them all, but I must acknowledge my indebtedness to several, some of whom still walk the earth:

My father and my mother, John Thomas Niles and Lula Sarah Niles
My wife, Rena
Mrs. Doris Ulmann
Dr. Carl Engel, formerly President of G. Schirmer, Inc.
Dr. George Lyman Kittredge, who gave me, among other things, an invaluable bibliography
Dr. Kenneth Wright, musicologist, University of Kentucky
Miss Helen Louise Smith, Johnson City, Tennessee
Miss Caroline Beauregard, formerly Supervisor of Public School Music, Louisville
The Right Reverend William R. Moody, Bishop of Lexington, Kentucky
Dr. William Ward, English Department, University of Kentucky
Dr. William H. Jansen, folklorist, University of Kentucky
Miss Katherine Pettit, co-founder of the Pine Mountain School
Mr. and Mrs. Barry Bingham, Louisville
Mrs. Marie Turner, Superintendent of Public Schools, Breathitt County, Kentucky
Miss Lula Hale, Homeplace, Ary, Kentucky
"Ma" Hibbler, Grand Hotel, Hazard, Kentucky
Mrs. Dickey, Drummers' Rest, Murphy, North Carolina
Dr. William J. Hutchins, formerly President of Berea College
Dr. and Mrs. Daniel Z. Gibson, Washington College, Chestertown, Maryland
Dr. Frank Dickey, President of the University of Kentucky
Miss Bertha Bauer, formerly Director of the Cincinnati Conservatory of Music
Mr. W. C. Diamond, guitarist, Lexington, Kentucky
Dr. Thomas D. Clark, University of Kentucky
Mr. J. Stanley Sheppard, St. Mark's School
Mr. Hewitt Pantaleoni, State University College of Education, Oneonta, New York
Miss Helen Phillips

# Contents

# Introduction

THE FINE PEOPLE, young and old, who sang the ballads found on the pages of this book, were the direct descendants of the hardy English settlers who came to the shores of the North American continent in the 17th and 18th centuries. The spaces in those sailing ships were small. They traveled light. But the men and women who crossed the stormy Atlantic in those early days came from a civilization rich in the tradition of ballad and carol singing, and although we have no records of such activities, it is safe to assume that once they came ashore in North America, the singing of the kind of native music they had inherited from their homeland was used to lighten their burdens and brighten what little leisure they had.

The same adventurous spirit which led these pioneers across the Atlantic continued to lead them, and their immediate descendants, farther and farther west. Disease, privation, or the American red man could not stop them. At great loss to life and personal comfort they crossed

Virginia and poured through the Cumberland Gap into the mountains of Kentucky. Parties traveling on foot, under the protection of James Robertson, and other groups led by John Sevier, crossed the Carolinas and set up the fortified villages in eastern Tennessee. Men on log rafts poled themselves down the turbulent Ohio, and when they were temporarily halted by the falls in that wide river, they paused long enough to build the palisades on Corn Island, and this settlement turned out to be the beginnings of Louisville, Kentucky.

Indeed, they were an industrious folk. The forests rang with the sound of the woodsman's axe, and the Indian warrior waited, ever ready with his flint-tipped arrows. Life was not easy in those early days. But the singing of the ballad and the carol, inherited from Elizabethan England, surely went on, and as years passed, there was more leisure, and as there was more leisure there was more time for singing and dancing. It must have been during this period that the dulcimer* (a homemade three-stringed instrument) came into use.

In 1772, Judge Richard Henderson engaged Pennsylvania-born Daniel Boone to explore the Kentucky country, to open the wilderness road, and to escort settlers into what is now the Bluegrass. In 1775 Boone entered upon the herculean task of assisting with the erection of the palisades at Boonesboro, a few miles from my home in Clark County. Soon after this, the coves, the valleys, and the ridges of the Appalachian Mountains were being populated. The cabins were far apart, but the ancestors of the men and women who sang the ballads to me were clearing the forest lands and planting their crops.

Historians tell us that the fort at Boonesboro, made up of 24 cabins and 4 blockhouses all connected in rectangular form with high palisades, was attacked by Indians many times but never taken. Time and decay finally destroyed it, and when the 20th century had come and I went about collecting my balladry and folklore, it had quite disappeared. But the turn of the 20th century found thousands of the descendants of those early pioneers scattered up and down the length and breadth of the Appalachians, still carrying on in almost complete isolation, living in all manner of houses and cabins, eking out a meager existence from the rocky soil, but still gay and willing to sing.

Some of these people lived in what we call "down houses" — that is, houses just this side of complete ruin. A few were slab-sided lean-tos with pounded earth or puncheon floors; some were cabins, and a few were one- or two-storied houses covered with poplar weatherboarding. But the homes I visited most often in the collection of folklore were cabins, and according to my notes they were usually about 20 to 22 feet long and from 14 to 16 feet wide. As a rule the ceiling was not more than 7 feet above the floor, with an upper room where the younger male members of the family slept. The downstairs room was literally a large bedroom, and sometimes there was a bed in each of the four corners. I was told that it took nearly 50 tall, straight trees to supply all the wooden parts of a single cabin.

The fireplace around which the "little gray wisps of women" sat and sang for me was the true center of all the cabin's activities. And if the family was large enough to need a double cabin, a dog-trot or breezeway connecting the two usually sheltered a loom and a spinning wheel, with a flax-hackle and a pair of cards† hanging on wooden pins on the wall nearby.

The beds in the older cabins were ofttimes covered with hand-loomed coverlids of great beauty, and at certain seasons of the year, the odor of the mildewed, fermenting indigo pot could be smelled from afar. It was in these indigo-pots that the womenfolk dyed their yarns to that indescribably beautiful blue found in so many of the coverlids.

In the earliest spring, the dogwood, peach, and plum trees bloomed outside the cabin door, and morning-glory vines, moon-vines, hollyhocks, zinnias, and other old-fashioned flowers grew about in great profusion as summer progressed.

---

* As one who has played the dulcimer much of his life and made all the dulcimers he uses, I am convinced that the traditional mountain dulcimer is a development of two instruments — one, the rebeck, a medieval English instrument of three strings played with a bow, and the other, the crowd, a Celtic instrument, having from 3 to 6 strings, also played with a bow. In my collection, I have a dulcimer of 4 strings, intended to be played with a bow; the bow, with a few remaining horsehairs, came with the instrument.

John Milton referred to the playing of the rebeck: "And the jocund rebecks sound," and Stephen Hawes (1472 to 1521), the English poet who was once a groom of the chamber to Henry VII, referred to the crowd in such a manner as to indicate that it was played with other instruments: "harpes, lutes, and crouddes right delycyous . . ."

In my lifetime I have made about 30 dulcimers. Only 5 of them proved successful — that is, playable. Of these 5, 3 are still in daily use. My dulcimers are made of Kentucky walnut, curly maple, spruce, mahogany, ebony, satinwood, wild cherry, ponderosa pine, and rosewood. They are put together with French rabbit-skin glue. The strings vary in length from 16 to 42 inches, and are made of steel, steel covered with bronze, and nylon covered with bronze and silver.

† Device to separate the fibers of wool or hemp.

Indeed, the location of long destroyed cabins may be rediscovered in the springtime by the blooming of the perennial "spring-pretties" planted by long dead hands — the daffodils, the tulips, the narcissi. Cabins of this kind housed many of the wonderful people who sang the ballads in this book.

At first my collection was a private family document. Being very young and having only a very limited view of the great world, I started it in a rather timid manner. Furthermore, only a very few people were interested in folklore collecting, and even they thought I was "quaint and cute." It was uphill from the beginning.

By the time I was 20 years of age (1912) well-informed scholars in Virginia, West Virginia, and North Carolina were collecting folklore, but I knew nothing of this. All I knew was that the tunes I encountered in those days were fascinating, and that when they were used to motivate the ballad texts *small* audiences listened.

So for many years my collection was a private family property, out of which I was selecting the ballads, the love songs, and the nursery rhymes I employed — at first in my early singing engagements and finally in my concert and lecture appearances. There were several reasons for keeping my collection private, and I thought them to be entirely valid. First among them was the feeling that publishing would be very unrewarding, because of the lack of public interest. And as I was making my collection at my own expense, I thought I deserved the first right to its use.

Although my first commonplace book (Notebook No. 2) was purchased as late as May. 1, 1908, I had already been writing down fragments of folklore, family and community music, proverbs, riddles, dialect speech, parts of revivalist sermons, my own poems and musical compositions, and even one ballad of 25 quatrains on the looseleaf pages of a school notebook. (This ballad, "Lord Bateman," Niles No. 22, was taken down on July 12, 1907, when, a stake driver and bush-cutter in a surveying party, I was just past 15 years of age.) Quite a few pages fell out of this notebook. I have no idea what was on the pages, but after I had repaired the book as best I could, I wrote the following: "If I had known that this book would need all this pasting, I would not have paid 10 cents for it, but would have offered 5 cents."

At the present time, this notebook contains 96 closely written pages of ballads, carols, love songs, a fragment of a handwritten rhyming dictionary, a family genealogy, certain weather signs and superstitions, and 40 pieces of priceless handwritten music. I say "priceless" because among these pages are the ones showing the original development of "Go 'Way from My Window" and "Black Is the Color of My True Love's Hair," which my publisher G. Schirmer, Inc., and I have used to establish the validity of my claim to their composition and copyright.

If there ever was a commonplace book or notebook indicated as No. 1, I have never found it. There *is* one indicated as Notebook No. 5, 1 + 1A. It is a tiny thing of 71 pages, measuring a scant 4 by 6 inches, and contains 12 ballads with music, 2 sonnets, some proverbs, many examples of dialect speech, cures, superstitions, and random notes. But I do not know what No. 5, 1 + 1A actually means.

My second notebook was once a publisher's dummy. A female-person first owned it and wrote her poems on its blank pages. I bought the book for five cents in Louisville, erased the former owner's poems and wrote my own over them. Later, I erased my own poems and wrote down the ballads, carols, love songs, and native lore I encountered in my field work. All together, I have 14 notebooks containing folklore. The pages of these books are covered, top to bottom, with tiny, faint, penciled notes. From these pages I first constructed my concert and lecture programs, and finally they became my source material when I wrote *The Ballad Book of John Jacob Niles*.

In 1935 I began to write a ballad book and a carol book simultaneously, hoping to have at least one manuscript to offer the publishers in 1937. The demands of the concert stage took so much of my time that I had to give up the carol book and concentrate on the ballads.

Meanwhile, G. Schirmer, Inc., had been publishing parts of my folklore collection in the form of small octavo pamphlets, and in 1940, RCA Victor presented me to the public in three albums of carols, ballads, and love songs.

Almost at once my imitators and an ever-increasing group of young ballad enthusiasts went about the disturbing business of pirating my collection by way of my published works and my recordings. In the spring of 1942 I gave up the writing of my ballad book, because I had concluded that a publication of my entire collection would only lead to wider piracies.

For more than 10 years thereafter, the ballad book lay quietly in several large brown envelopes, waiting the day when I thought I had employed my material sufficiently. I had collected it at great pains. No vastly rich foundation had helped me. I had financed the entire operation myself. Therefore, as I have said earlier here, I thought I should have first right to its use.

In 1953 I began the fifth revision of my material. In 1959, having been technically in retirement from the concert stage for two years, I submitted the eighth revision to Houghton Mifflin Company. Although I have suffered from many copyright infringements and have been honored by many imitators (some of whom have never been farther west of Manhattan Island than Manhattan Transfer, out in the Jersey meadows), I have an abiding satisfaction in the recollection of my father's statement concerning beginnings: "The eternal glory in all great things is to have laid the first stone." I did not lay the first stone, but I was present at the laying of that stone, and although I may not have had a trowel in my hand I was surely carrying hod.

My philosophy, however, was formulated slowly and at great pains. In fact, it was not until after I had concertized in England and Holland, and observed the school systems in these countries, and had traveled and performed in Scandinavia and been exposed to the concepts of nationalism prevalent there that I concluded that every man, woman, and child on earth had a right to be benefited, inspired, comforted, and assured by contact with the legend, the poetry, the prose writing, and the folk music arising from the language they speak or the race to which they belong. Insofar as the teaching of music is concerned, I found myself agreeing with Cecil J. Sharp, who said: "The primary purpose of education is to place the children of the present generation in possession of the cultural achievements of the past, or to put it another way, the aim of the educationist should not be to forge the first link of a new chain, but to add a fresh link to the already existing chain."

Lest I be misunderstood, may I hasten to assure the reader that I have always wanted my composed and collected music employed by the public, either privately in homes or publicly in schools and colleges and in concert halls, on the radio, and by television. But I strongly object when the singer, either through ignorance or misinformation, mistakes my composed love songs and carols for public-domain folk material, and when the aspiring collector, through a complete lack of ethics, publishes or records *any* of my material without my knowledge and consent.

As long ago as 1910 my father told me that our "old-timey family music came from the people, and it should go back to the people." Incidentally, he seemed to think that I might be one to help the process along.

The present ballad book is based on a small portion of the folklore I collected and wrote down in my field notebooks. I selected this portion after I was able to identify it with similar items found in the Child* collection. These items I

---

* Francis James Child was born in Boston on February 1, 1825, the son of a sailmaker. He attended Boston public schools, the Boston Latin School, and entered Harvard College. In 1846 he was graduated at the head of his class. He entered the service of the college immediately and continued in this service until the day of his death, September 11, 1896. First he taught mathematics, history, and political economy; then from 1849 to 1851 he traveled abroad and studied in Germany (Berlin and Göttingen). When he returned to Harvard College in 1851 he was appointed Boylston Professor of Rhetoric and Oratory and continued in this post for 25 years. On May 20, 1876, he was transferred to the newly established professorship of English literature. Some of his better-known works are: *Four Old*

have chosen to call the folklore classics — that is to say, ballads whose Old World origin has been clearly established.

The form of the ballad book is the outgrowth of considerable investigation. First I ran a questionnaire among the students in one of my classes, asking what sort of ballad book they would like best. Next I consulted with faculty members — English Department people interested in folklore — asking them what kind of text they would like to use in their teaching. I talked with college deans and presidents, and finally turned to scholars abroad. Of course my own feelings in the matter had quite a lot to do with it, and what my friends and neighbors thought became important, too. Ultimately I decided to follow the lead of Francis James Child — to treat each ballad individually by prefacing the text and the melodic material with a short, concentrated bit of what might pass for scholarly discussion. Then, deviating from Child, I decided to tell the story of my informant as fully as space would permit, following this with the text of the ballad as the informant sang it for me, and arrange to have the music immediately following.

In every case I have tried to create piano settings for the melodic material in such a way as to present the tune without disturbing the melodic line, and to preserve the modal quality, where it exists, at all costs. In almost every instance, the tune is found in the top line of the accompaniment. In a few cases I deviated from this process, because it seemed that a different method was more rewarding. The modal assignments found at the end of each setting concern the tune only, while the piano accompaniments may or may not coincide. Not being a guitarist, I worked out the guitar-chord symbols under the eye of an expert.

I have set only one verse of each ballad — for two very good reasons. First, I knew that if I set all the verses of each ballad it would make an endlessly long book. And second, I thought it would hamper the delights of variation —the interpolation of new words and the cunning twists of a new tune idea. Furthermore, the reader might want to sing several verses unaccompanied — and this would be a great idea.

My students and members of my audiences have asked me many times about the continual sadness of the ballad. Many good folk who are not overly informed musically refer to these ballads as "minor" or "in the sad minor." I discovered that the expression "in the sad minor" usually referred to a tune cast in the Aeolian or Dorian mode. And then I would try to explain that although the texts are truly sad the effect of sadness is compounded by the native folksinger's affection for the minor third. No one can deny the fact that the texts of the ballads are often tragic to an extraordinary extent, and this, added to the singer's continual use of the minor third, produces an unmatched but superb sadness.

There are those musicologists who will say

---

*Plays* (1848), *The Poetical Works of Edmund Spenser* (1855), "Observations on the Language of Chaucer" and "Observations on the Language of Gower's '*Confessio amantis*,'" published in the *Memoirs* of the American Academy of Arts and Sciences, NS, VIII, Pt. II (1863) and IX, Pt. II (1873), and *The English and Scottish Popular Ballads,* 10 parts in 5 large volumes, published 1882–97.

This latter work contains every version then available in print or manuscript of 305 distinct English and Scottish ballads, with an introduction, a history, and a bibliography concerning the piece under discussion, and a full account of parallels in foreign languages and traditions.

A condensation of this work, edited by Helen Child Sargent and George Lyman Kittredge, was issued in 1904, with an introduction by Kittredge, Child's pupil and associate. Child's monumental work, with its exhaustive collations, bibliographies, indices, etc., has become the standard work throughout the world wherever balladry is studied.

If the reader is interested in finding out more about this distinctive and gentle scholar, it is suggested that he read *A Scholar's Letters to a Young Lady.* In one of these letters, Child speaks of his few "superstitions," which he enumerates as "love of women, roses (including apple-blossoms), popular poetry, Shakspere, my friends, wild flowers, trees, violin music, *voila!*"

Through my acquaintance with his daughter, Miss Henrietta Child, I have concluded that Francis James Child was a man with a fine sense of humor, patience enough to appreciate good sense, and an aesthetic understanding of his contemporaries.

that with the establishment of Gregorian chant (*Cantilena Romana*), the golden age of the creation of a certain kind of music came to an end quite abruptly. This type of music is called monody, and is one in which a single voice sings a tragic ode, or where a group of singers sing entirely in unison. Although I do not agree with this idea, I shall leave it for my readers to decide, after they have heard and perhaps sung the melodic material in this book — all of which was created in the Southern Appalachian Mountains in the 19th and 20th centuries.

Seldom did I encounter the use of harmony in folk singing. However, I have heard folk hymns, carols, ballads, work songs, and nursery rhymes in which one voice sang the melodic line and others, numbering from 1 to 25, sang a monotone that occasionally harmonized. The effect was not unlike some of the results gained when a singer supports himself with dulcimer accompaniment, for the dulcimer actually produces as much dissonance as consonance.

On one of the doors of my house on Boone's Creek in Clark County, Kentucky, the following sentence has been carved in large, bold letters: "A ballad is a song that tells a story, or — to take it from the other point of view — a story told in song." This oft used statement is a quotation from the first few lines of George Lyman Kittredge's introduction to the Cambridge Edition of *English and Scottish Popular Ballads*. Although there is little or no agreement among scholars and students of ancient literature as to the historical background of some of the ballads, I am prepared to say that, so far as anyone has ever been able to tell, the ballad has no author. The teller of the story or the singer of the song must at the time of performance, if he is to be successful in the telling or the singing, appear to be the author, just as much as the long dead person, or persons, who first put the material into shape.

Since the beginning of time man has been trying to express himself. Indeed, we might almost say that the history of mankind is a record of these efforts. Occasionally, and for short periods, mankind has succeeded in this effort, and the measure of this success may be said to represent the level of his civilization at that moment. The development of a national culture may not appear to be a steady growing process, but is, rather, one that has long, blank periods, when artistic and cultural efforts seem to be lost under the dust of wars, invasions, pestilences, and changing tastes. By taking a long-range view of the wide picture of time, we see that a national culture is a tenacious thing, a recurrent thing, and a thing that is found in its best and purest form in the arts of the lowliest citizens — that is, the folk-art creations of a nation.

English folk balladry, and particularly folk-carol singing, suffered an enormous setback from the period of Oliver Cromwell's Commonwealth. The folk carol went underground, and seemed to be forgotten for 178 years. In 1647 the Puritan Parliament abolished Christmas as a heathen celebration, and, of course, there was no longer any reason to sing carols.

If we count time from the death of Chaucer, we might conclude that two-and-a-half centuries of folk-ballad and folk-carol creation went over the side in 1647. But this is not true, for there was a renaissance in due time and season. Neither the story of the birth of Jesus Christ nor the enduring, melodramatic legend of the Maid Freed from the Gallows could be avoided by the English and Scottish people forever. How those Puritan politicians must be turning over in their narrow graves as they observe the mass of ballad- and carol-singing going on today, not only at Christmas but at every season of the year! I could be mistaken, but I have always believed that the pioneer families who came into the Appalachian Mountains in the early days were not overly influenced by the thinking of the English Puritans or their American counterparts. The realities of frontier life in the Appalachian Mountains were stern enough without the angry voice of Hezekiah Woodward's 1656 tract denouncing the celebration of Christmas.

The ultimate result of creative thinking in the field of music — that is, composition — may appear to be magic, but it is not. So far as I have been able to tell, the only thing the composer has is what he has inherited, and no matter what modern garb he may employ to dress his ideas, underneath them are the inherited motifs of the past, and this past is studded with folk motifs. A very great English musicologist has said: "Music cannot be produced out of nothing."

After an exhaustive comparative study, I have concluded that the music in this book is an American product. So far, I have not been able to discover similar tunes in any of the standard books of collected English folk songs. The fact that the American ballad and carol tunes sound somewhat like the English and Scottish tunes is because their creators were somewhat alike. Both used a gapped scale. Both have also employed the Dorian, Mixolydian, Aeolian, and occasionally the Phrygian modes, and the reasons for their so doing would surely lead into a musicological controversy.

In Estonia I was told that the gapped scales came about because in very early times the minstrels sang their ballads or recounted the news of distant places in a monotone. As years passed, they discovered the dramatic possibilities of the fourth scale degree, and at last the five-tone, or pentatonic, scale evolved. Personally, I subscribe to this idea, and I offer this information for what it is worth, after hearing the rune singers of Finland and the Baltic States chant their magnificent versions of the *Kalevala*.

But let me repeat: this book does not contain my entire folklore collection. Out of more than 3000 interviews and thousands of notes, it contains only 110 items, and they are the ballad classics, coming to us from English and Scottish sources. Second, the melodic material employed by the native American folk singers *I have known* is entirely a native American product, though the texts are of ancient origin. Third, this melodic material is ofttimes modal, and, as my father said so rightly, "Our tunes have the God-given benefit of ending at the end." Seldom will one find an artificial, tacked-on tune ending, although the last line of the text may be repeated for strength and finality.

In the early days of my career as a collector of folklore, I discovered the importance of having the help of a native man or woman, who

understood something of the habits and tendencies of the community. In this way, I saved myself weeks of time. Even so, the number of false starts, "the backing and filling" I did were quite disturbing.

Naturally, I did not have time to settle down in a mountain community and wait for the folk singers to come to me. I had to go to them. Whenever I arrived in a new community I immediately made myself known to the county officials. This was done for two reasons. First, I wanted the officials to know why I was there and what I was seeking, so as to prevent the sheriff from taking a dim view of my operations. Then, I assumed that the potential ballad singers would be known to the local politicians.

I usually started at the top and went down the list, and as a rule the people at the bottom of the list were the most helpful. First, it was the county judge and the county sheriff. Next in order came the county school superintendent (he or she was usually helpful), the county health nurse (if there was one), the county agent, the county road supervisor, the county jailer, the county truant officer, and, last, the county dogcatcher. The dogcatchers were wonderful people. Being a foxhound fancier myself, I found that we had much in common.

But county officials were busy people, even in the sleepy mountain counties. If there was a political campaign going on, the politicians were more than willing. Out of election season, they were only mildly interested. This situation usually led me to engage a local character who had time on his hands and was willing to work for a small, stipulated fee. I referred to these characters as my "contact men."

One of my best contact men was a middle-aged person known to us all in Whitesburg, Kentucky, in 1932–1934 as "The Bat-Winger." A bat-wing, in local slang, was a flat half-pint bottle of some kind of alcoholic beverage. Thus, the man who made a trade of selling bat-wings was known as a bat-winger. It was the Bat-Winger who told me about Aunt Flory French, as colorful a person as I have ever encountered. At the same time, it was the Bat-Winger who convinced me that a singing bee-man named Chet Hawk would be willing and able to sing if I would only allow him to show me his bee-gums and purchase several combs of his tree-blossom honey.

The bee-yard was three miles beyond Isom, about seven from Whitesburg, as I recall, and I rode a mule all the way. It was a gray mule, and it was a gray day, and the honey man turned out to be gray-bearded and as glum and uncooperative as anyone I had ever met. The bees must have taken a signal from their owner. I was stung quite a few times. I did not purchase "a few combs of tree-blossom honey," but I did fall from the mule and land in a loblolly. And when I returned empty-handed to the hotel in Whitesburg, "the boys," who made a life of lounging on the front porch, raised a mild, derisive yell of amusement at my muddy appearance. The Bat-Winger was greatly crestfallen over this tragicomic interlude, but he went right on selling bat-wings and trying to locate willing folksingers. (His pay for the latter activity was one dollar a week and Sunday dinner at the Daniel Boone Hotel.)

In Hazard, Kentucky, I worked with a watery-eyed individual of great age named Poachy Gabbard. According to my notes, Poachy's fees were small, and the results of his efforts in the field of folklore were smaller. From a page of my notebook, I see that Poachy received fifty cents now and then.

Gabbard was something of a rustic philosopher. I remember how one day when he and I were driving along a rutted country road he asked me to stop a minute. The next thing I knew, Gabbard was out of my car, over a rail fence, and — in spite of his age — climbing a large peach tree. When he returned, laden with a dozen lovely peaches, I asked him if he thought the raiding of a farmer's peach tree was quite honest. "Aw, pshaw now, Mr. John," said Poachy, "a sip from an open bottle is never missed."

In the neighborhood of Jenkins, Kentucky, I engaged a disabled miner named Charlie Elrod. Charlie told me that he worked when the notion

struck him, but at other times he mostly rested. He worked at a strange and hazardous occupation. He was, in reality, a mine scavenger; he called it "gob-mining." This operation took him into abandoned or worked-out coal mines where, with a pick and wheelbarrow, he mined out the coal left in the walls and the supporting pillars. So far as I could tell, the supporting pillars were called "gobs." His speech was not clear, but I had him write down the word in my notebook. Charlie Elrod had never been married, because, he said, the womenfolk put blinders on a man as soon as they got their hands on him. I enjoyed riding about with Charlie, making notes on his life experience, but as an assistant he was completely unsuccessful.

Arlie Duckmer, ancient of days, part-time dogcatcher and local ward-heeler in Knoxville, Tennessee, was not only helpful but enormously amusing. As I remember him, he resembled Ichabod Crane, being extraordinarily thin. In fact, Arlie admitted that he was so thin he had to stand twice to make a shadow. He and I had a very interesting experience in the Knoxville public market, and it was through Arlie that I met the man who sang the ballad of "Judas." But I ultimately discovered that Arlie was a one-fault type: he drank to excess, when he could get it. He referred to the local homemade whiskey as "corn coffee," and in moments of great exhilaration he spoke in the unknown tongue.

In the back pages of one of my notebooks I kept a list of the ballads I had taken down, and this list was shown and explained to any interested party, and particularly to my so-called contact men. In this way I was able to give them an idea of the sort of thing I hoped to find. Never during my collecting days did I see any of the informative pamphlets recently issued by the folklore and dialect societies, under such titles as *A Method for Collecting Dialect* or *A Guide for the Collecting of Folklore* or *How to Identify Folk Tunes,* etc. I had none of these benefits. I made my own rules, and in my earliest days I was looked upon by educated people as "quaint and cute," and I was tolerated by the singing natives because I seemed to be an inoffensive youngster, who was occasionally amusing when he spoke and slightly entertaining when he sang. Finally, it was my singing of their own ballads that won the day, for when the natives found me, an outlander, so willing to sing, they usually were impelled to respond with whatever they knew.

The scholarly investigation of folklore has been going on for many years, and bids fair to continue at a still more important level, each new generation producing more gifted and more informed folklorists, folk singers and folk musicologists.

Although I have been singing "The Maid Freed from the Gallows," in one form or another, for nearly 40 years and have written and lectured about it considerably, only recently I discovered that in 1957 a new and exciting study of this ballad was made by a Finnish scholar named Iivar Kemppinen. His findings were published under the title of *The Maid to Be Ransomed: A Comparative Study of the Ballad.* I have not seen this work, but by way of a review written by Friedrich Ege of Helsinki, I find that Kemppinen concluded, after making a study of 1634 variants from many countries and linguistic areas, that the following is the basic structure of the plot:

The maid is weeping in the vessel of a stranger, bound for an unknown destination (in America, she is weeping because she is about to be hanged). She begs her father, mother, brother, and sister to produce some money and ransom her from aboard ship. They refuse. But her lover arrives and ransoms her, whereupon the maid curses her relations. Iivar Kemppinen tells us, further, that in his opinion the ballad we now know as "The Maid Freed from the Gallows" originated in southern Europe some time between the 12th and 13th centuries and is based on the same mythology from which Euripides drew in writing his play *Alcestis*. This play, written in 438 B.C., involves Admetos, King of Thessaly, who was doomed to die a premature death. Neither the King's mother nor his father, though quite aged, would die in his place, but the King's wife, Alcestis, makes the sacrifice, somewhat as the maid's beloved does in the ballad.

No, the last word in the scholarly investigation of the ballad will most likely never be written. New voices and new minds will always be ready to start where the men and women of my generation left off.

In conclusion, I must tell my readers that most of my ballad singers were simple people, never overly rich in the world's goods, usually living in the most frugal manner, most of them closely associated with agriculture. In the days before World War I many of them were housed in cabins of their own making and dressed in clothes which they had woven, out of yarn they had previously carded and spun.

No one could say that they lived by bread alone. In many cases there was not even an oversupply of bread. They were not interested in getting rich. Their charming, lack-a-daisy attitude toward everything gave them more leisure than their more industrious brethren in the lowlands, and a fair part of this leisure was spent in resting and dancing and singing. My desire to perpetuate their unique folk arts led me to them.

The reader may be struck, as he turns the pages of this book, by the frequent use of the adjectives "delightful" and "gay" applied to the people who sang these ballads for me. The use of these terms is not accidental, but reflects my own reaction to the stalwart gallantry of men and women, many of them advanced in years, whose high spirits were in such sharp contrast to their meager circumstances. The fact that they were poor among the poor may explain the lack of resentment and bitterness, at least in part, but a fuller explanation would have to take into account their innate dignity, which would not permit them to be anything less than gay — and consequently, delightful.

In my collecting years (more than 50 of them), I interviewed as many as 3000 people. Only a few more than 100 found their way into this book. On several occasions my disappointments were so keen that I almost gave up entirely. Heat, cold, food poisoning, lack of public interest, skin eruptions, stubborn horses and mules, snakebites and insect bites, automobiles stuck in mudholes, hotel fires, railroad wrecks, tornadoes, floods and dust storms — all these things came and went, but never in all my travels did I encounter a single person who was impolite or inhospitable. And if I had it all to do over again, I believe I would do it exactly the same way.

# THE BALLAD BOOK

OF

# JOHN JACOB NILES

Frankfort
to Louisville
60
Lexington
60
Versailles
Lawrenceburg
Winchester
BOOT HILL FARM
Boonesboro
Bardstown
Harrodsburg
25
Berea
Big Hill
Crab Orchard
McKee
Science Hill
Manchester
Somerset
27
Corbin
Barbour
Kentucky
Middlesbo
Jellico
Harrogate
Tennessee

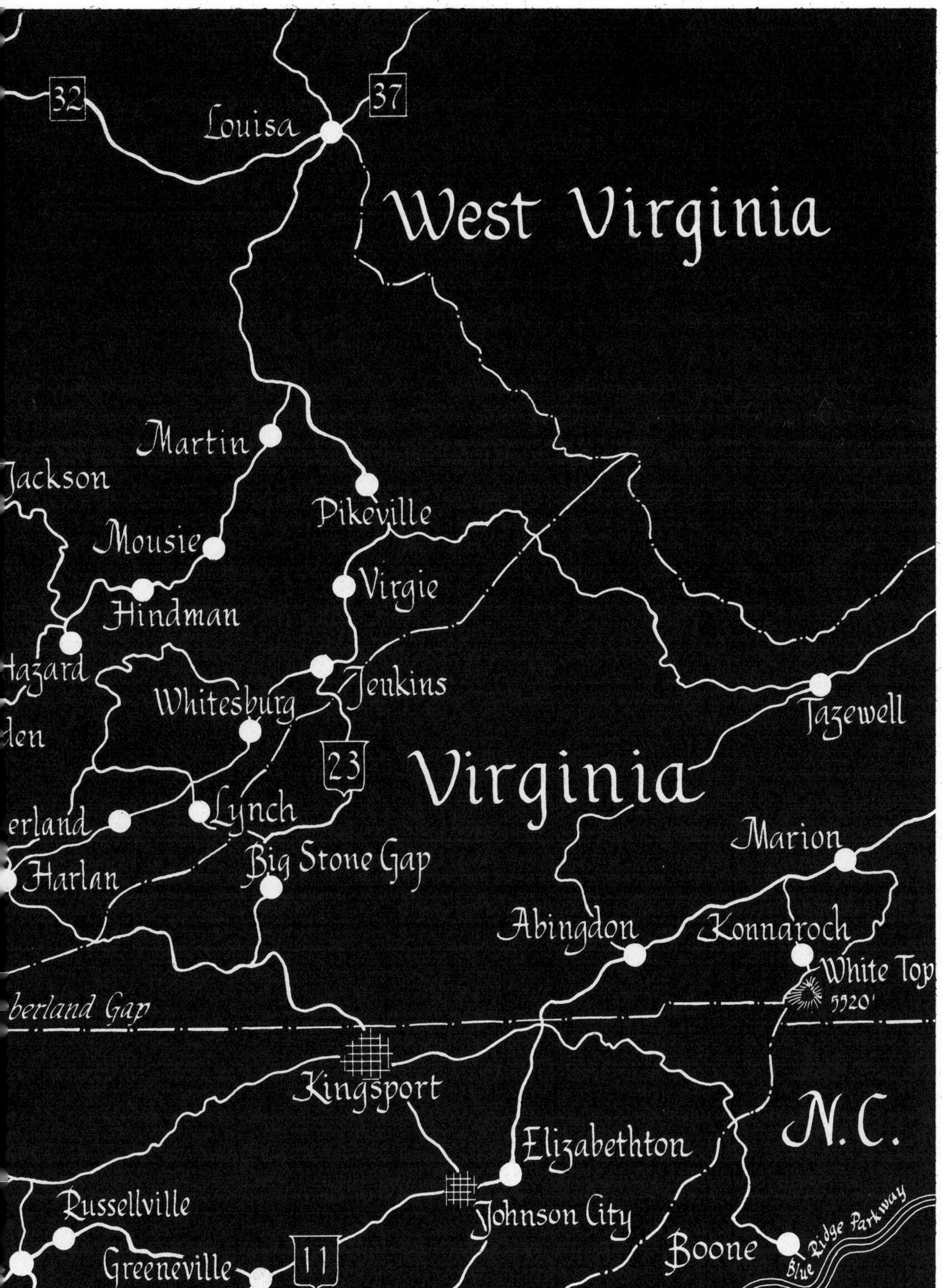
32
37
Louisa
West Virginia
Martin
Jackson
Pikeville
Mousie
Virgie
Hindman
Hazard
Jenkins
Whitesburg
Tazewell
23
Virginia
Lynch
Big Stone Gap
Harlan
Marion
Abingdon
Konnaroch
White Top
5520'
Kingsport
N.C.
Elizabethton
Russellville
Johnson City
Blue Ridge Parkway
Boone
Greeneville
11

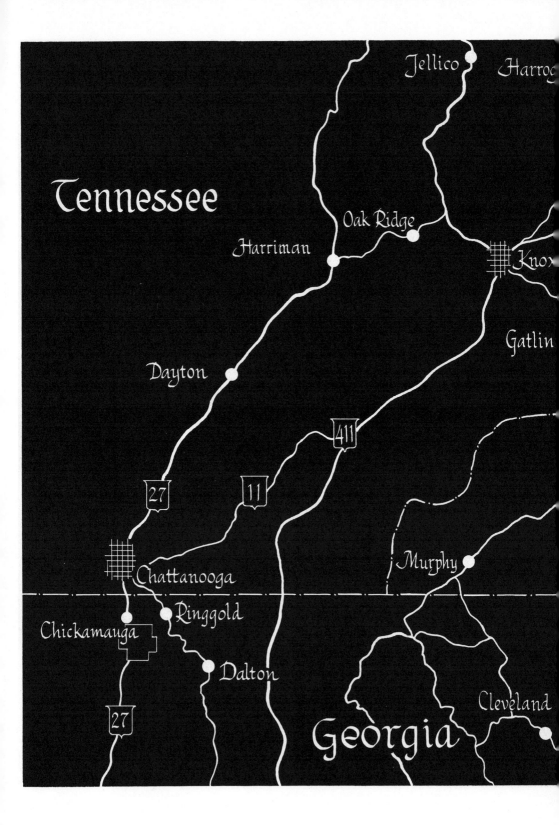

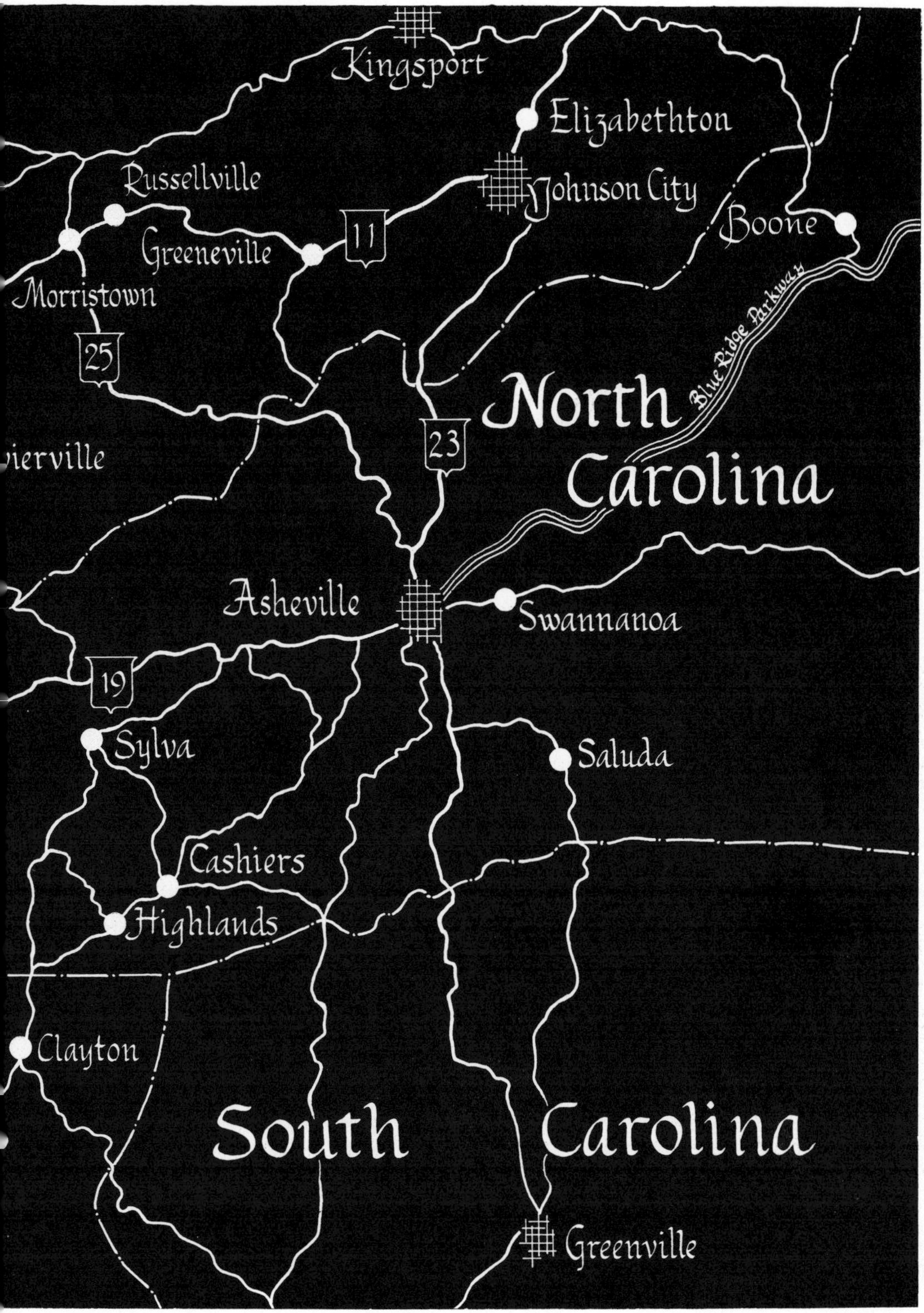
Kingsport
Elizabethton
Russellville
Johnson City
Boone
Greeneville
11
Morristown
25
Blue Ridge Parkway
North
Carolina
23
ierville
Asheville
Swannanoa
19
Sylva
Saluda
Cashiers
Highlands
Clayton
South
Carolina
Greenville

# Riddles Wisely Expounded

(Child No. 1)

The Devil's Questions

(Niles No. 1 A)

The Riddle Song

(Niles No. 1 B)

Piri-miri-dictum Domini

(Niles No. 1 C)

**R**IDDLING IS an almost universal art. And as James McNeill Whistler said in *Ten O'Clock,* "No hovel is safe from art, and no prince may depend upon it." A generation ago distinguished authorities on folklore could be found to say that Chinese people, Jewish people, and American Indians did not employ or understand riddles. It doesn't take much investigation, though, to discover riddles in Hebrew literature dating from great antiquity, and just in 1952 Ruth Rabin, writing in the *Journal of American Folklore,* gave some delightful examples of Yiddish folk songs which were variants of a riddle song sung in the United States. Miss Rabin also included five examples of riddles in folk songs coming from Lithuania, one of which was cumulative and very complicated.

It might be added that riddles in the Western world, whether spoken or sung, are quite simple when compared with those of the Near East and the Far East. This is particularly true of those coming from the United States. The Armenians, on the other hand, delight in some of the most complicated riddles in existence; they seem to go out of their way to make them unsolvable.

The Chinese have their own oriental way of riddling, and examples of their riddles have been discovered in considerable numbers. In the case of the American Indian, no less an authority than Dr. Archer Taylor has declared that "although our information is scanty, the American Indians have riddles of their own."

For general consideration, ballads containing riddles may be divided into three classifications. The first involves a situation where rivals offer to guess each other's riddles under penalty of forfeiting life or great treasure, an example being "The King and the Bishop," found later in this book as Niles No. 19. In the second classification, a suitor wins or loses a lady's hand by guessing riddles, and the third involves what we may call "the clever lass," who by her great knowledge and cunning saves her father's life, or wins a crown, or gets a prince who becomes her husband and ultimately becomes a king. In one case, the man asking the questions runs out of ideas and admits that he is at a loss to think up any more riddles, but, says he, "Let's get married anyway." True to tradition, the girl is overjoyed. They mount his horse and gallop away. If there were a script for all this, it would probably call for background music of wedding bells.

Although ballads based on riddling have been encountered many times in the Old World, they

1

are not widely distributed on the North American continent. In fact, we might say that they are very rare in our country, and this is particularly true of "Riddles Wisely Expounded." There may be some I have not encountered, but, so far as I can tell, only 5 examples of this ballad have been reported — a 4-stanza fragment from the state of Maine, a delightful 10-stanza text with music from Virginia, and the 3 versions offered herewith.

# The Devil's Questions

## (Niles No. 1 A)

IN THE SUMMER of 1933 (some of my notes are dated July 20 and 21) Hugh Stallcup, now dead and then a man in his seventies, sang me quite a few bits of folk music. He was fascinated with the supernatural, and had a wide understanding of weather signs and other backwoods superstitions. He told me a long yarn about a man he had known in his youth who could cure babies of certain lung and throat troubles by blowing in their mouths. The news of my "partial clairvoyance" had reached him, and he was impressed. He put me to the test, and, of course, I failed. My experience is that whatever clairvoyance a person has is an automatic device, operating on its own energy rather than a controlled skill that can be employed at will. But though I must have been a disappointment to Mr. Stallcup, he was surely not a disappointment to me.

He was interested in hunting animals, and particularly wild animals. The wilder they were, the more dangerous they were, the more interested he became. I well remember the yarn he told me of his Uncle Andles' combat with a wildcat. He called it a bobcat, and from his description, this bobcat must have had a mouthful of teeth not unlike a shark's. It seems that his uncle was walking through a wooded part of western North Carolina one evening, when suddenly he found himself face to face with a terrific bobcat. Now Uncle Andles had no rifle, no gun-pistol, not even a walking stick. But he was a man of great resourcefulness. He waited until the bobcat decided to spring. After the fashion of bob-

cats, this animal sprang with his mouth wide open. Uncle Andles rammed his fist into the bobcat's mouth and jammed his arm all the way through the animal's body, until he finally caught hold of the tail. Giving one gigantic pull, he turned the animal inside out. Later he skinned the carcass and sold the hide to a fur collector in Murphy, N. C., and made an Indian-style necklace from some of the smaller teeth.

Many of Hugh Stallcup's folk-music contributions were fragments concerning mistaken identity. He also sang songs about animals and Indians (the Cherokee reservation was not far away). One of the few songs he sang without interruption or variation was one he called "The Devil's Questions." I recognized his ballad as the first item in Child's collection, "Riddles Wisely Expounded," and tried to explain this to Hugh Stallcup — with no success. The fact that a somewhat similar ballad had been published somewhere off in the far world was beyond his concern. He would not have raised his eyes had I told him that the origins of his ballad could be found in manuscripts at Oxford University dating back to about A.D. 1450.

Nor was he interested in any quare-turned* furrin-body† who thought himself able to sing the old-timey music of Cherokee County, N. C. As it was with most native ballad singers I have encountered, first things came first. "The Devil's

---

* Foolish, half-witted.
† Person from some foreign place — that is, any place outside Cherokee County.

Questions" concerned a girl and the devil, and, as Stallcup explained it, "hit all goes to show that when a body deals with the devil, a body gets the devil's dealings."

Stallcup lived almost all of his life in and around Murphy, N. C. In fact he had been out of Cherokee County only twice. Once, at the turn of the century, he had made a trip to Abingdon, Va., to see a circus. There was a party of ten men, and they were very gay. They rode horses part of the way, buggies a little way, and a train the rest of the way. The trip to Abingdon took five days of steady travel. They saw the circus, and then, somewhat reluctantly, turned homeward.

The return trip took more than a week, allowing for a stopover in Asheville. Only eight of the original party of ten ever returned to Cherokee County. One managed to marry up with a widow-woman who had 75 of her own acres and a fine frame farmhouse painted white with red trim. The other punched a policeman and landed in the Asheville jailhouse on a disorderly conduct charge. He was never seen again in Cherokee County.

The Virginia text of this ballad ends happily, while the North Carolina version offered herewith ends tragically. How fortunate it would have been if the young girl in "The Devil's Questions" had named the devil for what he was. It would have been the end of him, for it is one of the rules of the game that naming the devil to his face destroys his power and sends him scurrying back to hell. This point is illustrated in a ballad found in the Child collection, indicated as No. 1 C, 19th verse:

> *As sune as she the fiend did name,*
> *He flew awa in a blazing flame.*

(Child took this ballad from page 647 of a manuscript collection brought together by a collector of wide reputation called Motherwell, and it was sung to collector Motherwell by a Mrs. Storie.)

Here follows Hugh Stallcup's ballad.

# The Devil's Questions
## (Niles No. 1 A)

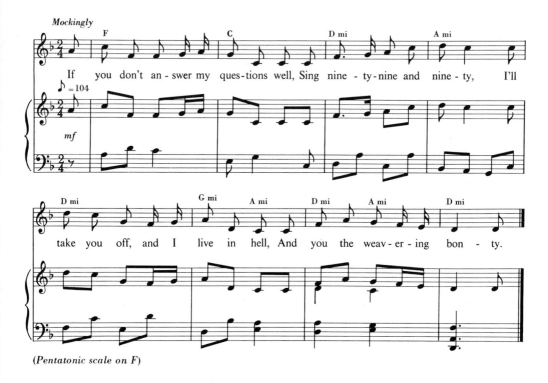

If you don't an-swer my ques-tions well, Sing nine - ty-nine and nine - ty, I'll take you off, and I live in hell, And you the weav-er-ing bon - ty.

*(Pentatonic scale on F)*

1. If you don't answer my questions well,
    Sing ninety-nine and ninety,
  I'll take you off, and I live in hell,
    And you the weavering bonty.*

2. Oh, what is whiter far than milk?
    Sing ninety-nine and ninety,
  And what is softer far than silk?
    And you the weavering bonty.

3. Oh, snow is whiter far than milk,
    Sing ninety-nine and ninety,
  And down is softer far than silk,
    And me the weavering bonty.

4. Oh, what is louder than a horn?
    Sing ninety-nine and ninety,
  And what is sharper than a thorn?
    And you the weavering bonty.

5. Oh, thunder's louder than a horn,
    Sing ninety-nine and ninety,
  And death is sharper than a thorn,
    And me the weavering bonty.

6. Oh, what is higher than a tree?
    Sing ninety-nine and ninety,
  And what is deeper than the sea?
    And you the weavering bonty.

* This was Stallcup's way of saying *bonny,* and although I did not ask him I believe that the term "weavering bonty" was intended to mean the "weaver's bonny."

7. Oh, heaven's higher than a tree,
       Sing ninety-nine and ninety,
   And hell is deeper than the sea,
       And me the weavering bonty.

8. Oh, what red fruit September grows?
       Sing ninety-nine and ninety,
   And what thing round the whole world goes?
       And you the weavering bonty.

9. The apple in September grows,
       Sing ninety-nine and ninety,
   And air around the whole world goes,
       And me the weavering bonty.

10. Oh, what is wicked man's repay?
        Sing ninety-nine and ninety,
    And what is worse than woman's way?
        And you the weavering bonty.

11. Now hell is wicked man's repay,
        Sing ninety-nine and ninety,
    And a she-devil's worse than woman's way,
        And me the weavering bonty.

12. Oh, you have answered my questions well,
        Sing ninety-nine and ninety,
    But I'll take you off, 'cause I live in hell,
        And you the weavering bonty.

# The Riddle Song

## (Niles No. 1 B)

ALTHOUGH "The Riddle Song" is a variant of Child No. 1, the riddling scheme employed is somewhat reminiscent of that found in Child No. 46 B, "Captain Wedderburn's Courtship." In this last ballad the tables are turned. The man captures the woman and takes her away with the idea of holy matrimony, but it is he who is asked to answer the questions. First, however, he tells her that "were 't na agen the law" he would "tak her to [his] ain bed, and lay her at the wa." Meanwhile, the supper bell is ringing, and the young woman replies:

*"Haud awa frae me, kind sir, I pray let go my hand;*
*The supper-bell it will be rung, nae langer maun I stand.*

*My father he'll na supper tak, gif I be missd awa;*
*Sae I'll na lie in your bed, at neither stock\* nor wa."*

The young woman is finally carried off to the Captain's "quartering-house" and put to bed. It is then that the questioning begins, with the Captain doing the answering. The ending is happy for all concerned: the Captain answers the questions, and the young woman, now Mrs. Wedderburn, lies next to the wall.

All these delightful complications are lost to us in the Kentucky "Riddle Song" as sung by Miss Wilma Creech of Pine Mountain, Ky., in the summer of 1933. The music is quite lovely.

\* Outside rail of the bedstead.

# The Riddle Song

## (Niles No. 1 B)

*In a storytelling manner*

"I gave my love a cher - ry that hath no stone, I gave my love a chick - en that hath no bone, I gave my love a thim - ble that hath no end, And I gave my love a ba - by that's no cry - in'."

*(Pentatonic scale on D)*

### The Riddle Song (Niles No. 1 B)

1. "I gave my love a cherry that hath no stone,
   I gave my love a chicken that hath no bone,
   I gave my love a thimble that hath no end,
   And I gave my love a baby that's no cryin'."

2. "How could there be a cherry that hath no stone?
   How could there be a chicken that hath no bone?
   How could there be a thimble that hath no end?
   How could there be a baby that's no cryin'?"

3. "A cherry when it's a-bloomin', it hath no stone.
   A chicken when it's a pippin, it hath no bone.
   A thimble when it's a-rollin', it hath no end.
   And a baby when it's a-sleepin', there's no cryin'."

# Piri-miri-dictum Domini

## (Niles No. 1 C)

AN INTERESTING VARIANT of the riddle-song idea is found below. Here we have a macaronic poem, most probably the result of the English people's fundamental stubbornness. When in the 16th century the Church of England banned the use of Latin in church services, a portion of the English population remained obdurate in the face of official orders and royal decrees, and that portion went right on using Latin whenever possible, particularly if it would irritate the authorities.

The hornbooks* and primers of Archbishop Cranmer's time led to a widespread acceptance of the English language as applied to religious service, though by no means all the people of England wanted their mother tongue used in the Church. Thirty years after Henry VIII became King of England in 1509, the first officially authorized English version of the Bible, called the Great Bible, appeared; it was followed in 1549 by the first *Book of Common Prayer*, authorized by the young king, Edward VI. Even so, and even then, there were those who preferred

* A hornbook was not a book at all, but a sheet of vellum, and later a sheet of paper, covered by a thin sheet of transparent horn and attached to a wooden frame with a small handle. On this paper, or vellum, was printed the alphabet in large and small letters, followed by lines of vowel and consonant combinations. Then followed the usual exorcism: "In the name of the Father, and of the Son, and of the Holy Ghost. *Amen.*" Next came the Lord's Prayer.

The hornbook was actually a primer, and was intended for the use of children. Paintings of the period which portray children often show them at play with hornbooks tied to their belts or girdles.

# Piri-miri-dictum Domini
## (Niles No. 1 C)

Gaily

I had three cous-ins o-ver the sea, Pi - ri - mi - ri - dic - tum Do - mi - ni. Three or four pres-ents sent they me, Pan - trum quar - trum pa - ra - dise stan - trum, Pi - ri - mi - ri - dic - tum Do - mi - ni.

(Major mode on C)

Latin, and proved once more that the law of the land was based on the willingness of the people to be governed.

This variant was taken down June 1934, at Berea, Ky., from the singing of Miss Cora L. Swift, who lived in Oberlin, Ohio. Miss Swift learned the song from Miss Phoebe M. Hayes, whose parents came from Massachusetts (where their ancestors landed in 1636) by way of Mendham, N. Y.

The text above, with a few minor changes, can be found in Halliwell's *Popular Rhymes and*

*Nursery Tales,* page 150. The main differences are in the Latin responses. The music was certainly created at a much later date.

For years macaronic poems — poems in English and Latin — were written, published, and sung. Some were religious, some were love poems; many were uninhibited and bawdy. It is not surprising that the idea of the riddle song was taken over and employed as the basis of a very effective set of macaronic lyrics. Today, as "Pari-miri-dictum Domini," it is widely sung in the schools of the United States, hog-Latin and all.

## Piri-miri-dictum Domini (Niles No. 1 C)

1. I had three cousins over the sea,
   *Piri-miri-dictum Domini.*
   Three or four presents sent they me,
   *Pantrum quartrum paradise stantrum,*
   *Piri-miri-dictum Domini.*

2. The first was a bird without a bone,
   *Piri-miri-dictum Domini.*
   The second was a cherry without a stone,
   *Pantrum quartrum paradise stantrum,*
   *Piri-miri-dictum Domini.*

3. The third was a book that no man 's read,
   The fourth was a blanket without a thread.

4. Can there be a bird without a bone?
   Can there be a cherry without a stone?

5. A bird in the egg's without a bone,
   A cherry in the bud's without a stone.

6. Can there be a book that no man 's read?
   Can there be a blanket without a thread?

7. A book in the press, that no man 's read,
   A blanket in the wool's without a thread.

# The Elfin Knight

(Child No. 2)

## My Father Gave Me an Acre of Ground
(Niles No. 2 A)

## The Parsley Vine
(Niles No. 2 B)

## The Shirt of Lace
(Niles No. 2 C)

THE SECOND BALLAD in this collection gives us an opportunity to observe what happened to the supernatural in the crossing of the North Atlantic. On short acquaintance one might conclude that the American text of "My Father Gave Me an Acre of Ground" could not be even remotely related to its ancestor "The Elfin Knight," 12 examples of which are given by Child from English and Scottish sources. The supernatural elements in the original have disappeared from the American version.

Indeed, the differences between the ancestor and the offspring are so marked that it would seem worthwhile to quote a portion of a Scottish text indicated by Child as No. 2 B:

> *My plaid awa, my plaid awa,*
> *And owre the hills and far awa,*
> *And far awa to Norrowa,*
> *My plaid shall not be blawn awa.*

> 1. *The Elphin knight sits on yon hill,*
>    Ba, ba, ba, lillie ba
>    *He blaws his horn baith loud and shrill.*
>    The wind hath blawn my plaid awa.

> 2. *He blaws it east, he blaws it west,*
>    Ba, ba, ba, lillie ba
>    *He blaws it where he liketh best.*
>    The wind hath blawn my plaid awa.

> 3. *"I wish that horn were in my kist,\**
>    *Yea, and the knight in my arms niest."†*

> 4. *She had no sooner these words said,*
>    *Than the knight came to her bed.*

Oh, it's very easy to see that in the first 5 verses of this Scottish example a great many things happened in a very short while. In the vernacular of the Southern Appalachians, we might say, "She hoped he was a-comin', but she didn't expect him all to-oncet."

There he was, though, appearing by magic — the Elfin Knight, horn and all. And as the ballad unfolds, we discover this knight to be quite a gentleman. He even tries to talk the lass out of a hasty marriage.

The first evidence of any relation between the Scottish original and the American variants appears with the 11th numbered verse. It is here that the Scottish lass (who, we suppose, is by this time sitting up in her bed) declares herself to be the owner of an acre of untilled land:

> *"I have an aiker of good ley land,*
> *Which lyeth low by yon sea strand."*

It would appear that the lass is offering this in-

* Chest.    † Nearby.

11

formation as bait, but when she proposes that the Elfin Knight work the land, till it, plant a crop and cultivate it, the gentleman loses interest. Then follows a series of impossible tests — impossible for both parties concerned — a plain sark or a bridal sark being the prize:

*"And when that ye have done your wark,*
*Come back to me, and ye'll get your sark."*

Now "sark" is an antique word coming to us in a rather roundabout manner, through Old English, Old Norse, and original Teutonic, and it represents a garment somewhat like a shirt or chemise, worn next to the skin. In the hands of present-day ballad singers, the "sark" of the original ballad turns out to be a simple cambric shirt.

But the Elfin Knight, with the cunning of his kind, rejects the opportunity of becoming a landed squire, and bows himself out, saying that he "would not quit his plaid for his life" because he uses it "to cover and comfort his seven children and his wife."

The supernatural, being exactly what it is, never can stand analysis or logic. It can hardly stand the light of day. The native ballad singers in the Southern Appalachians may have been superstitious, given to hants (haunts) and charms, but the supernatural in the *fullest* sense has never been *entirely* accepted. This is possibly why the 3 variants of "The Elfin Knight" offered herewith contain no reference to a lusty, hill-topping, full-grown elf with a taste for magical music played shrilly on a horn.

# My Father Gave Me an Acre of Ground

## (Niles No. 2 A)

IN HAMBLEN COUNTY, Tenn., in May 1934, I encountered Simeon B. Coffee. He had been fishing. In fact he was greatly interested in fish. He had even worked, on occasion, at a fish hatchery. He was born in Knoxville, where he had lived much of his life, but he had left the place because "there were too many people and too much noise." He was quite proud to relate that he had been a WPA worker in 1932 and 1933. He was not married. He had seen many men who had "driven their ducks to a bad market" and married up with tiresome females. "To tell the truth," said he, "many women are witches." I said yes and no, and waited for further information on this vital subject. Finally, we both nodded our heads in what seemed to be agreement, and I thought that the discussion was closed. But I was mistaken. Almost at once Mr. Coffee launched into the telling of one witch story after another.

According to Mr. Coffee, witches could do the following things with no trouble at all —

1. Cause cows to go dry
2. Cause horses to throw shoes
3. Cause wheels to come off wagons and buggies, even in wet weather
4. Cause children to stutter
5. Cause milk to sour
6. Cause vinegar mothers to mildew
7. Cause sickness and death in human persons
8. Transfer themselves into animals at will.

This last piece of witchery was illustrated by an extended tale, which most readers will recognize as a well-established folk legend. Mr. Coffee told it this way:

It seems that sometime around the turn of the century a young man lived not far from Witt, Tenn. — a young man who farmed a reasonably fertile piece of land and supported himself and his widowed mother. His barns bulged with hay, his cribs were filled with shucked-out corn, and his cows waded in deep pasture grass. This young man (his name was Yancy) and his mother lived well.

During the summer of that year there had been a protracted camp meeting at Bear's Lick Spring church. It was at this camp meeting that our young Mr. Yancy met a bright-eyed, pink-cheeked girl, of whom he became enamored. Sarah lived just over the top of the hill. Twenty minutes of reasonable walking took him to her door.

As Indian summer came, Yancy's visits to Sarah's home became more frequent, and his mother was worried for fear her son should marry up with this woman-person and bring her home to the comfortable farmhouse, and bring complications with her. It was in early October when Yancy had his first encounter with a great antlered deer that blocked the path to Miss Sarah's house. At the first encounter, Yancy went home. But when on his next visit the deer once more blocked his path, Yancy, who had provided himself with a rifle, shot at the deer. The shooting, as he saw it, would serve two purposes — it would rid him of a nuisance and supply him with venison. But no matter how often Yancy fired, he was unable to kill the deer.

With the approach of cold weather, the cattle and hog buyers came through the country, and it was one of these worldly-wise men who advised Yancy on how to destroy the deer: he was to melt down a silver coin and fire it point-blank into the deer's heart. This was the sure and only way.

The following day Yancy melted down a silver dollar, molded it into a bullet, and when next he met the deer and fired the bullet into the animal's heart, the deer fell dead. Yancy went on to visit Miss Sarah, proposed marriage to her, was accepted, and with joy in his heart returned home through the dark. When he came to the place where the deer had fallen, no deer lay on the ground. Nor was there any sign of the combat that had taken place. Troubled, Yancy walked on home. The farmhouse door stood wide open. On the floor lay Yancy's mother, quite dead, with a bullet hole just over her heart. Probing the wound with his pocketknife, Yancy found the silver bullet he had molded.

Mr. Coffee was silent for quite a while after telling his story. Finally, returning from the realm of fantasy, he went on to the singing of something quite as fabulous — namely, "The Elfin Knight."

Mr. Coffee was a thin, homely little man with a thin, though accurate, little voice. In his early days he had often sung in church choirs and at camp meetings, but as years passed he thought there was too much noise in camp meetings — "too much noise and not enough Jesus Christ." He owned a copy of *The Sacred Harp*,* the shape-note hymnbook, but he did not know where it was at the time I saw him. He said it was the same book his great-grandfather had used in 1850 (?). If this was indeed a fact, it might have

---

* *The Sacred Harp* is a songbook measuring 9¾" wide, 5¼" high, and 1¼" thick. The original edition contained 263 tightly packed pages of hymns and other sacred music. Some pages contained two numbers. It was compiled by Benjamin Franklin White and published in 1844 in Philadelphia. In his preface White states: "Many efforts have been made to please the public with a collection of sacred music; and none but those who make the effort know how difficult it is to accomplish this task."

B. F. White succeeded beyond his wildest dreams. His book, *The Sacred Harp*, a collection of psalm and hymn tunes, odes and anthems, sold more than a million copies before his century turned. It is still selling in a slightly larger format.

*The Sacred Harp* was not a church hymnal, though its contents are religious songs. It was usually referred to as "old Baptist music," but it was never really adopted by the Baptist church. It was, and still is, widely used at the Interstate Sacred Harp Singing Association meetings, and at gatherings called Old Folks' Shape-Note Singing Meetings. Most of the music in the original editions was set up in three-part harmony and the notes were of different shapes — squares, triangles, circles, half-moons, etc. They were occasionally called "buckwheat notes," because some of them really resembled grains of buckwheat. The late George Pullen Jackson of Nashville is accepted as the world authority on shape-note music and *The Sacred Harp*. His works are found in every library of importance.

# My Father Gave Me an Acre of Ground

## (Niles No. 2 A)

Lightly

My fa - ther gave me an a - cre of ground, I - vy, sing i - vo - ry, My fa - ther gave me an a - cre of ground, Pars - ley, rose - mar - y, ___ and thyme, My fa - ther gave me an a - cre of ground, Be - twixt the sea - side all ___ a - round, And she shall be a lov - er of mine,

Pars - ley, rose - mar - y, ___ and thyme.

*(Dorian mode on B)*

1. My father gave me an acre of ground,
   *Ivy, sing ivory,*
   My father gave me an acre of ground,
   *Parsley, rosemary, and thyme,*
   My father gave me an acre of ground,
   Betwixt the seaside all around,
   *And she shall be a lover of mine,*
   *Parsley, rosemary, and thyme.*

2. He made a plowing-share out of leather,
   *Ivy, sing ivory,*
   He made a plowing-share out of leather,
   *Parsley, rosemary, and thyme,*
   He made a plowing-share out of leather,
   And he harrowed it down with a white turkey's
         feather,
   *And she shall be a lover of mine,*
   *Parsley, rosemary, and thyme.*

3. He planted hit down with Hickory King,*
   And laid it by with a red robin's wing.

4. If you would make me a cambric shirt,
   All woven around with no needle work.

5. If you would wash and dry hit well,
   Where ne'er a drap of water fell.

6. If you would dry hit on a thorn,
   That blossomed when King John was born.

7. And when the corn is cut and bound,
   I'll wear my shirt in yonders town.

8. And when 'tis done all speedily,
   Plaid or no plaid, married we'll be.

been a first edition. I offered to purchase the book and gave him a small advance as earnest money. I never did get the book, however, because he could not find it. "Most likely fell into the fish-hatcher's pond," said he sadly. I dis- covered in 1940 that Mr. Coffee was dead.

Above is his contribution. It has become known as the Tennessee version of "The Elfin Knight."

* A variety of wide-grained white field corn, planted extensively in the Southern mountains.

# The Parsley Vine

## (Niles No. 2 B)

*(Minor mode on D)*

1. My uncle gave me an acre of ground,
     Parsley hangs upon the vine,
   My uncle gave me an acre of ground,
   The poorest I did ever find,
     Where the parsley hangs upon the vine.

2. My uncle gave me an old gray mare,
     Parsley hangs upon the vine,
   My uncle gave me an old gray mare,
   Who wouldn't work and didn't care,
     When the parsley hangs upon the vine.

3. My lover gave me a linny smock,
  Parsley hangs upon the vine,
  My lover gave me a linny smock,
  But on her door I would not knock,
    'Cause the parsley hangs upon the vine.

4. My uncle took my plaid away,
  Parsley hangs upon the vine,
  My uncle took my plaid away,
  In spite of totter and head of gray,
    And the parsley hangs upon the vine.

# The Parsley Vine

## (Niles No. 2 B)

THE SINGER of these verses, Carter Patterson, was an engaging vagabond. On the morning of July 5, 1908, when he sang "The Parsley Vine" for me, he was suffering slightly from the celebration of the Fourth of July. He and all the other numerous Pattersons lived a few miles from Jeffersontown, Ky., in a series of tin shacks by a creek. There were many children, large and small, and, of course, the traditional beautiful daughter of about 16 summers. The daughter was a waitress in a nearby summer hotel. Carter was a woodsman and a stake maker and a stake driver. As such, he was my assistant. We were both engaged by the county surveyor.

The Pattersons were experts in woods lore. Carter had a name for every weed and wildflower in the forest. He knew the flower and plant superstitions, how they could be used as cures, and which ones were safe to eat. He told me of a long dead relative who could poison a "humanperson" with a scrap of wild mushroom no larger than a man's fingernail. It was all in knowing which mushroom was edible and which one was poisonous.

# The Shirt of Lace

## (Niles No. 2 C)

UNCLE BROTHER PATTERSON (that is the way his name appeared on the county engineer's paybook) was Carter Patterson's brother. He was much older than the other men in the family, and he was much more silent. The others were full of words and fun but Uncle Brother was on the sad side, as a rule. He had been a cattle drover as a young man, and had once owned a very fine farm; but he ran afoul of the law and lost it all. It seems that there was some bloodshed in a

# The Shirt of Lace
## (Niles No. 2 C)

**Gently**

A mi / F / A mi / D mi

Oh, wa-ter where there is no well, — Vin-y flow'r and rose-may tree, —

A mi / F / A mi / D mi / A mi

Wa-ter where there is no well, — What name will my true love

G / A mi / D mi / E mi

tell? Vin-y flow'r and rose-may tree. —

**mp**

♩ = 60

**(Minor mode on A)**

saloon in the old Haymarket section of Louisville, Ky., in the winter of 1880. According to Uncle Brother's story, it was a sort of drunken brawl over some strayed cattle. Uncle Brother came out alive, but when the law took leave of him, the century had turned. He spent the remainder of his life living as a vagabond, doing occasional odd jobs and working in the forests. He had heard his noisy relatives sing the rather uninteresting "Parsley Vine" song, and to establish his position as a singer he took me aside and sang "The Shirt of Lace" very quietly and accurately. None of the Patterson men could read or write.

My notes say: "A very interesting melodic line. The music in the family came from a Patterson grandmother, who emigrated from Virginia at the end of the War Between the States." The date of this is August 20, 1908, Jeffersontown, Jefferson County, Ky.

## The Shirt of Lace (Niles No. 2 C)

1. Oh, water where there is no well,
    *Viny flow'r and rosemay tree,*
   Water where there is no well,
   What name will my true love tell?
    *Viny flow'r and rosemay tree.*

2. Oh, valley where no sun do fall,
    *Viny flow'r and rosemay tree,*
   Valley where no sun do fall,
   Grows no crop, no spring, no fall,
    *Viny flow'r and rosemay tree.*

3. If you should wash my linsey dress,
   If you wash my linsey dress,
   And hang it in my mother's press.

4. If you should wash my shirt of lace,
   If you wash my shirt of lace,
   Be sure the buttons be in place.

5. And then my acre 'side the sea,
   Then my acre 'side the sea,
   Will be halved up, my love, with thee.

# 3

# The False Knight upon the Road

(Child No. 3)

## The Smart Schoolboy
(Niles No. 3)

THIS BALLAD is not often encountered; not more than a dozen examples have been reported from the United States. At first it might be concluded that its rarity is the result of the supernatural situation, the devil appearing as a knight on the road. But other ballads involving the supernatural are occasionally encountered.

Here we find a smart little schoolboy outwitting the devil himself and, we may assume, going off to school quite gaily. In one American text the schoolboy calmly throws the devil in a nearby well and then departs for school. The boy wins

out, of course, because he stands his ground, and by a process called "flyting" (to flyte means to dispute, to debate, to scold, to flout, or to mock) turns the devil's device back on the demon and in reality, outnonpluses the devil. Finally, we must remember that there was a time when no one could trust to scolding or flyting for foiling a witch — unless he knew more words; and in the case of the smart schoolboy, he would have been carried off to hell had he not been sturdy and brave and full of words, and also of answers.

## The Smart Schoolboy

### (Niles No. 3)

"THE FALSE KNIGHT UPON THE ROAD" was known to the singer Preston Wolford of Powell County, Va., as "The Smart Schoolboy." I came upon this man Wolford in a strange way. I had been searching the towns around Coeburn, Va., for a man named Adams who was reputed to be one of the great woodcarvers in all that country. He had been injured in a coal-mine explosion, and woodcarving was his sole means of making a livelihood. I had visited the towns of Dante, St.

Paul, Tom's Creek, Coeburn, and Norton, but had not found him. Finally, I was told that the woodcarver Adams might be found living near Pattonsville. At Pattonsville no one seemed to know anything about a disabled coal miner named Adams who had turned woodcarver. So I turned off in the direction of Middlesboro, Ky., hoping to get there by nightfall.

Just outside Pattonsville I encountered a man trying to drive a very much broken-down auto-

# The Smart Schoolboy

## ( Niles No. 3 )

*Demandingly*

"Oh — where be ye go - ing?" Said the knight — on the road. "I be go - ing to school," Said the boy as he stood. And he stood and he stood And 'twas well — that he stood. "I be go - ing to school," Said the boy — as he stood.

*(Major mode on F)*

mobile to which a truck body had been added. He asked me to push him up a little hill so that he might roll down the other side and thereby start his motor. The motor did start, and later we met at the tiny village of Dot, Va.

It was here that I discovered Mr. Wolford to be quite a singer. He was a dance caller on Saturday nights and a small-time farmer by day. On his farm he raised the usual corn crop. (The date of our meeting was springtime 1935.) He

crooners on the radio, and his
something of an imitation of
wever, he did stay on the pitch
anted to go up to New York and
in the world of radio singing. I
nst this move. He was enjoying
rd in southwestern Virginia; the
New York City might not be so
bene

Preston Wolford had been married, but he did not know where his wife was at the moment.

What ballad singing he did was remembered music once sung by his granny on his mother's side. She had been born a McVaine.

He sang quite a few songs for me, but his version of "The False Knight upon the Road" was the only thing I took down. His other songs were either westerns or the more synthetic hillbilly ditties he learned by way of the radio. I might add that in 1956 I discovered the woodcarver named Adams living in retirement in Florida.

## The Smart Schoolboy (Niles No. 3)

1. "Oh where be ye going?"
*Said the knight on the road.*
"I be going to school,"
*Said the boy as he stood.*

   *And he stood and he stood*
   *And 'twas well that he stood.*
   "I be going to school,"
   *Said the boy as he stood.*

2. "Oh what do ye there?"
*Said the knight on the road.*
"I read from my book,"
*Said the boy as he stood.*

   *And he stood and he stood*
   *And 'twas well that he stood.*
   "I read from my book,"
   *Said the boy as he stood.*

3. "Oh what have ye got?"
" 'Tis a bait of bread and cheese."

4. "Oh pray give me some."
"Oh no, not a crumb."

5. "I hear your school bell."
"Hit's a-ringing you to hell."

# Lady Isabel and the Elf-Knight

(Child No. 4)

## Lady Ishbel and Her Parrot
### (Niles No. 4 A)
## King William's Son
### (Niles No. 4 B)
## The Courting of Aramalee
### (Niles No. 4 C)

CHILD TELLS US that this ballad has obtained the widest circulation of all ballads. (He was speaking of circulation in the Old World. In the United States and Canada, I would say, "Barbary Ellen" is by far the most widely circulated and the best known.) However, Child has traced "Lady Isabel and the Elf-Knight" to Scandinavia, Poland, southern and northern Germany, and even into the Latin countries. To this I can add, from my own investigations in Finland and Estonia, that it is well known in both these countries, in folk tradition. In Estonia there is a tribe known as the Setu people. It is a small tribe, and they speak a language of their own which is quite unlike the official Estonian. These Setus, employing the manner of the rune singers of Finland, tell a story following the lines of Lady Isabel's adventures almost exactly, the chief singer telling the story and the chorus joining hands in the best rune-singer tradition and chanting a monotonous musical background.

In almost every case a young woman of the nobility or upper gentry is charmed out of her good senses by a man (a knight), who proves to be a full-grown elf possessing supernatural powers. In some cases the elf casts a charm by singing; in others, he gets his results by persistence and the speaking voice. After he has followed the young woman until she can no longer raise a hand in resistance, she follows *him* and takes his advice. Later, when the young woman is confronted with death at the knight's hand, she employs a little trickery, saving her own life and destroying the elf-knight in the bargain.

In the German versions a handy brother rushes forth and saves the hapless maiden. In some French and Italian texts hunger and thirst are added to the situation, and in one instance there is a long ride during which neither party speaks.

Scholars have been toying with the idea that "Lady Isabel and the Elf-Knight" is derived from the biblical story of Judith and Holofernes. This could be true, although there are certain definite differences. Lady Isabel came home from this odd elopement riding one horse and leading another and, we hope, carrying the bag containing a portion of her father's gold and another bag containing her mother's fee, and on arrival made great effort to enter the family castle without attracting any attention — though the noisy, talkative parrot was a handicap. Judith, on the other hand, came home with pomp and ceremony, carrying the head of Holofernes in what is

24

described as a meat bag. Lady Isabel saved what was left of her honor, the bag of gold, the fee, and two fine horses. Judith saved her people.

The Flemish version of "Lady Isabel and the Elf-Knight" (communicated in 1836 by one Willems to *Mone's Anzeiger* in 38 two-line stanzas) follows the general outlines of the Lady Isabel–Judith and Holofernes legend up to a point, but this Flemish version presents some interesting variations. Instead of the young woman's slipping away quietly and secretly (as she surely does in the American and English-Scottish versions), she asks her father's permission to go away with the elf-knight. She fails in this, and then she goes to her father confessor, who strangely grants her request.

The short scene at the end of most American and English-Scottish versions concerning the parrot was perhaps created as an additional and final hurdle. Talking birds are not unknown to balladry. We find one at the end of "Young Hunting" (Child No. 68), where the feathered friend attempts to expose the young lady and is bribed into silence by the promise of a cage made of golden wires. We never discover whether delivery was made on this promise.

# Lady Ishbel and Her Parrot

## (Niles No. 4 A)

In July 1934 a charming old lady named Mrs. Hattie Melton sang this ballad for me. Mrs. Melton lived near Allanstand, N. C., which is about seven miles from Asheville. She had been visiting her sister-in-law for several days, helping with the canning of green beans. The bean crop ripened slowly that year, and Mrs. Melton, not being employed with canning, entertained us with singing. She and I swapped songs and ballads. She had been a singer all her life and was very proud of the fact that she could sing many hymns and ballads (she called them "old-timey songs") from memory. She could read and write and had some faint memory of Cecil Sharp's* visit, which she calculated to have been about fifteen years earlier.

In two counties in central Kentucky the motif of the legend of "Lady Isabel and the Elf-Knight" remains in stories concerning the early struggles between whites and Indians. In one case, several white traders capture or entice an Indian princess away from her tribe. Later these white traders try to kill the girl, but are destroyed themselves in the attempt. In another case, a white girl is involved with an Indian brave. The white girl, perhaps a clever-lass type, outwits the Indian. The ghosts of these girls and their victims are persistent figures walking the roads of Boone Creek country in Clark and Fayette Counties, Ky.

Commenting on the song she had sung for me, Mrs. Melton vouchsafed this information: "I tell you, a woman-person has just got to watch her step when she's dealing with a man. Nowadays menfolk will promise a woman anything. They'll

* Cecil J. Sharp and Mrs. Olive Dame Campbell co-authored a collection of folk songs entitled *English Folk Songs from the Southern Appalachians*. Mrs. Campbell, wife of John C. Campbell, representative for the Southern Highland Division of the Russell Sage Foundation, began her collection as early as 1907. Cecil Sharp, who was an Englishman, worked in the Southern mountains forty-six weeks during the summer months of 1916, 1917, and 1918. The ultimate published collection, edited by Maud Karpeles (Oxford University Press, 1932), contained 273 songs and ballads and 968 tunes. Among these are ballads traceable to 45 of the Child ballads, as compared to the 65 such ballads represented in this book. It should be remembered, however, that while the Campbell-Sharp collection was made in a comparatively short time, the Niles collection started in 1907 and covered over 50 years thereafter.

# Lady Ishbel and Her Parrot

## (Niles No. 4 A)

*(Pentatonic scale on D)*

promise her the moon, and when the woman-person gets the moon, she finds out it ain't even made of green cheese."

Hattie Melton was known as an excellent cook. She told me quite a few things about cooking green beans. First, you had to start with the right sort of beans. According to Mrs. Melton, Kentucky Wonder was one of the greatest of all beans. The Valentine was fair, the Marrowfat was better. The stringless beans were nice to talk about and looked powerful good in seed catalogs, but you had to string 'em just the same.

Now the Lazy-Wife Pole was grand as a cornfield bean, and the October, or Cranberry, bean was wonderful for shelling out. Of course, if you liked shellies, then the crowder pea was the most prolific and the easiest to open. I listened and my mouth watered.

"No bean is fit to eat if it's not properly cooked," said Hattie. "These watery, soupy, limp beans young brides cook in cities should be lawed agin — then no man would have to eat 'em! You can use fat back, hog jowl, side meat, butter, or even beef to flavor and season beans, but be sure to use something. And add a small red pepper-pod to the beans. . . . And if they look tough, boil 'em twice, the first time with a little baking soda in the water . . . and don't oversalt the beans . . . and serve 'em hot with buttermilk biscuits and honey. . . . Old ham tastes mighty good with well-cooked green beans. In that case, a body ought to turn out a batch of beaten biscuits — you know, fifty licks for homefolks and a hundred licks for company."

By this time I was dying of hunger. It was noon, so we had dinner, and the food was quite wonderful. There were green beans and buttermilk biscuits.

Here follows the ballad as sung by Hattie Melton on July 30, 1934.

## Lady Ishbel and Her Parrot (Niles No. 4 A)

1. He followed her up and he followed her
      down,
      He followed her where she lay,
   And she not havin' the strength to withstand,
      Nor the breath to say him nay.

2. "Go fetch me a sack of the old lord's gold,
      And most of your mama's fee,
   And a pited hoss and an iron-gray,
      From your stable of thirty-and-three."

3. If Ishbel did ride at the villian's side,
      With the gold and her mama's fee,
   She was ridin' far off to the broad seaside,
      Where married she would be.

4. "Get down, get down, my right pretty miss,
      Your hour has come, I see,
   For here I've drownded nine young ladies
      gay,
      And you the tenth one will be.

5. "Pull off, pull off that shiny silk gown,
      And them right pretty rings you own,
   For women's clothes cost too much gold
      To rest in the salt sea foam."

6. "It's turn, oh turn, oh turn your head,
      And look at yon green-growin' tree,
   For if I doff my shiny silk gown,
      A naked lady you'll see."

7. He turnèd his face around about,
      To look at that green-growin' tree,
   And she grabbed him round the middle so
      small,
      And she flicked him into the sea.

8. "Lay there, false villian, lay cold and dead,
      Lay there in room of me,
   For it's nine gay ladies you've drownded here,
      But the tenth one drownded ye."

9. Her pited hoss tuck her right quickly home,
      She led the iron-gray,
   And when she entered her father's hall,
      The sky was breakin' day.

10. "Speak none of my pranks, my right pretty
      poll,
      Else I'll make you out a liar.
   But if you be wise, your cage shall be made
      Of pretty golden wire."

# King William's Son

## (Niles No. 4 B)

*(Dorian mode on E)*

# King William's Son

## (Niles No. 4 B)

THIS interesting version of "Lady Isabel and the Elf-Knight" was sung to me in the summer of 1936 by a tall, angular woman of great age who lived in western North Carolina. She did not wish to have her name associated with anything that might get into print because of certain family difficulties and embarrassments brought down upon her by her children. In spite of all her troubles, she had a great sense of humor and was ready to laugh at almost everything, including herself.

She used the word "hide" in "King William's Son" — possibly for the sake of rhyme, but more probably, I think, for humor's sake. "If a body wants to be glum-faced," said she, "there always be lots of reasons for it. Why, if I worked at it, I could be as sour as any straddle-pole politician in Franklin, North Carolina."

I later discovered that one of her brothers had enjoyed the benefits of county office for a number of years by being what she called a "smollygooster" — one who manages to come out on top no matter which side wins. This had given her a negative point of view concerning politics and politicians.

I came away with a great admiration for this white-haired, motherly woman, who seemed to be living entirely alone, save for a pair of little boy grandchildren. "Them cute little fellers playin' out yonder in that cow-stomp* are my only partners now," she said. "They's young enough to mind me, and they ain't old enough to be a botherment — not yet."

Her singing was not overly consistent, but her melodic material was very fine, and she was a most willing singer.

## King William's Son

1. Of all the sons King William had,
   Prince Jamie was the worst,
   And what made the sorrow even more,
   Prince Jamie was the first.

2. He sang his song to Isabel,
   A song like none did sing,
   And she did follow him away,
   A very silly thing.

3. They wandered over hill and dale,
   They came upon the sea,
   "Light down, light down, fair Isabel,
   And give your clothes to me."

4. "Hit's turn, oh turn your head away,
   And look at yonder sea.
   I do not wish to have it said
   I let you see my bare body."

5. "Oh turn, oh turn your head away,
   Behold the yon seaside,
   And do not look this way a bit
   Or you'll see me in my hide."

6. And as he stood a-waiting
   And a-looking o'er the lea,
   She grabbed him by his slender hips
   And pitched him in the sea.

7. "Oh save me, save me from this death,
   And when the King is dead,
   I will be King Jamie
   And you'll be queen instead."

8. "If you could lie to nine young maids,
   You'll lie as quick to me,
   But soon the fish will eat your meat
   Instead of eating me."

9. She mounted quick the dapple gray,
   And then she led the black
   Across the fields and pastures,
   A-homing she rode back.

10. "Where have you been and what have you done,
    Your horse is all a-sweat?
    Your father looked the castle o'er
    And hasn't found you yet."

11. "If you would only hold your tongue,
    You'll never have to lie.
    My father ne'er must ever know
    How near I come to die.

12. "No talk, no talk, my pretty poll,
    It be the break of day."
    "The cat was at my cage's door,
    And you shooed her away."

13. "Well said, my parrot bird, well said,
    No cat shall bother thee,
    And thy cage shall be made of beaten gold
    Instead of the willow tree."

* A cool, dusty place under a tree where cows rest in summer and stamp at flies.

# The Courting of Aramalee

## (Niles No. 4 C)

HERE ARE 10 two-line stanzas which tell the deathless story of Lady Isabel and her knight. They were recited (not sung) by Mrs. Pet Fugate who was visiting and assisting at a stir-off on Fugate's Fork, near Hardshell, Ky. Mrs. Fugate was ancient of days, but very gay. She was quite proud of her recitation and gave it with spirit. The menfolk deserted the operation of the stir-off, which is the traditional squeezing and boiling of the sorghum juice,* to listen to the legend of a man whose courting brought him to grief.

Here is Mrs. Fugate's way of telling the story of Lady Isabel and the elf-knight.

### The Courting of Aramalee

1. He courted her above, he courted her below,
   He showed her ways of courtin', the first she ever did know.

2. She tried to send him on his way, she chased him over the lea,
   But never a bit would he ever go for a-courtin' of Aramalee.

3. He said, "Go get your father's gold, go get your mother's fee,
   And saddle a horse for a man to ride and one for a fine lady."

4. She mounted herself on a deep dark roan, himself on a medium gray,
   And after two hours twill midnight, they quietly rode away.

5. "Light down, light down, fair Aramalee, beside this cliff of rocks,
   For here is where I kill the girls who ride away with me.

6. "Pull off that pretty silken gown and the cord that round it goes,
   For a naked girl will drown as quick as one a-wearin' clothes.

7. "Pull off the gown, pull off the rings, and give them unto me,
   For they are much too costly to rot in the salt, salt sea."

8. "It's turn, oh turn, your head away and look at yonder sea,
   'Cause if I take my dresses off, a naked girl you'll see."

9. "I've seen nine naked ladies here, and you the tenth will be,
   But just to please a princess, I'll look at yonder sea."

10. He turned his head around about, she pushed him quickly in,
    And rode off to her castle to make up for her sin.

* The green sorghum, which looks much like corn before it matures, is cut down with a corn-knife and fed into a horse-drawn squeezer. The horse walks around in a circle to operate the squeezer, and the entire process is a sort of festival. There is usually a certain small amount of distilled corn juice drunk by the menfolk, and the womenfolk prepare huge dinners out in the open. The fact that the scum on the top of the boiling cane juice is removed with a long-handled scraper gives the operation its name of "stir-off." The odor of the boiling cane juice, combined with the smoke of woodfires and the smells of the food in the kettles, is something one will never forget.

# 5

# Earl Brand

(Child No. 7)

## Lord William's Death
(Niles No. 5 A)

## William and Ellen
(Niles No. 5 B)

## Brandywine
(Niles No. 5 C)

"LORD WILLIAM'S DEATH" stems from a parent ballad entitled "Earl Brand," indicated in Child's collection as No. 7, and at the same time is very near the Douglas tragedy, so dear to the heart of Sir Walter Scott.

There are two other versions of "Earl Brand" in this collection — "William and Ellen" and "Brandywine." They follow the outlines of "Earl Brand" and the Douglas tragedy, too, with the added complications of a talking horse and the disaster precipitated by the eloping girl when she "names" her lover in a moment of great emergency.

The English and Scottish versions do not contain this so-called "death-naming" situation, but the lines "name me not to death, though thou see me bleed" (or a similar statement following along the lines of this idea) are found in nearly every Danish, Icelandic, Norwegian, Swedish, Estonian, and German ballad telling the story of "Earl Brand."

While in the Baltic States in 1936 and 1937 I was told by an Estonian folklorist that the end results — the American versions of "Earl Brand," the 5 versions in Child's collection, and the uncounted texts from Scandinavia, Iceland, Denmark, the Baltic States, and Finland — do no

doubt derive from a medieval legend brought into Estonia by the German Knights of the Sword. The Estonians suggest that the German knights brought their long-ago ancestors a legend not unlike the German counterpart known as "Graf Friedrich," wherein the bride, as she is returning from her wedding, falls from her horse and is mortally injured. Her father captures the heartbroken young husband, kills him, and, as an added indignity, drags his body behind his horse. The miracle of the flowers happens at once. Lilies spring up and bloom where the young husband is buried. Some Estonians claim that the lilies were laid out in such a way as to spell the words "Here lies one of God's best loved" or "He was loved of God." Others claim that the words were written on the lilies.

A substantial part of this legend crossed the narrow Baltic Sea, and was localized, made over, and adopted by the Finns, the Swedes, the Norwegians, the Danes, and the Icelanders. In some places it was "Hildebrand and Hilde"; in others, "Ribold and Guldborg"; and in still others it was known as "Ribbalds kvaeði." A century later it turned up in England and Scotland and was called either "Earl Brand" or "The Douglas Tragedy." In America many versions of "Earl Brand" have been encountered, one of which is called "Brandy-wine."

Thus we have Graf Friedrich, Hildebrand and Hilde, Earl Brand, and finally Brandywine; and the legends told throughout centuries of telling, involving many languages and climes, are as similar as the names involved — Hildebrand, Earl Brand, and Brandywine.

# Lord William's Death

## (Niles No. 5 A)

SOLOMON and Beth Holcolm of Whitesburg, Ky., knew this version of the ballad of "Earl Brand" as "Lord William's Death," and they argued considerably during the singing of it. Once it seemed that they would never come to the end of a rather pointless discussion. So far as I could observe, this was a strange situation in the Holcolm family, because they usually agreed nicely. In this instance, each offered a small portion of the text and then claimed that the part offered by the other was incorrect. Much of the disagreement concerned the advice and counsel offered by Lord William's horse. Finally, they got together on both text and tune. It was a matter of being patient with a wonderful pair of old people, who were also quite ill.

The melodic material was a modal tune, and one of the most beautiful. Before the singing began, Solomon wanted it understood that he might insert something concerning "a watery cross." Beth would have none of it. I now realize that Solomon Holcolm remembered a version of "Earl Brand" more nearly like the one I took down from an inmate of the Breathitt County (Ky.) jailhouse in 1913. (This is offered later as No. 5 C.)

Another point Solomon wanted settled was this troublesome business of not using names. It would seem that Solomon was better informed on the magical power of a combatant's remaining unnamed. This idea never occurred to Beth, and as she was a very strong personality, she carried the day. In the Icelandic version of this ballad the hero named Ribbald and the heroine, Gull-brún, find themselves confronted with an outraged father, eleven brothers, and seven brothers-in-law. The hero calmly ties his horse and directs his stolen bride to take up her sewing, and then three times forbids her to name him by his name during the coming battle. Richard Wagner has Lohengrin warn Elsa only twice in a similar situation. Of course, Lohengrin had only one adversary, while poor Ribbald fought and destroyed nineteen foes before he was felled because Gullbrún cried out his name. In the Holcolm version, the only possible reference to the speaking of the name is found in stanza 7, where the girl is said to "hold so silent."

Finally, the singing began, and I sat still as a mouse, listening and writing in my small notebook. As I look back to that day, I believe I never expected them to sing the ballad to the end. But they did. There were a few halts and some sharp discussions — sharp for those two old people. Neighbors walked by and stopped to watch, wonderingly. I feared they might try to get into the performance, but they did not. I finally took down 15 verses and asked for repeats on several of them.

When at last I had finished with my notes and was trying to thank the Holcolms and tell them goodbye, Solomon took me aside and gave me some fatherly advice about getting along with women-persons. He told me that when he was a young man he used to sing "Lord William's Death" in a much different manner. But time had taught him to make peace with a woman whenever he could, and that was why he let his wife have her way. In his early days, Solomon said, there was a talking horse in the ballad, and a wise talking horse it was, too. But nowadays, "People hain't got no interest in talkin' animals of any kind, and particularly, talkin' horses."

Solomon walked with me to the front gate, and there he unfolded a tale about a talking horse and a talking dog. I had heard my father tell the same tale with certain additions and variations, but I took down Solomon's version eagerly. It seems that two of Solomon's friends were driving into Whitesburg from the direction of Hazard, Ky. They were bringing some ginseng plants to a so-called "sang" buyer. They were driving a good-looking 16-hand horse to a light wagon, and as they drove along they were discussing politics. On the side of the road about five miles from town they saw a largish shepherd-type dog, standing quite still, with one of his paws pointed upward.

"Jump up, jump up," said Fred.

The dog jumped up and sat on the floor of the wagon, between the two men.

At first there was a deep silence. Then the dog spoke up and said, "It's been a dry fall."

"That's right," said the driver. "Been a dry summer, too."

"If it don't soon take to rainin'," continued the dog, "the corn crop won't be worth shockin'. Then there'll be no shelter or food for the small furry beasties. No game, no huntin' . . . It'll be bad . . ."

"That's right," Fred agreed. Turning to his companion, he whispered, "This dog is *talkin'* to me!" His companion nodded, quite speechless.

Finally, they came to the bridge.

"I'll get down here," said the dog politely.

"Whoa, Julius Caesar, whoa!" said Fred.

"Thanks ever so much," said the dog. "It was

"Good morning," said the dog. "Be you fine men goin' into Hazard?"

The occupants of the wagon heard the dog speak, but they were so surprised that they made no move to stop.

"I say," cried the dog, "could you give me a lift into Hazard?"

Whereupon Fred, who was driving, said, "Whoa, Julius Caesar!"

"I'm just goin' as far as the bridge, before you come to the graveyard. I'm on my way to visit some friends, and . . ."

very kind of you-all. I'll move on now and look up my friends." And he trotted off in the direction of some buildings on the right.

Fred looked at his companion in complete consternation. "Charlie, did you hear that? The dog was talkin' to me!"

But before Charlie could answer, Fred's horse, Julius Caesar, swung his head around and said, "Well, and what's so awful unusual about that?"

Here, then, are the verses of "Lord William's Death":

# Lord William's Death

## (Niles No. 5 A)

"A-wake, ye sev-en sleep-ers, And take a warn-ing of me:— I will not have— your eld-est girl, But the wee— one rides with me, fa la la, The wee one rides with me, fa la le, By the lit-tle Bin-o-ry."—

*(Dorian mode on C)*

1. "Awake, ye seven sleepers,
   And take a warning of me:
   I will not have your eldest girl,
   But the wee one rides with me, fa la la,
   The wee one rides with me, fa la le,
   By the little Binory."

2. "Rised up, my seven sons,
   Put on your armor bright,
   No man shall say that a steward's son
   Took my daughter away by night, fa la la,
   Took my daughter away by night, fa la le,
   By the little Binory."

3. "I thank you, sir, I thank you,
   But it can plainly be seen
   That I could not be a steward's son
   With my mother quite a queen, fa la la,
   With my mother quite a queen, fa la le,
   By the little Binory."

4. He mounted her on a milk-white horse,
   Himself on a dapple gray,
   And he swung his bugle horn down at his side
   And so went singing away, fa la la,
   And so went singing away, fa la le,
   By the little Binory.

5. They had not gone a furlong
   When he cast his eyes around,
   And there came her father and all seven brothers,
   Came trippling over the ground, fa la la,
   Came trippling over the ground, fa la le,
   By the little Binory.

6. "Light down, light down, fair Ellen,
   And hold my gray by the rein,
   While I do play with your father dear
   And all seven brothers again, fa la la,
   And all seven brothers again, fa la le,
   By the little Binory."

7. She held, she held so silent,
   And never shed a tear
   Until she saw her brothers fall
   And the father who loved her so dear, fa la la,
   And the father who loved her so dear, fa la le,
   By the little Binory.

8. "Hold hard, hold hard, Lord William,
   Your hand so strong and so sore,
   For I could have many lovers true,
   But fathers I never have more, fa la la,
   But fathers I never have more, fa la le,
   By the little Binory."

9. The milk-white horse she mounted
   Himself on the dapple gray,
   And with his buckler low down at his side,
   They sadly rode away, fa la la,
   They sadly rode away, fa la le,
   By the little Binory.

10. They rode to his mother's castle
    And loudly tingled the ring,
    Saying: "Mother awake or Mother asleep,
    Oh pray come let us in, fa la la,
    Oh pray come let us in, fa la le,
    By the little Binory."

11. "Oh Sister dear, go make my bed,
    For my wounds are deep and sore.
    Oh Mother dear, come bind up my head,
    For you never will bind it more, fa la la,
    For you never will bind it more, fa la le,
    By the little Binory."

12. It was three hours till morning,
    The cocks began to crow,
    When seven wounds Lord William had,
    Began his blood to flow, fa la la,
    Began his blood to flow, fa la le,
    By the little Binory.

13. Now William died like hit was today,
    Fair Ellen she died of a morrow.
    Lord William died of his wounds so sore,
    Fair Ellen she died of sorrow, fa la la,
    Fair Ellen she died of sorrow, fa la le,
    By the little Binory.

14. They lay fair Ellen in the near churchyard,
    Lord William just beside her,
    And from his heart grew a red, red rose,
    And from her heart a briar, fa la la,
    And from her heart a briar, fa la le,
    By the little Binory.

15. They grew so close to the church's wall
    Till they could not grow no higher,
    They grew till they tied a true-lovers' knot,
    With the red rose a-hugging the briar, fa la la,
    With the red rose a-hugging the briar, fa la le,
    By the little Binory.

# William and Ellen

## (Niles No. 5 B)

(*Minor mode on F*)

1. Lord William fetchèd up his bride,
   He fetchèd up his horse,
   Said: "If we fail at the watery ford,
   We'll suffer then a loss."
   We'll suffer then a loss, a loss,

2. His horse's name was Pointed Star,
   And then he quickly said,
   "If you don't call me by my name,
   We'll leave them all cold dead, cold dead,
   We'll leave them all cold dead."

3. "Oh Ellen, Ellen, tell me true,
   'Tis now you must decide,
   It's go back to your mother dear
   Or stay and die my bride, my bride,
   Or stay and die my bride."

4. There was no wedding on that day,
   No wedding on that night,
   For they were dead and laid to rest
   With chant and candlelight, light, light,
   With chant and candlelight.

5. His mother died account of grief,
   Of sorrow died his bride,
   And there they laid the three to rest
   In churchyard side by side, side, side,
   In churchyard side by side.

6. Come all young men and ladies,
   Who yearn for love's delight,
   Remember how Lord William's rose
   Hugged Ellen's briar so tight, so tight,
   Hugged Ellen's briar so tight.

# William and Ellen

## (Niles No. 5 B)

In a blacksmith shop in Hazard, Ky., on April 7, 1913, I encountered a group of men who were celebrating an election victory. As well as I can remember, it concerned the election of a county school superintendent. I sang for them, and they sang for me. In my field notebook I find the results of that day, copied and dated July 4, 1916. It all stems from the singing of Red Jules Napier and Black Jules Napier, both blacksmith's helpers, and Mr. Chester Staffer, a onetime schoolteacher in the neighborhood of Cumberland, Ky. The Napier boys (locally pronounced "Napper") were foils for one another. They could have been end men in a minstrel show. Mr. Staffer prompted the performance and corrected the singers when they got off the melodic line. There was a considerable amount of good-natured argument and fun; at one point, there was a bit of name calling, but the Brothers Napier decided to take Mr. Staffer's advice, and after that all went well. I think I should say that they always addressed the onetime schoolteacher as *Mr.* Staffer.

The Napier boys had been singers all their days, having been members of a "singing meeting" where hymns of the *Sacred Harp* and *Southern Harmony* variety were sung. But when they were away from church groups, they were noisy, combative, and amusing. They treated me with great consideration. I think this was because I was "well related" in the southeastern Kentucky counties, being blood-kin to the Tollivers. The itinerant Mr. Staffer, their constant companion, was a well-informed person who worked on a farm near Cumberland and also in a ginseng arbor near Hazard.

Some years later I discovered that the Napier boys got into some local family trouble (the word "feud" is not generally accepted in the mountains), and went to Oklahoma for safety. I never saw Mr. Staffer again.

# Brandywine

## (Niles No. 5 C)

*(Minor mode on G)*

1. "Oh Brandywine, my Brandywine,
   Why did you steal my pearl?
   Why did you ride the countryside
   And rune my youngest girl?
   And rune my youngest girl?"

2. Oh, they traveled far, and they traveled fast,
   And never stopped in between,
   Because his father was a king
   And his mother a Quaker queen.
   *(repeat last line of each verse)*

3. He spake unto his faithful horse,
   And speaking, thus spake he:
   "Pray carry us over this watery creek,
   And your name unsaid shall be."

4. Oh, they crossèd o'er the watery creek,
   And once on t'other side,
   Her father's men were a-waiting there
   With their horses neatly tied.

5. "Oh come, my dear, and come you quick,
   And hold the horse I ride,
   And never name me by my name
   If you would be my bride."

6. "Oh Brandywine, for love of me,
   Hold your hand so sore,
   For if my people all are dead,
   I'll ne'er have people more."

7. He knockèd on his mother's door,
   He cried to be let in:
   "Oh Mother, I am wounded more
   Than ever man has been."

8. He died before the cocks did crow,
   She died before the dawn,
   And just as day was breaking,
   His mother, too, was gone.

9. They buried them a-side by side,
   And when the rose and briar
   Had reached the top, they tied a knot
   'Cause they couldn't go no higher.

# Brandywine

## (Niles No. 5 C)

JUBIE GABBARD had struck a railway conductor, and in the hot month of July 1913 he was jail-hampered in Breathitt County, Ky. There must have been more than a charge of "striking," but I never went into it. The railway conductor in question was not overly popular in Jackson, the county seat of Breathitt, and so in some quarters Jubie Gabbard was looked upon as a kind of public benefactor. Gabbard was later released, because no one would testify except the railway conductor.

"Yes," Jubie said to me, "I've done a lot of sittin' in jails and courthouses, and I've decided that there be three kinds of folks in courtrooms. First, there's them as has just been elected to office. Then there be those who is cravin' to get theirselves elected — and there's a lot of back-slappin' and handshakin' among 'em. But the third kind of folks is the sorriest of all. They is the folks who want to get out of jail, and they is the backslappinest backslappers of 'em all. I'm one of 'em, friend, and I know."

As a singer Jubie was noisy and inaccurate, but full of gusto. In spite of the tragic quality of his text, he managed to make the first verse definitely funny through his use of the word "ruin," which he pronounced "rune." The word itself is not unusual in the mountains, being employed to indicate that a young woman's reputation has been hopelessly damaged. The tune Gabbard used is exceptionally fine.

Note that in the third verse the taboo against the use of the proper name is extended to the horse. And, in the fifth verse, true to tradition, Brandywine asks his bride not to mention his name. The puzzling reference to "Quaker queen" in verse 2 is probably a corruption of "quite a queen."

# 6

# The Fair Flower of Northumberland

(Child No. 9)

## The Deceivèd Girl
(Niles No. 6 A)
## The Sinful Maiden
(Niles No. 6 B)
## Sin's Reward
(Niles No. 6 C)

THIS BALLAD, formerly popular in Scotland, usually concerns a lady of high position who makes the error of falling in love with an imprisoned man and then helping him to escape. The lady supplies horses and money for the trip.

The lady has indeed been deceived. She has been promised marriage and the treatment of a great lady. When she at last discovers that the promises are false, the lady offers to be the servant of the man she hoped to marry, but she will not be his mistress. She finally gets back to her original home and is taken back into the family and is comforted, and almost honored, in the manner of the prodigal son.

The three fragmentary versions of this ballad in my collection came from singers who hoped they were teaching a lesson by singing the verses. One of my informants was an ardent shape-note singer. Another was a revivalist. The third was Solomon Holcolm, who was teasing his wife.

## The Deceivèd Girl

### (Niles No. 6 A)

LIKE MANY another unemployed person in 1932, Taylor Mullens was making a living as an odd-jobs man. He collected wild ginseng, and he worked in a bed of cultivated ginseng near Hazard, Ky. He was a member of a very large family of folks. One can find branches of the Mullens family all through the southeastern counties of Kentucky. This particular member of the clan was a small man, and rather shy. His voice was faint and his singing was inaccurate, but he stuck to his text, never changing a word in five or six performances. He was a church member and loved to sing hymns. Although he didn't own a shape-note hymnal, he loved to sing with the shape-note singers. One may note the hymnlike nature of his melody.

40

I got in touch with this man through "Ma" Hibbler, the owner of several hotels in Hazard. She had employed him in the past and had discovered that he sang at his work. I didn't even have to look him up. Mrs. Hibbler sent out word, and the next day there was Taylor Mullens, hat in hand, ready to "make talk." It was the easiest folklore collecting I had done in some time.

I sang for him, of course, to get things under way, and the entire hotel lobby filled up with a continually moving audience. But Taylor remained a little shy about singing and took to telling me about himself. While assuring me of his high standing as a law-abiding citizen, he also boasted a bit about his knowledge of the jailhouses in the surrounding counties. He said that he was willing to take an oath that he had never been jail-hampered, but, at the same time, he claimed to know quite a lot about such places. His knowledge came, according to his statement, from carrying messages and small gifts of food to inmates of the county jails. Said Mullens: "Mr. John, jails all smell alike. They is a stink to 'em a body can never forget. No matter how they wash 'em — and they wash 'em little enough — they stink just the same." I had been in and out of almost every jail in the southeastern counties of Kentucky, jailhouses being excellent repositories of singers, and I knew Mullens was right.

A crony type who was sitting nearby, listening to Mullens, was greatly amused at Mullens's statement concerning the messages and small gifts he had brought to prisoners. "Messages and small gifts!" laughed the crony. "Why, mister,

that Taylor Mullens once took a hacksaw, a file, and a small wrecking bar right past the turnkey here in Hazard, and handed 'em to a cousin of his'n." Mullens never bothered to contradict this statement, and I assumed it to be true.

I asked him about the ginseng business, and he said it was slow. And then he added, "Hit's a pain." With an eye toward an increased market for wild roots and herbs, he asked me if city people drank "sassafack" tea. I had to discourage him on this score, for I thought that few city people ever drank it, and those few were people who had grown up in the country and had discovered the delights of sassafras tea as children on the farm.

"Hit's a great drink," Mullens declared. "Hit's good for the old man's disease, hit'll help the diabeter, hit's good for the kidney, hit'll thin the blood . . . why, mister, hit'll do you good and help you, too."

He assured me that he could dig, wash, split, and tie a hundred bundles of sassafras root in a day. Though I was greatly given to sassafras tea, a hundred bundles of the root were more than I could encompass.

Finally, when I began to wonder whether I was trying to assemble a collection of folklore or a treatise on wild medicinal herbs, my informant went to singing in a shy, inaccurate manner. But it was a beginning, and before noon of that day I had a clear copy of a ballad which Mullens called "The Deceivèd Maiden." It was, in fact, a native version of "The Fair Flower of Northumberland."

Here are Taylor Mullens's verses and his tune:

# The Deceivèd Girl

## (Niles No. 6 A)

(Major mode on F)

1. As she walked past the jailhouse door,
   She spied a man with head hung low,
   And all because of bolts and bars,
   His homeland he would never know.

2. "I am a prisoner far from home,
   But if you'll only steal the key,
   I'll take you where the grass grows green,
   And make of you a great lady."

3. "I cannot go, I will not go,
   And be your great lady,
   For you have got a Scotland wife,
   And you've got babies three."

4. She's done to her father's stable,
   She's done to her mother's till,
   She's got the jailhouse key so large,
   And she's galloped o'er the hill.

5. And as they galloped o'er the plain,
   It was "my dearling dear,"
   But as they came to Scotland,
   Well changèd was this cheer.

6. "Oh pity, pity, pity, please,
   As I did pity thee,
   Or fling me from your castle's walls
   And break my slim body."

7. "But how can I have pity
   When you are just a whore?
   Now get you back to England
   Where I'll see you no more!"

8. "Oh false and faithless knight," said she,
   "I'll to my father's door,
   And he will prove to Scotland
   That I have never been whore."

9. Her mother, who was truly queen,
   She gently then did smile:
   "You're not the first, nor only one,
   The Scotsmen did beguile."

10. Come all ye maidens, young and old,
    Pray come, be warned of me —
    Scots were never, never true,
    And Scots will never be.

# The Sinful Maiden

## (Niles No. 6 B)

ON JULY 5, 1932, it was dreadfully hot in Whitesburg, Ky., and Solomon Holcolm was engaged in teasing his wife Beth. The burden of the teasing was the waywardness of females generally. So long as the Holcolms were not singing the same song, they got on quite well. In the case of "The Sinful Maiden," Aunt Beth sat back with a small smile on her lips, and never said a word. Solomon finally concluded that there was no way for a woman-person to answer the facts in "The Sinful Maiden." I can testify

that, on this occasion, no answer was attempted.

After the singing was over, and I had sung 16 verses of "Barb'ry Ellen," Solomon said: "This-here ballad about the sinful maiden is a backward thing. Hit never tells what sinful thing she up and done. Now lettin' a man outa jail is no sin. Matter of fact, Holy Writ is full of times when men got let outa jail when the jailer wasn't a-lookin'. No, hit's not the lettin' outa jail that matters; hit's what happened after that jail-hampered feller got out . . . I always did say that

# The Sinful Maiden
## (Niles No. 6 B)

(Minor mode on A)

1. As she walked by the jailhouse,
   She heard a fellow say:
   "It's getting awful lonesome here,
   I'd like to get away."

2. Then, as she was a silly one,
   And in her nonage, too,
   She stole the key and let him out,
   A thing she'd often rue.

3. "Oh Mother and oh Father,
   He said I'd be his wife.
   He said he'd love and cherish me
   As long as I had life.

4. "But now I'm coming home to you,
   And I hope you'll let me in,
   And soon forget the day that I
   Committed all this sin."

girls had no business a-hangin' around jailhouses, even when the jailer was handy and a-lookin' on."

Solomon Holcolm offered all this information in the hope that Aunt Beth would make some comment, but she held her peace.

# Sin's Reward

## (Niles No. 6 C)

THIS SONG was taken down from the singing of Preacher Marcum, who was carrying on a "tent preaching" (a protracted meeting) near Clay City, Ky., in July 1932. His home was in Breathitt County, in the Leatherwood district. He demanded to sing the song privately for me because there were words in it that would offend a Christian woman. It was the only "ballard" he would sing, and he made the exception because "Sin's Reward" possessed a powerful moral.

The melodic material was either not taken down or it was lost; at least, it does not appear on the page with the text. Here we have a version of "The Fair Flower of Northumberland" in which revenge is promised — a feature that does not appear in any of the original versions in Child's collection: the young lady's father "will repay." When Preacher Marcum came to the evil word, he lowered his voice to a whisper.

## Sin's Reward

1. As she did pass the jailhouse
   She heard a man make moan,
   "I am a prisoner far from friends,
   And I am sad and lone."
2. "I'd like to help you, my kind sir,
   I'd like to do you well,
   But you have wife and chil-der-en,
   'Tis simple for to tell."

3. She helped him to his freedom,
   She helped him to a horse,
   She helped herself to trouble,
   Her honor was a loss.

4. He was a gay deceiver,
   She should have known before,
   Now for her care and trouble,
   She's got to be a whore.

5. "Come back, my child, my only one,
   And harken what I say,
   The ills this prisoner did you
   Your father will repay."

# 7

# The Twa Sisters

(Child No. 10)

### The Old Lord by the Northern Sea
(Niles No. 7 A)

### Bowie, Bowerie
(Niles No. 7 B)

### The Little Drownded Girl
(Niles No. 7 C)

THE SUPERNATURAL elements in this ballad are found in nearly all the English, Scottish, Danish, Swedish, Norwegian, Icelandic, Finnish, Estonian, Lithuanian, Slovak, Polish, German, and Spanish versions. In America the supernatural is found very rarely; in fact, out of scores and scores of versions of "The Twa Sisters" known to Americans by oral tradition, I have encountered only two in which the supernatural plays a part — one from the state of Maine and one from North Carolina.

None of the 3 versions of "The Twa Sisters" found in this collection has even the slightest reference to the supernatural. The melodic material is, however, of the highest order.

The many reported discoveries of "The Twa Sisters" in America are indicated on succeeding pages. It would be a great service to musicians generally if all the melodies could be transcribed and preserved. A detailed study of this ballad has been made by Paul G. Brewster of Indiana University.

## The Old Lord by the Northern Sea
### (Niles No. 7 A)

UNDER DATE OF August 1933 in my field notebook I discover that Miss Doanie Fugate sang a delightful version of the justly famous ballad entitled "The Twa Sisters." Further information about Miss Fugate was as follows: "about 13 years of age, quite fat and gay." She lived in the Lost Creek community of Breathitt County,

Ky. In my field notes I marked the fact that Miss Fugate sang a full 4th measure. Prior to meeting her, I had been trying to dance to almost the same melodic material, but always felt there was a measure lost somewhere. Miss Fugate was the first singer I encountered who filled out the 4th measure.

# The Old Lord by the Northern Sea

## (Niles No. 7 A)

*Brightly*

There lived an old lord by the North-ern Sea, Bow down, _____ There lived an old lord by the North-ern Sea, The boughs they bend_ to me; _____ There lived an old lord by the North-ern Sea, And he had daugh-ters one, two, three, That will be true, true to my love, Love and my love will be true to me.

*(Major mode on F)*

# The Old Lord by the Northern Sea
## (Niles No. 7 A)

1. There lived an old lord by the Northern Sea,
   *Bow down,*
   There lived an old lord by the Northern Sea,
   *The boughs they bend to me;*
   There lived an old lord by the Northern Sea,
   And he had daughters one, two, three,
   *That will be true, true to my love,*
   *Love and my love will be true to me.*

2. A young man come a-courtin' there,
   *Bow down,*
   A young man come a-courtin' there,
   *The boughs they bend to me;*
   A young man come a-courtin' there,
   His natural choice was the young and the fair,
   *That will be true, true to my love,*
   *Love and my love will be true to me.*

3. He gave his love a gay gold ring,
   And the family thought 'twas a sinful thing.

4. He gave his love a beaver hat,
   The ugly sister thought hard of that.

5. "Oh Sister fair, let's we walk out,
   And venture where ships go sailing about."

6. They walkèd near the salty brim,
   And the mean one pushed the fair one in.

7. "Oh Sister dear, pray lend thy hand,
   And I will give thee my farming land."

8. "I'll neither lend thee hand nor glove,
   But I will have thine own true love."

9. Away she sank as the current ran,
   And into the miller's race she swam.

10. The miller said, "If you'll give me a groat,
    I'll fish you out by your petticoat."

11. He robbed her of her gay gold ring,
    And then he pushed her in agin.

12. The miller was hung for what he take,
    And the ugly sister was burned at the stake.

# Bowie, Bowerie

## (Niles No. 7 B)

(Dorian mode on F)

1. *Bow-ie bow-er-ie,*
   A lord once lived by the deep blue sea,
   He had daughters one, two, three,
   *Bow-ie bow-er-ie bow-ie,*
   *Bow-er-ie bow down-er-ie.*

2. *Bow-ie bow-er-ie,*
   A young knight came his court to pay,
   He did choose the beauty and the gay,
   *Bow-ie bow-er-ie bow-ie,*
   *Bow-er-ie bow down-er-ie.*

3. The daughters walked on ocean's rim,
   The mean one pushed the beauty in.

4. "If you will lend your lily-white hand,
   I'll give you my fee and my land."

5. "I'll neither lend you either hand,
   'Cause I will have your lover and your land."

6. The miller pushed her farther in,
   He wanted of her silly* pin.

7. And when she died, the fiddles played,
   Her father heard how she had been slayed.†

8. The miller and the ugly one
   Hanged for the murder they had done.

# Bowie, Bowerie

## (Niles No. 7 B)

IT WAS a soft-spoken, bewhiskered old man named Arlie Tolliver who sang "Bowie, Bowerie" at Cumberland, Ky., on July 12, 1932. Here we find a shortened version of the great ballad of "The Twa Sisters." Child gives two versions running to 28 verses. In this variant the story is told in 8 verses. Arlie Tolliver was old and bent with years, but his singing voice was clear and accurate. Before he would start singing, however, I had to sing for about an hour. After that, it was not easy to stop him.

I gave him a twist of chewing tobacco, which he seemed to prize very much. Later, when I was getting ready to take my leave, he took me aside and said: "I wonder — be they any drinkin' liquor in that fancy-lookin' automobile of yourn?" I told him no, and reminded him that it was against the law to transport drinkin' liquor in automobiles, plain or fancy. He looked disappointed and said, "I was only a-askin'."

# The Little Drownded Girl

## (Niles No. 7 C)

IT WAS in front of the Hatcher Hotel in Pikeville, Ky., and the date was July 16, 1932, and the singer was named Pat (Patterson) Whetmore, and the ballad was a very interesting version of

"The Twa Sisters." As soon as he began to sing, I realized that he must have had some form of musical experience. He sang accurately, and though his tune was not overly original, it was

* Silver.

† This verse could be construed as a reference to the supernatural. In some of the original versions, bones from the slain maiden's body are made into a harp, and the harp sings out the story of the murder.

# The Little Drownded Girl

## (Niles No. 7 C)

*(Major mode on D)*

graceful, and he sang it very charmingly.

On further investigation I discovered that Pat Whetmore had been a dance caller all his life and had recently been as far away as Prestonsburg, Paintsville, and Louisa, either playing fiddle for dances or calling sets. He was about 55 years of age, unmarried, and had a slight limp. Here follows Pat Whetmore's way of singing "The Twa Sisters," which he called "The Little Drownded Girl."

# The Little Drownded Girl
## (Niles No. 7 C)

1. *Derry derry down and around the old piney tree,*
   I know a lord who lived by the Northern Sea,
   He had daughters by one and by two, three,
   *Derry derry down and around the old piney tree.*

2. *Derry derry down and around the old piney tree,*
   "Sister, fish me out of the raging sea,
   You may have my own true lover-ee."
   *Derry derry down and around the old piney tree.*

3. She did swim around so heartily,
   Until she sank and she did drowndery.

4. She was stripped to her bare body,
   For her gold and her watches and her fee.

5. They hanged the sister and the miller-ee,
   On a scaffold 'side of the deep blue sea.

# The Cruel Brother

(Child No. 11)

## Brother's Revenge

### (Niles No. 8)

ONE OF the first things a criminal investigator does in trying to solve a crime is to establish a motive: Why was the crime committed? In the case of "Brother's Revenge," which is in reality "The Cruel Brother," Child No. 11, we have no way of establishing the reason for the crime. A brother stabs his sister on her wedding day as she is leaving on her honeymoon.

By inference the ballad tells us that the brother was not consulted about this marriage. The mother, the father, and the sister of the bride were asked and their consent obtained. The brother was left out. Thus, jealousy may have been the motive, but this seems unlikely. The

facts behind the ballad of "The Cruel Brother" may include incest.

This ballad has not often been reported in the United States. For that matter, although it is widespread in the Old World, it has not been encountered or reported many times in any one country. It is a limited part of the oral tradition of Italy, Denmark, Finland, France, Portugal, and Spain.

Attempts have been made to associate this ballad with the widely known German ballad of "Graf Friedrich," but the ballad of "Earl Brand" seems to be a closer parallel to "Graf Friedrich."

## Brother's Revenge

### (Niles No. 8)

"BROTHER'S REVENGE" was sung by Granny Holcolm (no close kin to the Holcolms of Whitesburg) in Kingdom Come Valley, Harlan County, Ky., on July 7, 1932. In those days, getting in and out of Kingdom Come Valley involved driving a car over a road better suited to oxcarts. Furthermore, there was no way of getting food or fuel once you left the main high-

way (U.S. Route 119). The food generously offered by the local people was heavy and not overly digestible. The wise visitor carried his own provisions.

Granny Holcolm was of great age. Her neighbors said, "She's up in age." Some said she was "nigh on to 95." She was greatly bent with years and arthritis. She had very clear memories of

# Brother's Revenge

## (Niles No. 8)

*(Dorian mode on E)*

the War Between the States. Her grandson teased her, saying she had "fit Indians." She had lived through all the family wars of the valley, made famous by John Fox, Jr., in "The Little Shepherd of Kingdom Come." When asked whether she had ever encountered Mr. Fox, she said she had not, and that she had never heard

the word "fox" applied to a man — "foxy" perhaps, but never the word "fox" alone. She had a fine sense of humor and was said to have been a great beauty in her youth — "in her flash," as her family put it.

At first Granny Holcolm recited the verses of "Brother's Revenge," and then she sang the entire ballad. At one point, several members of her family put on a great show of being shocked. Granny Holcolm said: "I'm a-singin' the ballad for this young man the way I know it to be, and if you people can't stummick it, then get out of earshot." And she continued with her head held high.

## Brother's Revenge (Niles No. 8)

1. Three fine maids did play at ball,
   *Il-e-o-lay and a lullay gay,*
   Three fine maids did play at ball,
   Came three lords and wooèd them all,
   *Il-e-o-lay and a lullay gay.*

2. The first young lord was dressed in yellow,
   *Il-e-o-lay and a lullay gay,*
   The first young lord was dressed in yellow,
   "Come, fair maid, and be my marrow."*
   *Il-e-o-lay and a lullay gay.*

3. The second lord was dressed in red,
   "Come, fair maid, and grace my bed."

4. The last of the lords was dressed in green,
   "Come, fair maid, and be my queen."

5. "You must ask my father dear,
   Mother, too, who did me bear."

6. "I have asked them one and all,
   Save Sister Anne and Brother John."

7. Father dear did lead her down,
   Mother, sister kissed her crown.

8. John did place her on her steed
   Ere he did the cruel deed.

9. "Kiss me, Sister, ere you part."
   As he kissed, he stabbed her heart.

10. "Would that I were on yonder stile,
    That I might rest and bleed a while.

11. "Carry me to yon little green hill,
    That I might rest and make my will."

12. "What will you give your father dear?"
    "The milk-white steed that carried me here."

13. "What will you give your mother own?"
    "She may have my blood-stained gown."

14. "What will you give your brother John?"
    "A gallow's pin to hang him on!"

---

* A companion, partner, or mate (about 1440).

# Lord Randal

(Child No. 12)

Jimmy Randal
(Niles No. 9 A)

Tiranti, My Love
(Niles No. 9 B)

Sir Walter Scott, who has been alternately cursed and blessed by modern folklorists, made an equivocal, almost timid statement (I mean timid, for Sir Walter) concerning the possible origin of the legend behind the great tragic ballad of "Lord Randal." Scott said: "I think it is not impossible that this ballad may have originally regarded the death of Thomas Randolph, or Randal, Earl of Murray, nephew of Robert Bruce, and the Governor of Scotland, who died at Musselburgh in 1332."

An English priest was implicated in the plot — an English priest who prepared what was called a "cankered confection." This was eaten by Thomas Randolph at a feast at Wemyss by the sea. Thereupon Thomas Randolph died slowly and painfully. Scott continues, declaring: "The substitution of some venomous reptile for food, or putting it into liquor, was anciently supposed to be a common mode of administering poison." We might add that poisoning was a time-honored method of disposing of one's enemies.

But 116 years before the death of Thomas Randolph, Governor of Scotland, an unhappy, unsuccessful, world-weary king named John, being set upon by a French invasion, crossed an inlet from The Wash late one October day, lost all the royal English treasury, and his crown, in a sudden rush of the tide, and in a heartbroken way turned his horse northward in the direction of the Cistercian monastery at Swineshead. Although he was already suffering from dysentery, on arrival he sat down to a heavy meal, topping it off with some peaches and a great tankard of ale.

He was suddenly taken violently ill and declared that the monks had poisoned him. Not even the Abbot of Croxton, who was greatly talented in the physic of the day, could save the King. John was finally moved to the palace of the Bishop of Lincoln at Newark, and there he died on October 19, 1216.

Almost at once a legend sprang up concerning the King's death. It concerned one of the Cistercian brothers, who was said to have added the blood of a toad to the tankard of ale, and being forced by the King to drink first, went into the monastery garden and died immediately. This situation was taken up by Shakespeare and used in the final scenes of the play *King John*.

We find, however, from the writings of the Countess Evelyn Martinengo-Cesaresco, that in 17th-century Italy the plot material and almost the exact lines of the dialogue between mother and son in "Lord Randal" appear in an Italian popular folk ballad. The dates of this discovery are 1629 in Verona and 1656 in Florence.

The Countess Martinengo-Cesaresco suggests that what we now call "Lord Randal" might have started out as the report of a crime in the Middle Ages and traveled from Italy to England and Scotland by way of the continual interchange of populations — that is, by way of the crusaders, pilgrims, church dignitaries, and their hosts of guards, servants, and supernumeraries. Owing to the similarity of the questions and answers, the Countess makes bold to declare that the ballad moved across the world in song form and not as a disjointed spoken legend. She further calls attention to the fact that wherever the ballad appears, there is usually a cooked eel in it somewhere, and this item is taken as the means of poisoning.

I have investigated 52 American versions of the ballad of "Lord Randal," and I have found that 40 of them indicate that the poisoning was accomplished by way of cooked eels. The remaining 12 mention cold poison, snake heads, parsnips, and other less interesting dishes. To increase their indigestibility, the eels are nearly always fried, and the frying compound varies all the way from butter to soap grease.

The very name "Lord Randal" is rather arbitrary, because the word "Randal" appears very rarely in the verses of the ballad. Some of the more interesting names are: Johnny Randolph; Johnny Randal; Johnny Ramsey; Henry, My Son; McDonald; Willie, Oh Willie; Johnny Reeler; Johnny Reelsey; John Willow; Johnny Elzie; Tiranti, My Son; Jimmy Randal; Charley Harley, My Son; Sweet Nelson, My Boy; King Henry; Laird Rowlands; My Own Pretty Boy; My Bonny Wee Croodlin' Doo; Fair Andrew, My Son; Oh Billy, My Boy.

The ballad of "Lord Randal" is very widely distributed. Besides the English-Scottish, Italian, and American versions already mentioned, evidences of this ballad have been reported from Germany, Holland, Scandinavia, the Baltic States, Iceland, the Setu people, the Magyars, and the Wends.

# Jimmy Randal

## (Niles No. 9 A)

THIS VERSION of "Lord Randal" was taken from the singing of Solomon and Beth Holcolm in Whitesburg, Ky., on July 8, 1932. The singers were in agreement all the while.

# Jimmy Randal

## (Niles No. 9 A)

*(Dorian mode on G)*

1. "Oh where have you been, Jimmy Randal, my son,
   Oh where have you rovèd, my oldest dear one?"
   "Oh Mither, oh Mither, go make my bed soon,
   'Cause my courtin' has sicked me and I fain would lay doon."

2. "What had you for supper, Jimmy Randal, my son,
   What had you for supper, my oldest dear one?"
   "Some fried eels and parsnips, go make my bed soon,
   'Cause my courtin' has sicked me and I fain would lay doon."

3. "What will you give me, Jimmy Randal, my son,
   What will you your mother, my oldest dear one?"
   "My house and my lands, Mither, make my bed soon,
   'Cause my courtin' has sicked me and I fain would lay doon."

4. "What will you your father, Jimmy Randal, my son,
   What will you your father, my oldest dear one?"
   "My wagon and team, Mither, make my bed soon,
   'Cause my courtin' has sicked me and I fain would lay doon."

5. "What will you your brother, Jimmy Randal, my son,
   What will you your brother, my oldest dear one?"
   "My horn and my hound, Mither, make my bed soon,
   'Cause my courtin' has sicked me and I fain would lay doon."

6. "What will you your sweetheart, Jimmy Randal, my son,
   What will you your sweetheart, my oldest dear one?"
   "Bullrushes, bullrushes, and them all parched brown,
   'Cause she gave me the pizen that I did drink down."

7. "And when you are dead, Jimmy Randal, my son,
   And when you are dead, my oldest dear one?"
   "Go dig me a grave 'side my grandfather's son,
   'Cause my courtin' has sicked me and I fain would lay doon."

# Tiranti, My Love

### (Niles No. 9 B)

THE SINGER, Mrs. Molly Ratliff, was 68 years of age, and she lived in Madison County, Ky. She had been at the loom as a weaver since her 14th year. Born in Clay County and brought up in Madison County, she had married a Mr. Ratliff, who came from Breathitt County. She had 9 living children, 32 grandchildren, and 1 great-grandchild. She had sung "Tiranti, My Love" in

# Tiranti, My Love

## (Niles No. 9 B)

(*Minor mode on A*)

her youth, with many more verses than the four she could recall on May 15, 1934.

The singer pronounced the first syllable of "Tiranti" with a long *i* (as in "lie"), with great emphasis on this syllable. Her sense of humor led her to make the entire performance a little bit funny. However, her tune is one of the finest.

# Tiranti, My Love (Niles No. 9 B)

1. "Oh where have you been, Tiranti, my love,
   And why are you home so soon?"
   "It's I've been a-courting, oh Mother dear,
   And I'm dying to lie down."

2. "What did you eat, Tiranti, my love,
   What did you eat, my son?"
   "Some pizened eels, oh Mother dear,
   But I ate only one."

3. "One eel is enough, my little son,
   Yes, one will surely do.
   But two would be too many eels
   For one bonny boy like you.

4. "Oh what will you give the great lady
   Who was to you untrue?"
   "A strong piece of rope for hanging, for hanging,
   And that will hardly do."

# Edward

(Child No. 13)

## The Murdered Brother

(Niles No. 10)

T HE BALLAD of "Edward" has long been considered (to quote Child) "one of the noblest and most sterling specimens of the popular ballad." In spite of all this, the ballad is not widespread. In fact, it is more often found in oral tradition in America than in the parent countries of England and Scotland. "Edward" is found in Sweden, Denmark, Finland, and Germany. In each of these countries, the story is told almost exactly as it is told in the English and Scottish versions. The title of the Finnish ballad, "Brother-Murderer," is not so far from the title indicated by my North Carolina informant — "The Murdered Brother."

There is an odd similarity between certain portions of "Edward" and the ballad "Lizie Wan," but this can never dim the beauty of this short, powerful example of popular balladry.

## The Murdered Brother

(Niles No. 10)

ALTHOUGH the singer called her ballad "The Murdered Brother," it is beyond all doubt the truly great ballad of "Edward." The notes were taken down on August 2, 1934, in Saluda, N. C., from the singing and recitation of Aunt Selina Metcalf. Before she began to sing, she said: "Would you like to hear me tell the story of 'The Murdered Brother'?" I said I would rather hear her sing it. But she quickly went into the recitation of the verses. I believe she did this to rehearse her performance a bit. Once she had begun to sing, she never varied from text or tune. She admitted to 77 years, but she looked much older. In another notebook I have found her age indicated as unknown.

Aunt Selina's husband, Uncle George Metcalf, was a basketweaver and even made trunk baskets, with tops and hinges and locks. He said he was born at Travelers Rest, N. C. He seemed to be even older than his wife Selina.

Uncle George told me that he had been a nighttime fox hunter ever since he was "knee-high to a duck." He thought that nighttime fox hunting was being destroyed by the daytime fox hunters. I reminded him that daytime fox hunting was not overly benefited by the nighttime operations.

# The Murdered Brother
## (Niles No. 10)

(Dorian mode on D)

# The Murdered Brother (Niles No. 10)

1. "How come that blood on your own coat sleeve?
   Little son, pray come tell me."
   "It is the blood of that skinny greyhound
   That tracèd the fox for me,
   That tracèd the fox for me."

2. "Too pale, too pale for that skinny greyhound,
   Too pale, little son, too pale."
   "It is the blood of that old gray mare
   That plowèd the corn for me."
   (*repeat last line of each verse*)

3. "Too red, too red for that old gray mare,
   Too red, little son, too red."
   "It is the blood of your youngest son,
   And the truth I have told to you."

4. "Oh what, oh what, fell ye out about?
   Little son, pray come tell me."
   " 'Twas over a wand, and a withy-withy wand
   That never could be a tree."

5. "Oh what will you do when your father comes home?
   Little son, pray come tell me."
   "My foot I will place on an old oakum boat
   And sail me across the sea."

6. "Oh what will you do with your newly wed wife?
   Little son, pray come tell me."
   "I'll save her the grief, and I'll save her the pain,
   And take her for company."

7. "Oh what will you do with your sweet little boy?
   Little son, pray come tell me."
   "I'll leave him alone for to wait and to wonder
   What's come of his mammy and me."

8. "When will you come back to your mother again?
   Little son, pray come tell me."
   "When the moon and the sun and the stars set together,
   And that will never be."

He admitted this, reluctantly. Selina listened to our discussion with considerable interest. Finally, turning to me, she said: "Be you a daytime or a nighttime fox hunter?" I admitted I favored the daytime variety. "Well now," she said, "I'm pleasured to hear it. A daytime fox hunter is a great comfort to a woman. This nighttime fox hunting gives a woman a lonely bed." I was marveling at this 77-year-old woman who yearned for a man to grace her bed, when Aunt Selina went on, and rather sadly, too: "Once a man gets into the habit of this nighttime fox hunting, he'd a heap rather listen to the music of the hounds than to hear his old wife snore."

It is interesting to note how these two wonderful old people had taken what they remembered of the great ballad "Edward" and localized it with the introduction of the old gray mare and the plowing of corn — and with the omission of the hawk, whose blood is credited with the stain in some of the Old World versions. In the hunting of fox, I have not encountered the use of greyhounds, at least not in the United States. However, the greyhound appears in Child's texts and is probably a carryover from England and Scotland.

According to my notes, here are the text and tune of "Edward" as the Metcalfs sang it to me 25 years ago in Saluda. When the singing was over, I made a few additional notes, folded up my books, and took my leave. Once I looked back and saw that they had gone to work again, weaving on the opposite ends of a large trunk-type basket. I never saw them again.

# 11

# Babylon; or, The Bonnie Banks o Fordie

(Child No. 14)

## Bonny Farday

(Niles No. 11)

**F**IVE VERSIONS of this ballad appear in the Child collection, and it has been encountered in Denmark, Sweden, Norway, Iceland, and the Faroe Islands. On our continent it is not too widespread, though a few examples have been found in Newfoundland, Maine, Vermont, Virginia, Tennessee, North Carolina, and, as in the following example, in Kentucky. The story of this ballad is told more fully and effectively in the tradition of the Scandinavian countries, but even here it is not often encountered.

The Scandinavian versions are almost all more violent, more bloody, and more tragic than the English-Scottish-American counterparts. Even so, the Kentucky text presents 14 verses of the starkest tragedy, interspersed with refrains concerning the "jury flower and rosemary" (probably a corruption of "dewy flower"). The melodic material is natural and delightful, if not of the most important kind.

## Bonny Farday

(Niles No. 11)

THIS KENTUCKY variant of the tragic ballad of "Babylon; or, The Bonnie Banks o Fordie" was sung on July 2, 1932, on the sidewalk near the Hibbler Hotel in Hazard, Ky. The singer was named Preston Little, and he was assisted by a friend named Roscoe Phipps. Phipps made only a few suggestions, and these in so low a voice as to be inaudible to me. Preston Little did not know how old he was, but he said he came from Owsley County, and as a young man he had sung much "old-timey" music. He said his friend Phipps once sang in a church choir. They made quite a picture, both having white whiskers.

After the singing was over, I proposed that Mr. Little and Mr. Phipps come into the hotel and have a bite of food with me (I referred to it as a "bait" of food). "Better not do it," said Mr. Little, and Mr. Phipps nodded assent. "You

# Bonny Farday

## (Niles No. 11)

**Tenderly reminiscent**

Three fine la - dies lived in a bow'r - y, Ju - ry flow'r and rose - mar - y,

Three fine la - dies lived in a bow'r - y, They went forth in a

field that was flow'r - y, Ju - ry flow'r and rose - mar - y. ____

*(Minor mode on E)*

see, Mr. John, we hain't got no womenfolk to look after us. Our clothes hain't much to brag on, and we hain't shaved. Fact is, my friend Roscoe Phipps hain't shaved in thirty years. He quit shavin' the day his wife left 'im. She said he was a drunk-man and a ne'er-do-weel. Roscoe didn't much want to support her. She was always a-hankerin' fer things. As a feller says, Mr. John, hit takes two fools to make a bad bargain."

Mr. Phipps's eyes lighted up, and once I thought he would speak in an audible voice, but he merely smiled. They were both unbelievably old. Later I discovered that they lived in a cellar and had their meals at a Methodist preacher's back door. "Good meals, too," said Mr. Little, his head on a side. "Good meals, considerin' the hard times we're a-livin' in."

Here are the verses and the tune of the tragic ballad of "Bonny Farday." Of course, Preston Little did the singing, but, as well as I can remember, the silent partner, Roscoe Phipps, prompted him once or twice.

## Bonny Farday (Niles No. 11)

1. Three fine ladies lived in a bow'ry,
   *Jury flow'r and rosemary,*
   Three fine ladies lived in a bow'ry,
   They went forth in a field that was flow'ry,
   *Jury flow'r and rosemary.*

2. They pulled flow'rs by two, by three,
   *Jury flow'r and rosemary,*
   They pulled flow'rs by two, by three.
   A man come, bent on a robbery,
   *Jury flow'r and rosemary.*

3. He asked one sister would she wife.
   He robbed her of her own sweet life.

4. He buried her so tenderly
   To keep the flowers company.

5. He took the second by the hand,
   He made her lightly step and stand.

6. He asked this sister would she wife,
   Or would she die by his wee knife.

7. She would not wife, she would not bide,
   So at that robber's hand she died.

8. So like the first he laid her by,
   To keep the flowers company.

9. He took the wee one by the hand,
   She would not step, she would not stand.

10. Said, "I'll not marry such as you,
    Who killed my sisters one and two.

11. "Among my kin my brother strong
    Will kill you for this very wrong."

12. "What name, what name, what name, my fay?"
    "My brother's name is Bonny Farday."

13. "Oh Sister dear, what can I do
    But kill myself in room of you?

14. "Come dig my grave full wide and deep
    And place my sisters at my feet."

# Hind Horn

(Child No. 17)

## The Pale Ring
(Niles No. 12 A)

## The Jeweled Ring
(Niles No. 12 B)

"THE PALE RING" is really the cheerful ballad of "Hind Horn." I say cheerful because the ballad has a happy ending. The synthetic, sentimental drivel of modern soap opera cannot even compete with the plot complications of the original legend of "Hind Horn." In olden times, this legend had a story line developed in three long narrative poems, or romances. The first of these, "King Horn," is no doubt from the latter part of the 13th century and runs to 1550 short verses. The second, possibly from the 14th century, is called "Horn et Rymenhild" and covers 5250 verses; and the third, also from the 14th century, is called "Horn Childe and Maiden Rimnild" and is told in almost 100 twelve-line stanzas.

The vast complications of a 5000-verse poem could hardly be reduced to 10 short couplets, but the portion of the idea which could be absorbed, understood, and remembered by the English and Scottish people who immigrated to North America three hundred years ago remains in the American versions of today.

The original story behind the ballad of "Hind Horn" is somewhat after this fashion: a young man, Hind Horn, usually a born Scotsman, has served his king an apprenticeship of seven years. Meanwhile, he has fallen in love with the King's daughter, sometimes called Jean or Princess

Jean. For reasons undisclosed, the King is angered with Hind Horn and sends him off to sea — again, for a period of seven years. Before his departure, his sweetheart gives him a ring containing a magic stone. So long as she is faithful to him, the ring will retain its lustrous color; but it will turn pale and lifeless if she loves another man. One fine day Hind Horn discovers that the ring has turned pale and wan, and he starts for home at once. He exchanges clothing with a ragged beggar when he finds out that his sweetheart Jean has indeed married another and that the wedding feast has already lasted anywhere from 8 to 42 days. Jean, however, will not go to the wedding bed until she has the final word on the fate of Hind Horn. In beggar's clothing, Hind Horn approaches the castle and asks for a drink of wine. The new bride comes down, gives the man the drink, and as he drinks, he slips the ring into the cup. Jean recognizes her true love, although he is dressed in rags, and takes him to her heart, and there is a happy ending for a change. Nothing is said about the husband whom the bride wedded, and nearly bedded. Presumably, he wasn't so gay.

The French version of this romance is six times as long as the 13th-century English gest of 1550 verses. These 10,000 French verses in a modern translation with proper illustrations might become a best-seller. Of course, they would have to be made over into prose if a wide public were expected to read the book. I make this statement because the story contains the elements thought to be important for the success of a piece of fiction — plot and suspense.

A list of the countries where the legend has been reported would simply be a list of all the countries of continental Europe, Scandinavia, Russia, and, of course, the British Isles. In spite of all this, it is very rare in the United States.

# The Pale Ring

## (Niles No. 12 A)

"THE PALE RING" was sung by James Duff on the courthouse lawn at Hazard, Ky., on a Sunday afternoon of July 1932. He sang the 5th verse several times and employed the word "tress" alternately with the word "hair." Finally he decided that "hair" was the better choice. His singing of the melodic line was accurate, and his use of the raised 6th and 7th was clear at all times. He was amused to discover that I had spent the previous night in the county jail, interviewing the drunks and brawlers.

The only other evidence of this ballad I have ever encountered is a single verse sung by the Mulleneoux family in Jefferson County, Ky.

James Duff was a willing singer so far as the first performance was concerned, but he was reluctant to sing anything over the second time, and did so only at my insistence. I wanted to ask him to sing the 9th verse a second time, but he was getting weary, and there were several other numbers yet to write down. So I contented myself with the word "not" though it did sound somewhat like "na." He was delighted with the last verse. "They did things direct in them days," said he with a knowing smile on his leathery face.

It was rumored about that James Duff had once aspired to the ministry. A friend of his said, "Why, Jimmy was *that* anxious to become a preacher that he even learned to read and write." This was in 1872, when he had just turned 20. Duff had some very clear memories

of the War Between the States, referring to the entire operation as "a power of coat-turnin' and bush-whackin'." Before the evening was over he sang a fragment of a carol which I later developed into "When Jesus Lived in Galilee." James Duff was full of contradictions. At one time, he would appear to be an embittered old man; and later he could be both amusing and poetic.

In 1912 the Consolidation Coal Company had discovered a rich vein of coal on his farm, and from that date for many years onward Duff enjoyed a limited form of comfort. The same friend who had commented on his ambitions for the ministry said: "Yep, Jimmy had money in the bank. Once owned an automobile . . ."

Just as I was about to put away my notebooks, Duff asked, "Stranger, do you know a play-party song about the rabbit and the hunter?" I said no, and opened my field notebook. Duff sang in stentorian tones:

*"Rabbit, rabbit, where you goin'?"*
*"No time to talk 'cause there's a man just behin',*
*With a gun, and a pistol, and a great big knife,*
*Tryin' fer to kill me in the middle of my life,*
    *Oh Lordie, Lordie, Lordie."*

James Duff had quite an audience as he sat on the courthouse lawn at Hazard, on that hot Sunday afternoon so many years ago, and sang the following verses:

# The Pale Ring

## (Niles No. 12 A)

*(Melodic minor mode on E)*

1. When this ring is pale and wan,
   *Fa-le-la-le lu-le-la,*
   When this ring is pale and wan,
   Then my true love will be gone.

2. Once he look his jewel on,
   *Fa-le-la-le lu-le-la,*
   Once he look his jewel on,
   Saw that his was pale and wan.

3. When he came to her fine hall,
   He was dressed in scarlet all.

4. There he cast off scarlet red,
   There he begged for his bread.

5. When the bride tripped down the stair,
   See the lovely golden hair.

6. See the wineglass in her hand
   For the poor old beggarman.

7. As he drank the lastest drop,
   Dropped the ring in from the top.

8. "Got ye it by sea or land,
   Or off drownded man's cold hand?"

9. " 'Twas not* got by sea or land,
   But did come from your dear hand."

10. Off the beggar's rags he shed,
    Hind Horn took the bride to bed.

* Perhaps "na" for "not."

# The Jeweled Ring

## (Niles No. 12 B)

FROM THE SINGING of some members of the Mulleneoux family in Jefferson County, Ky. The music to "The Jeweled Ring" was either lost or never taken down. The date was August 12, 1908. The Mulleneoux family, and particularly Pete Mulleneoux, will be discussed in connection with the ballads "Oh Judy, My Judy" (Niles No. 16 C) and "Two Old Crows" (Niles No. 17 C).

### The Jeweled Ring

My jeweled ring is pale and wan,
My true love is surely gone.
When my love is married up,
She will find it in her wine cup.

# 13

# Sir Lionel

(Child No. 18)

**Old Bangum**
(Niles No. 13 A)

**Rurey Bain**
(Niles No. 13 B)

**Bangum and the Bo'**
(Niles No. 13 C)

THE SWINE BALLAD of "Sir Lionel" appears in this collection as "Old Bangum," "Rurey Bain," and "Bangum and the Bo'." Killing wild boars was a favorite pastime for the knightly figures of ancient legend. The English and Scottish texts offered by Child are not all complete, but they do tell essentially the same story. In some instances, the rescue of a fair lady provides the motivation for the slaying of the boar — a situation that is missing in the American counterparts.

Anyone who has seen an enraged wild boar — or, for that matter, an enraged tame boar — will understand the problems confronting the boar's adversary. In my life I have seen both wild and tame boars, and I believe that when enraged they are as terrifying as a Bengal tiger or a medium tank.

In the American texts Old Bangum fights the boar only four hours. In the Old World, the battle goes on for days, and at one point the victorious knight requires 30 days to recover from his wounds. As a rule, the American texts are very short, and the only subject under discussion is the actual battle between the man and the boar and the woman who owned the boar.

# Old Bangum

(Niles No. 13 A)

ELLA WILSON, onetime slave and a truly wonderful elderly person, sang this ballad for me. (She also sang "The Hangman," Niles No. 39 A, and in this connection, more information about Ella Wilson will be found.) She was very ill when she sang "Old Bangum," and I made the journey up to her cabin, northwest of the village of Murphy, N. C., to bring her food, drink, medicine, and soap. She was very helpful, and perhaps one of the most willing singers I ever encountered. The time was August 1936, and my notes indicate a hot, overcast day.

# Old Bangum

## ( Niles No. 13 A )

(Minor mode on F)

## Old Bangum (Niles No. 13 A)

1. Old Bangum he did hunt and ride,
   *Cairo kimbo dillie-down-day-o,*
   Old Bangum he did hunt and ride,
   *Cairo kimbo dillie,*
   Old Bangum he did hunt and ride,
   Sword and pistol by his side,
   *Cairo kimbo dillie-down-day,*
   *Cairo dillie-down-day-o.*

2. They be a wild bo' in dese woods,
   *Cairo kimbo dillie-down-day-o,*
   They be a wild bo' in dese woods,
   *Cairo kimbo dillie,*
   They be a wild bo' in dese woods,
   Eats men and women, drinks dey blood,
   *Cairo kimbo dillie-down-day,*
   *Cairo dillie-down-day-o.*

3. Bangum fired his pistol off,
   Bo' he didn't more than cough.

4. Bangum pulled his mighty knife,
   Swore he'd take that wild bo's life.

5. Bo' he make a mighty sound,
   Tromp dose bushes all around.

6. Fit four hours in one day,
   Bo' he bled and sunk away.

7. When dat woman fit and flew,
   Bangum cut her through and through.

# Rurey Bain

## (Niles No. 13 B)

THE SINGER, Walter McCoy, was a handyman. In some parts of the world he might have been called a man of all work. He claimed to own a gold mine and, for a small sum, offered me digging rights. I did not take up the offer, being otherwise engaged; furthermore, the clerk at the Highlands Country Club (N. C.) warned me of the rattlesnake danger. It was very pleasant at Highlands, and I was delighted to make the acquaintance of Mr. McCoy and hear him sing his variant of the great ballad "Sir Lionel." He called it "Rurey Bain," or "Crazy Sal and Her Pig." My mind went back to the almost forgotten pig-woman who had been so famous for a season in the old Hall-Mills murder trial.

Mr. McCoy was the only singer I have ever met who had the disturbing habit of singing his verses in the wrong order. He actually sang the verses of "Rurey Bain" as follows: 1, 4, 2, 3, 6, 5. Then he went back and sang them in the correct order.

In this ballad we find a man fighting with a magical sword made of silver and tipped with gold, suggesting that both the boar and his mistress had supernatural powers, for it is against such adversaries that weapons of precious metal are in order. Even so, Rurey Bain dies, and in true ballad style he, the boar, and the boar's mistress are buried in a common grave.

# Rurey Bain

## (Niles No. 13 B)

*(Minor mode on G)*

1. Crazy Sal, she lived in a wood,
   She owned the wildest pig.
   His legs were long, his backbone sharp,
   His tushes powerful big, big, big,
   His tushes powerful big.

2. Young Rurey Bain he drew his spear,
   Then with a mighty roar,
   Thrashing down the tallest trees
   Here come this mighty boar, boar, boar,
   Here come this mighty boar.

3. Then Rurey drew his pointed sword
   And swung with all his might,
   And there the boar lay moanin',
   His head was cut off quite, quite, quite,
   His head was cut off quite.

4. "Why did you kill my lovely boar?
   He always did me good,
   A-wandering where the nuts did fall,
   A-rooting for his food, food, food,
   A-rooting for his food."

5. A many a man had fit that boar
   With swords, some new, some old.
   But Rurey Bain had a silver blade
   All tipped with a point of gold, gold, gold,
   All tipped with a point of gold.

6. Now when the fight was ended,
   Crazy Sal was slain,
   And they buried the boar and his mistress
   With the body of Rurey Bain, Bain, Bain,
   With the body of Rurey Bain.

# Bangum and the Bo'
## (Niles No. 13 C)

JUST ACROSS the street from the hotel in Morristown, Tenn., there was a filling station with car washing as a sideline. One of the car washers was a colored man of undetermined age named Eddie Stiles. In early June 1934 Eddie Stiles washed my car and discovered that I was interested in the music of the countryside. He at once went into the singing of a rather disconnected version of "Sir Lionel." Both text and tune varied from time to time, but by taking him through his song several times I finally got 3 verses down on paper.

He said his mother (then dead twenty years) used to sing about "Old Bangum" and also about "The Hangman's Rope." In Eddie Stiles's version, the battle between Bangum and the boar is fought offstage, as it were, and all we discover is that Bangum arrives in view with the bo'-hog on his shoulder. From this I assume that Bangum was a person of great strength. A wild boar, weighing from 200 to 300 pounds on foot, would be a formidable load once killed.

After considerable backing and filling, my car was properly washed, and I paid Eddie, thinking the transaction was over. Again I was mistaken. Eddie took me aside and said: "I've got a girl who don't think much of me. She's stuck on a banjo-picker who works daytimes at the hotel. How about me takin' you and one of your dulcimers over to see her? You could sing her into thinkin' well of me . . ."

I talked Eddie out of this plan by proposing another, whereby he was to bring his girl friend to the gas station and I would sing for her there. Eddie seemed to think well of the new plan. He said, " 'Course, you ain't in no position to beat my time 'cause you is white and she is colored, and then you's goin' on your way in the mornin'."

I went back to the hotel, thought it all over, paid my bill, and moved on through the night to Asheville, N. C. What happened to Eddie Stiles and his lady friend I never knew.

This is how Eddie Stiles sang "Bangum and the Bo' ":

# Bangum and the Bo'

## (Niles No. 13 C)

Bang-um come out of de wood,— Bo'— on he shoul-der. Bang-um he— was ver - y young, Dat— bo' was more old - er.—

*(Minor mode on A)*

1. Bangum come out of de wood,
   Bo' on he shoulder.
   Bangum he was very young,
   Dat bo' was more older.

2. Pray, brother, brother pray.
   I am sanctify,
   Ask Ole Bangum when I die.
   Pray, brother, brother pray.

3. Oh, white man he lef',
   Ole Bangum he right,
   Forty-four when I fight.
   Pray, brother, brother pray.

# 14

# The Cruel Mother

(Child No. 20)

### Three Little Babies
(Niles No. 14 A)
### The Lady of York
(Niles No. 14 B)

O F THE 13 texts of "The Cruel Mother" offered by Child, less than half are complete. The ballad has been encountered many times in America, and very seldom is the story told fully. Until 1870 it had not been encountered in Denmark. That year, however, a folklore collector, working in Jutland, reported the ballad twice, and the similarity between the versions from Scotland and Jutland is surprising. One of these Danish texts runs to 18 verses and tells the story in its entirety. Although Child refers to the German and Wendish versions as "probable variations" of the English, Scottish, and Irish texts, we must admit that these "probable variations" are widespread and might be of equal antiquity.

With a few local changes, the story is almost the same wherever it is encountered. An unmarried girl of some importance produces issue — sometimes as many as three children. She destroys them, and although their feet are tied to prevent their walking as ghosts, they appear, denounce their mother, and make some dire prophecies concerning her future here and hereafter. In some of the Teutonic texts the devil himself appears and takes the hapless mother off with him. In America it is, as one of my informants said, "the tale of a child-killing female who tried to palm herself off as an honest person."

# Three Little Babies

(Niles No. 14 A)

THIS VERSION of "The Cruel Mother," entitled "Three Little Babies," was sung to me on July 16, 1936, by Granny Hannah Smith, who lived at a place called Willscott Mountain in Cherokee County, N. C. At first, the singer's pitch on the A-flats and B-flats was variable. This was especially true with the A-flat in the 2nd and 10th measures. After the 2nd verse, however, and in all the repetitions, Granny Smith's singing was very accurate. Later in the same day, she taught me her version of "The Cuckoo."

# Three Little Babies

## (Niles No. 14 A)

*Forebodingly*

Three lit - tle ba - bies danc - in' at the ball, Down by the green - wood side - ee - o, "Oh babes, oh babes, if you was mine, All a - lone, a - lone, a - lone, I'd dress you up in silk so fine, Down by the green - wood side - ee - o."

*(Mixolydian and major modes on C)*

### Three Little Babies (Niles No. 14 A)

1. Three little babies dancin' at the ball,
   *Down by the greenwood side-ee-o,*
   "Oh babes, oh babes, if you was mine,
   *All alone, alone, alone,*
   I'd dress you up in silk so fine,
   *Down by the greenwood side-ee-o."*

2. "Oh Mother dear, when we were yourn,
   *Down by the greenwood side-ee-o,*
   You had nothing to wrap us in,
   *All alone, alone, alone,*
   'Cept an old apron, and that right thin,
   *Down by the greenwood side-ee-o.*

3. "You leaned yourself against an oak,
   And then you leaned against a thorn,
   Falsehearted mother, we were born.

4. "You took a penknife keen and sharp,
   And placed that penknife to our heart,
   And prayed to the Lord we would depart.

5. "You buried us under a marble stone,
   You buried us under a marble stone,
   And prayed to the Lord hit would never be
   known."

# The Lady of York

## (Niles No. 14 B)

IN JUNE 1934, at a place about five miles from Trade, Tenn., I encountered a lacemaker named Aunt Didie Netherly, who was nearing 90 and was still working regularly, turning out enough handmade lace to support herself and several menfolk quite adequately. The menfolk never appeared. I was under the impression that Aunt Didie gave the orders in the Netherly cabin. I also observed that she spoke disparagingly of all males. She had the delightful habit of offering advice and gratuitous information without any advance notice. Once she said to me: "A skeleton is a man with his insides out and his outsides off." Her statement, humorous though it was, had no relation whatever to the previous conversation.

She told me that she had been baptized in her 86th year, that she was now 87½ years old, and had not cussed a single cuss since baptism. She also said she had made enough tied lace in her lifetime to stretch from Trade to Oregon. One of her enterprises was the making of Battenberg lace. It is made of linen tape sewed onto a paper design and connected with the most intricate kind of threadwork.

Her bitterness concerning the people in her community expressed itself in her frequent narration of the famous "drap-sucker" yarn — a story in which a man is made out a fool by a piece of machinery. She is even credited with having invented the tale.

This is how Aunt Didie told the story of the drap-sucker: "Once upon a time there be a tore-down person in these parts, a tore-down person name of Smathers, who owned an old patched-up automobile that had been turned into a kind of bus. Now this bus operated over some very pore roads in the back end of our county. Fact

# The Lady of York

## (Niles No. 14 B)

*(Minor mode on A)*

of the matter is, this bus operated in some places where a self-respecting mule would be 'shamed to go. Of course, the bus was out of order most of the time. The plugs burned out, and the gears stripped, and the bottom of the crankcase got knocked loose, so as to lose most of the oil, and somehow that caused the motor to get hotter than it should, and then the bearings burned out . . .

"One day this pore tore-down bus operator, name of Smathers, and his patched-up bus was stalled on the side of Hogback Mountain. The bus was full of impatient people. They wanted to get to Willowstand before sundown. There was a lot of mutterin' and squabblin' and pushin' goin' on inside that bus.

"So Mr. Smathers lifted up the hood of his injine and said, real sad like: 'Folks, I reckon we come to the end of the bus business, 'cause this injine is nothin' but a drap-sucker. Hit sucks over a drap of gas, and hit fires and stops, and then if I crank hard enough, hit'll suck over another drap of gas, and hit'll fire and stop again. Hit's a pure drap-sucker, and not unlike some folks I know, human drap-suckers just like this wore-out injine o' mine. They suck up a drap of gas and they fire and stop, and if someone is handy to crank 'em up, they'll suck and fire — and stop. Over and over again. Drap-suckers they are — always needin' some other body to crank 'em.' "

When she sang "The Lady of York," however, Aunt Didie seemed to be a different kind of person. For a few moments she could forget her 87 years of poverty and slim rewards. "The Lady of York" was, in fact, "The Cruel Mother." She had reduced the text to 9 verses, action-packed and tragic. Her melodic material, while not of the very best, was managed clearly and accurately. She was a willing informant.

At the conclusion of the song I thanked Aunt Didie, and started to take my leave, but she, following her process of uttering disassociated statements, turned to me and said: "Young man, I want you to know that hit takes a liar to raise gourds." This was a widely accepted old wives' tale, but coming from Aunt Didie Netherly, it sounded quite a lot like Holy Writ.

Here are the verses of her version of "The Cruel Mother":

## The Lady of York (Niles No. 14 B)

1. A great lady livèd all in York,
       *Allay, allay, and all alone,*
   A great lady livèd all in York,
   And she was much loved by her father's clerk,*
       *While the babes are under the marble stone.*

2. She went into the deep oak wood,
       *Allay, allay, and all alone,*
   She went into the deep oak wood,
   And birthed her babes as best she could,
       *While the babes are under the marble stone.*

3. She leanèd the oak, she leaned the thorn,
   Fornenst† the sky her babes were born.

4. She took her dress off o'er her head
   To wrap up her babes when they were dead.

5. She walkèd in her bowery hall,
   The fairest maid of maidens all.

6. "Come, pretty boys, what play at ball,
   I'll dress you up in satlins‡ all."

7. "Oh Mother dear, when we were thine,
   You robbed us of our life divine.

8. "You have some clothes in every press,
   But we were wropped in your bloody dress.

9. "Oh mother dear, hell is so deep,
   And lossèd souls in hell do weep."

---

* Aunt Didie made no attempt to rhyme "clerk" with "York."          † Opposite to, against or under.          ‡ Satins.

# 15

# The Maid and the Palmer

(Child No. 21)

## Seven Years

(Niles No. 15)

Although this ballad is found in the Faroe Islands, Finland, Norway, Sweden, Iceland, Denmark, Moravia, among the Wends, in France, Germany, and Spain, it has been encountered only once in England, once (as far as I have been able to tell) in a fragment from Scotland and once, again in fragmentary form, in the United States.

Modern theology is unwilling to admit that Mary Magdalene (Luke 8:2) and the woman of Capurnaum (Luke 7:37–50) are one and the same. Neither is it safe to say that the woman of Samaria (John 4:9–29) may be confused with either of the above. But the ballad muse is not subject to theological regulations. In the ballad, the Magdalen and the Samaritan woman are confounded and compounded, with "The Maid and the Palmer" as the result.

The extravagant acts of penance required in the Scandinavian versions of this ballad seem as nothing compared with the demands made in the English text and in the Scottish and American fragments. It is to be regretted that no music came with the American version.

The following was written in 1674 concerning a palmer: "The pilgrim had some home or dwelling place, but the palmer had none. The pilgrim traveled to some certain designed place,

but the palmer to all places. The pilgrim went on his own charges, but the palmer professed willful poverty and went upon alms."

A palmer can be defined as an itinerant monk under a perpetual vow of poverty or a perpetual pilgrim newly returned from the Holy Land, in token of which he carried a palm branch or palm leaf. Living as they did by begging, palmers became quite expert at it.

In the Child text of "The Maid and the Palmer" (which derives from the Percy MS), the story is along these lines: an old palmer meets a maid at the well and asks for a drink of water. She refuses, saying she has neither "cupp nor cann" for the purpose. He replies that if her lover came from Rome, she would soon find cups and cans in abundance. She declares that she has no lover; whereupon the palmer reminds her that she has borne nine children and killed them all. The maid repents forthwith and begs the palmer to assign her penance. He tells her that seven years she shall be a steppingstone,

*"Other seaven a clapper in a bell*
*Other 7 to lead an ape in hell."*

At the end of the 21-year penance, she is to return home, with her sins forgiven.

# Seven Years

## (Niles No. 15)

THESE VERSES were recited, not sung, to me by a young member of the Holcolm family in Kingdom Come Valley — a girl about nine years old. Everyone else had either sung or told some tall tale, and the little girl felt she should make a contribution to the day. The result was a 3-stanza version of "The Maid and the Palmer." The child's grandmother said that the three verses had come from an uncle, whose name, unfortunately, I did not get.

This is obviously a condensation of Child No. 21. In the original ballad, the palmer claims that the maid has slain 9 babies. In Kingdom Come, the number is reduced to 3. Portions of the refrain are somewhat alike, and the penance demanded in the American version is similar to the palmer's. The promise in the original ballad that, once the penance is performed, the maid will again be a maiden, is lost to us. No doubt it was more than Kentuckians could believe.

## Seven Years

1. "Seven years you shall atone,
   Derry leggo, derry don,
   Your body be a steppingstone,
   Derry leggo downie.

2. "For your sins be as the sea,
   Derry leggo, derry don,
   You did slew your babies three,
   Derry leggo downie."

3. "Though my sins be as the sea,
   Derry leggo, derry don,
   I make a stone for thee,
   Derry leggo downie."

The date was July 7, 1932, and there was the promise of more rain in the air. Earlier on the same morning, I had taken down several important ballads. They were long and involved, and I was weary when I started down the mountain in the direction of Whitesburg and some lunch.

# 16

# Judas

(Child No. 23)

## Judas
(Niles No. 16 A)

## Judas and Jesus
(Niles No. 16 B)

## Oh Judy, My Judy
(Niles No. 16 C)

EVER SINCE the crucifixion of Jesus Christ, a few people in every century have believed that Judas Iscariot did not intend to do Christ a great wrong. They base this conclusion on Judas's reaction to the news that Christ had been convicted and sentenced by Pontius Pilate. We know from Holy Writ that Judas tried to return the thirty pieces of silver, and when this failed, threw the money into the synagogue and destroyed himself by hanging.

During the second century a sectarian gospel was written in the name of Judas. It represented the work and the belief of a group of gnostics called the Cainites. The Cainites apparently believed that Judas committed the betrayal in the hope that Christ would bring about a world-shaking miracle, saving himself from the cross and the nation from the Romans.

We know about this sectarian gospel through the writings of the theologian Irenaeus, Bishop of Lyons, who was born in about A.D. 130, listened to the preaching of Polycarp in Smyrna (as a small child), knew men who had, in turn, known St. John the Disciple, did a great missionary work at Lyons, wrote extensively, and died at an unknown date, possibly around the turn of the 3rd century, martyred under Septimius Severus.

Most of what is written about Judas Iscariot is conjecture. We know from John 13:29 and 30 that Jesus said to Judas, "Buy those things that we have need of against the feast; or, that he should give something to the poor." Following these instructions, Judas went out into the night, and it must have been at this time that he made the arrangements for the betrayal.

The 13th-century text of the ballad of Judas — and apparently the only text coming to us from antiquity — goes into many details not found in the Bible, principally Judas's sister, the discussion with Pilate, and the loss of the money. Later versions of the ballad must have retained these features of the original, which reappear in the American text.

# Judas

## (Niles No. 16 A)

THIS SONG came to me from the singing of a "yarb doctor"* named Mayberry Thomas, a resident of Knoxville, Tenn. When I first knew him in 1929, he and two of his cronies had a little stand in the unused end of the Knoxville public market, where they sold roots, herbs, a liquid made from wild-cherry bark, dried mullen leaves, sassafras, ginseng, March snow-water, the dried root of dandelion, dried jack-in-the-pulpit, love-charm powders, and dozens of similar items. Each dried herb or root was laid out on a scrap of newspaper. The liquids were offered in an odd collection of discarded half-pint whiskey bottles. It was as picturesque a drugstore as one could imagine.

Mayberry Thomas and his two assistants were bearded and somewhat bent but gay and twinkle-eyed and ever ready for fun. In fact, they made so much noise and their sly banter upset the female clientele of the public market so much that they were finally ejected from their corner. From that day on they became pushcart peddlers, with every salable thing they possessed piled onto a rickety, flat-topped wagon. The three old men provided the motive power.

In August 1933 their out-of-doors location was on a street just beside the market. They unloaded their wares and spread them out on an old tarpaulin (pronounced "tarpoleon"), each collection of roots and herbs on its separate scrap of newspaper. They must have had a peddler's license among them, for I observed the local police pass by the herb stand, smile knowingly, and move on.

One of Mayberry Thomas's colleagues told me quietly that the boss (Mr. Thomas) had been "learned to be a preacher" and had preached diligently but with little success. "His vineyard was in and about Maryville, Tennessee," said the bearded informant, "but treckly† he found out that in preachin', like in a lot of other hard-workin' jobs, they was not much fun and very little pay." There was a long pause, and then this gem came out: "Young man, a preacher never gits no rest. When he's a preachin', he sure is a-workin', and when he ain't a-preachin', he has to go right on soundin' and lookin' like the Bible . . . hit ain't no fun."

Mayberry Thomas admitted that in his youth, some verses not unlike the text of his ballad about Judas were sold on broadside sheets‡ by colored preachers in the neighborhood of Chattanooga. He also said that a teacher of shape-note hymn singing named Pushmire once taught the song of Judas and sang it with great energy and noise. "Pushmire's voice was loud and harsh," Thomas said, "and he had a mouthful of store-boughten teeth which clicked and clacked like a snare-drum." He smiled as he remembered his youth, and said, "I ain't no singer . . . not any more, but if my pardners will take care of the trade, I'll sing what I know about Judas."

It took most of the afternoon, but my rewards were rich. Occasionally, he fumbled with the text, but his Dorian scale was accurate, and never once did he change key.

When the singing was over, I asked Mayberry Thomas about his wares. I was especially interested in his love-charm powder. He kept this item hidden, he said, "because of the bothersome old females in this town who want to jail-hamper us." After I assured him that I did not live in

---

* Herb doctor.                                                                  † A corruption of "directly."

‡ The German for this type of imprint is *fliegende Blätter;* the French term is *feuilles volantes*. Broadsides were employed from the very beginning of printing for royal proclamations and papal indulgences. In England, where the broadside had its chief home, they were used for dissemination of the dying speeches and last confessions of criminals, for personal statements and political agitation, and, chiefly, for the publication of ballads. Technically, a broadside is a broadsheet — that is, a single sheet of paper with printed matter found only on one side. The broadside is important in the history of English literature because, in addition to the ballads, the poems of several great English writers, such as Dryden, first appeared in broadside form.

# Judas

## (Niles No. 16 A)

*Reverently*

'Twas___ in the mer - ry___ month___ of May, The
East - er time was near, Our Je - sus to dear
Ju - das said: "I fear my time is
near, is near, I fear my time is near."

*(Dorian mode on G)*

Knoxville and would be gone within twenty-four hours, he admitted that the love powders were made out of pink powdered sugar with a bit of calomel and jalap added. "Of course," he said slyly, "I always sprinkle a drap or two of ten-cent-store perfume onto each powder." A love powder contained what seemed to me to be a teaspoonful. Thomas assured me that he added as much calomel and jalap as he could pick up on the end of his pocketknife. I discovered that love powders sold best on Saturday afternoons and evenings, in the spring of the year.

Here is how Mayberry Thomas remembered the text and tune of "Judas."

## Judas (Niles No. 16 A)

1. 'Twas in the merry month of May,
   The Easter time was near,
   Our Jesus to dear Judas said:
   "I fear my time is near, is near,
   I fear my time is near."

2. "How near, how near, how near, my Lord,
   How near your time, how near?"
   "Thou knowest well, dear Judas,
   Thou knowest well, I fear, I fear,
   Thou knowest well I fear."

3. "Go take thou pieces of silver,
   Take thou pieces of gold,
   Go take them to Jerusalem
   Where bread and meat is sold, is sold,
   Where bread and meat is sold.

4. "Nor tarry long upon the way,
   Nor seek out folk or foe,
   But take your silver pieces
   And to the market go, market go,
   And to the market go."

5. Now Judas had one sister,
   An evil sister she,
   She hated gentle Jesus
   For His Christianity-ee-ee,
   For His Christianity.

6. "Thou shouldst be stonèd, Judas,
   With large stones and with small,
   Thou shouldst be stoned for trusting
   This false prophet of all, of all,
   This false prophet of all."

7. Now Judas took a little rest,
   He took a nap of sleep,
   He laid his head in his sister's lap,
   And there he slept so deep, so deep,
   And there he slept so deep.

8. When Judas woke from sleep and rest,
   He sought his sister dear:
   "Pray help me find my silver,
   'Tis lost, 'tis lost, I fear, I fear,
   'Tis lost, 'tis lost, I fear."

9. Then quickly up spake Pilate,
   Then quickly up spake he:
   "Come sell the prophet Jesus,
   Come sell him unto me, unto me,
   Come sell him unto me."

10. "I will not sell my Jesus,
    Unless it be for meat,
    To feed my hungry brethren
    Who have no meat to eat, to eat,
    Who have no meat to eat."

11. "Oh silence, Peter, silence,
    Silence, for well I know,
    Three times thou wilt deny me,
    Afore the cock doth crow, doth crow,
    Afore the cock doth crow."

# Judas and Jesus
## (Niles No. 16 B)

*In a broad, stately manner*

Ju - das 'trayed Je - sus, and Je - sus hung the cross, ___ Yes, Ju - das 'trayed Je - sus, what a loss, what a loss! ___ Ju - das 'trayed Je - sus and died by his own hand, ___ Oh trou - ble, oh trou - ble, in the Ho - ly Land.

(Minor mode on F♯)

# Judas and Jesus

## (Niles No. 16 B)

ON JUNE 19, 1909, Harkus and Tillie Whitman stopped stacking wood in a charcoal pit and sang me their version of the ballad concerning the betrayal of Jesus Christ. They called it "Judas and Jesus," and it proves to be a distant relative of the original ballad on the same subject. They were kin to the charcoal-burning Mulleneoux family, and they also made their own corn liquor. This distillate was as foul a drink as man ever took. At the same time, both Whitmans were faithful in their attendance at the tent meeting being held not far from Benny Benkirk's saloon at the crossroads, in the south end of Jefferson County, Ky. They called themselves "foot-washers," and made quite a lot of the revivals and tent meetings of the summer of 1909.

The Whitmans had one very pretty daughter of 16 summers, and she had recently run off with a fence-wire drummer. (A drummer was a salesman.) The drummer wore attractive, citified clothes, and he convinced Miss Whitman that she should go to St. Louis with him, foregoing the usual benefits of clergy. According to legend, the two of them intended to take the downriver boat for Cairo, Ill., where they planned to change boats and go up the Mississippi to St. Louis.

They did depart on a night in July 1909. No one ever heard of them again. Harkus Whitman kept a shotgun handy to use on the fence-wire drummer, but the drummer apparently realized that he would be in danger of his life in Jefferson County and no doubt moved his territory to Indiana or even Illinois.

Knowing that the Whitmans had lost their daughter to a fence-wire salesman, I did not expect them to be over full of song. But with the delightful detachment of simple people, they did sing, and I made my notes as rapidly as ever I could. Later I tried to trace the Whitmans' verses to some origin. First I looked through the local hymnbooks, and then through both *The Sacred Harp* and *The Southern Harmony,* but to no avail. In 1909 I had never heard of Francis J. Child.

The text is reminiscent of some of the chantlike sermons in song, usually concerning the cruci-fixion, given by Negro preachers. I was told that some of these preachers were occasionally offer-ing a "hymn" concerning Judas, printed on a broadside sheet. I never saw any of these broadsides.

Here is the way the Whitmans, man and wife, sang "Judas."

## Judas and Jesus

1. Judas 'trayed Jesus, and Jesus hung the cross,
   Yes, Judas 'trayed Jesus, what a loss, what a loss!
   Judas 'trayed Jesus and died by his own hand,
   Oh trouble, oh trouble, in the Holy Land.

2. It was the night of the very last supper,
   They were in a room called the small room upper.
   Jesus said, "Judas, you will 'tray me today,
   Oh Judas, you will 'tray me for gold and for pay."

3. Jesus said, "Peter, you will sure 'tray me,
   But not for pay and not for fee."
   Jesus said, "Come, the cross is on the hill.
   I go to the hanging, 'tis my Father's will."

# Oh Judy, My Judy

## (Niles No. 16 C)

*Slowly and deliberately*

"Oh Ju - dy, my Ju - dy, hit's time that I go, I know you will 'tray me though I love you so. Go take of this mon - ey and buy us some meat, Our breth - ern are hun - gry, got noth - ing to eat."

*(Major mode on G and minor mode on E)*

# Oh Judy, My Judy

## (Niles No. 16 C)

THIS IS FROM the singing of Pete Mulleneoux, who burned charcoal and raised wonderful watermelons for the Louisville market. He lived in a section of Jefferson County, Ky., called the "Wet Woods." On July 4, 1909, the day his text and tune were taken down, he reached 75 years of age. I noted that he owned a copy of *The Sacred Harp,* first published in 1844. He was related in some way to the Whitmans, who lived about two miles away. (Some additional information about this man and his interesting way of life will be found in the discussion of the "Two Old Crows," Niles No. 17 C.)

Mulleneoux's singing of "Oh Judy, My Judy" reminded me of the manner employed by shape-note singers: there was no legato in his performance; it was rather noisy, and in some places even rough. However, it was more a storytelling than a singing performance, and it lacked the religious feeling of the shape-note hymns.

## Oh Judy, My Judy

1. "Oh Judy, my Judy, hit's time that I go,
   I know you will 'tray me though I love you so.
   Go take of this money and buy us some meat,
   Our brethern are hungry, got nothing to eat."

2. For pieces of silver, for pieces of gold,
   Our sweet brother Jesus to soldiers was sold.
   "Oh Judy, oh Judy, today I will die,
   Upon that high hill where the wild birds do fly.

3. "Oh Judy, oh Judy, it's you will die, too,
   Because you did 'tray me when you might-a been true.
   Oh Judy, oh Judy, don't try to deny,
   You sold me to soldiers, and now I must die."

# The Three Ravens

(Child No. 26)

## Lovers' Farewell
### (Niles No. 17 A)
## Willie McGee McGaw
### (Niles No. 17 B)
## Two Old Crows
### (Niles No. 17 C)

WILLIAM CHAPPELL, 19th-century editor and writer (who properly emphasized the necessary relation between words and music in old songs and ballads), brought out a work called *Popular Music of the Olden Time,* in which he tells us that in his time, the ballad of "The Three Ravens" was still so popular in some parts of England and Scotland, that he had "been favored with a variety of copies of it written down from memory; all differing in some respects, both as to words and tune . . ."

This ballad is not often encountered in folk tradition in the United States. However, it has been, and still is, widely sung by men's glee clubs under the burlesque title of "Willie McGee McGaw."

## Lovers' Farewell
### (Niles No. 17 A)

THIS DELIGHTFUL fragment is no doubt what Child would call "a traditionary form of 'The Three Ravens.'" "Lovers' Farewell," like "The Twa Corbies" and other variants, is in fact the corrupted remains of an original ballad.

The text and tune of "Lovers' Farewell" came to me from the singing of a schoolteacher named Miss Alice Wetmore. She was originally from northeastern Alabama, and had been teaching school most recently near Martin, Ky. She had friends or relations in the Line Fork community of Kingdom Come Valley, and was on her way there when I encountered her sitting on the front porch of Aunt Beth Holcolm's home in Whitesburg, Ky.

I sang a little, and so did Aunt Beth, and finally Miss Wetmore came forth with this little gem. Miss Wetmore's performance was very faint but accurate. I never did discover where she learned the ballad. We planned what we

# Lovers' Farewell

## (Niles No. 17 A)

*Gently*

My lov-er did come ere— e-ven-song, And he give me— a fare-well, But the wars that took him to the Low— Coun-try He nev-er a word did— tell, But the wars that took him to the Low— Coun-try He nev-er a word did— tell.

*(Minor mode on G)*

called a "singing bee," but the "singing bee" never took place.

Aunt Beth had been arguing Miss Wetmore into staying with her a while. "Yes," said she, "I've been sweet-talkin' Alice into restin' her things and stoppin' the night with me, but I hain't gettin' nowhere. The roads into Kingdom Come will be middlin' poor after that rain last night."

Miss Wetmore smiled a weary smile and said nothing.

"Why, honey," continued Aunt Beth, "that rain last night was a pure trash-mover. Hit was even a gully-washer and a toad-floater."

We all laughed a bit. I made some notes on Aunt Beth's way of describing a downpour of rain, and Miss Wetmore told us goodbye. I never saw her again.

## Lovers' Farewell (Niles No. 17 A)

1. My lover did come ere evensong,
   And he give me a farewell,
   But the wars that took him to the Low Country
   He never a word did tell,
       But the wars that took him to the Low Country
       He never a word did tell.

2. Oh, he did go to the bloody wars,
   His lance and his shield a-glisten,
   While his lady did weep in her bowing-room,
   And none was there to listen.
       (*repeat last 2 lines of each verse*)

3. Down fell he there, and there to die,
   In the wet of the Low Country,
   And no man knows that he lies there
   But his horse and his hound and his lady Mary.

4. Oh, he may sleep in an open grave,
   Where raven fly and flutter,
   But I will wake on my pallet of grief
   And many a cry will utter.

# Willie McGee McGaw

## (Niles No. 17 B)

*With gay abandon*

Three old crows sat on a tree, Caw, caw, —— caw,

Three old crows sat on a tree, Wil - lie Mc - Gee Mc - Gaw.

Three old crows sat on a tree, They was black as black could be, ——

Wil - lie Mc - Gee Mc - Gee Mc - Gaw, Wil - lie Mc - Gee Mc - Gaw.

*(Dorian mode on D)*

# Willie McGee McGaw

## (Niles No. 17 B)

THIS PIECE of nonsense was sung in my family, for the purpose of creating humor, when I was a boy. Although the situation is not the most amusing, "Willie McGee McGaw" never failed to get a laugh. There were more than 5 verses, but after the 5th verse it was all foolishness and gibberish.

### Willie McGee McGaw

1. Three old crows sat on a tree,
   *Caw, caw, caw,*
   Three old crows sat on a tree,
   *Willie McGee McGaw.*
   Three old crows sat on a tree,
   They was black as black could be,
   *Willie McGee McGee McGaw,*
   *Willie McGee McGaw.*

2. "I know where we find some food,"
   *Caw, caw, caw,*
   "I know where we find some food,"
   *Willie McGee McGaw.*
   "I know where we find some food,
   Yonder in the cool green wood."
   *Willie McGee McGee McGaw,*
   *Willie McGee McGaw.*

3. "Come and taste it, you can tell
   It is cookèd very well."

4. Mr. Crow to Miz Crow said:
   "I will eat it, live or dead."

5. Horse and rider side by side,
   It was morning when they died.

# Two Old Crows

## (Niles No. 17 C)

BY 1909 the number of crows had been reduced to two crows, or rather, two old crows. At any rate, that was the number in the version sung by Pete Mulleneoux, who lived on the edges of the Wet Woods in Jefferson County, Ky. He was 75 years of age and delightfully noisy, and his rough performance was definitely funny, if one can accept humor in the tradition of the medieval *danse macabre*.

Mulleneoux, being related to the Whitmans, was naturally concerned over the disappearance of the Whitman girl. (This sad affair was dis-

# The Two Old Crows

## (Niles No. 17 C)

Boisterously

Two old crows sat on a tree, Lord-y, hop-di, had-di-ho,

Two old crows sat on a tree, Black and ug-ly as they could be, ___

Lord-y, hop-di, had-di-ho.

*(Major mode on C)*

cussed quite fully in the commentary on "Judas and Jesus," No. 16 B.)

"That Whitman girl," said Pete, "was always a truth-careless sort. And she was always a-sky-larkin' and a-rampagin' about, even at the tent meetings up at Benny Benkirk's corner. Every time she saw a new man, she went to battin' her eyes like a toad in a hailstorm. So when that fence-wire salesman with his high-button shoes come along, Jerushy Whitman was a goner."

After a long pause, he continued. "She'll never come back. Her pa might as lief put the shotgun away. No, she'll never come back . . . Pretty thing, she was."

A small portion of Mulleneoux's income came from the manufacture of homemade whiskey. His best customer was the owner of the tavern at the crossroads, a few miles away. The tavern-keeper had a cunning way of retailing the Mulleneoux distillate. Bottles of this product were kept in a gunny sack, submerged in a pond just behind the tavern building. A rope on the sack was attached to a homemade derrick. This was nothing more than a long pole mounted on a fence post; when one end was depressed, the other end came up and could be swung around to the edge of the pond. Then the bottles containing Mulleneoux's highly desirable drink could be removed from the dripping gunny sack and brought into the tavern.

When a customer appeared at the tavern and expressed a preference for the homemade product, the keeper would say to his assistant, "Oppie, take a walk."

This was the signal for the recovery of a pint. But if the keeper said "Oppie, take two walks," Oppie came back with a quart.

Here are Mulleneoux's text and tune:

## Two Old Crows (Niles No. 17 C)

1. Two old crows sat on a tree,
     Lordy, hopdi, haddi-ho,
   Two old crows sat on a tree,
   Black and ugly as they could be,
     Lordy, hopdi, haddi-ho.

2. He-crow said: "Well, I'll be beat,"
     Lordy, hopdi, haddi-ho,
   He-crow said: "Well, I'll be beat,
   What have we got to eat for meat?"
     Lordy, hopdi, haddi-ho.

3. She-crow to old he-crow said:
     Lordy, hopdi, haddi-ho,
   She-crow to old he-crow said:
   "I know where there's a body not long dead,"
     Lordy, hopdi, haddi-ho.

4. "Press our feet upon his shin,"
     Lordy, hopdi, haddi-ho,
   "Press our feet upon his shin,
   Pick his bones as clean as a pin,"
     Lordy, hopdi, haddi-ho.

# 18

# The Marriage of Sir Gawain

(Child No. 31)

## Sir Gaunie and the Witch

(Niles No. 18)

WHEREVER this Arthurian legend is encountered, the cast of characters is almost always the same. First we have a king or prince, then a knightly member of the king's court (he may be a relative or a friend). These two are then pitted against a bold, robber baron type and his sister, who although young and beautiful, has been stepmother-bewitched into the foulest-appearing female known to man, or at least to legend.

The robber baron (himself somewhat bewitched) demands the answer to what seems to be the most difficult of questions: "What do women most desire?" Failing to answer, the king will lose his life. But the answer is offered by the misshapen bewitched sister, who, in return, demands marriage to the king or one of his knights. Marriage to the knight is arranged at great pains, and the ugly bride is restored to her natural beauty that night, just after the wedding. No legendary situation paid greater rewards where so little was expected.

Two very interesting items from the New England states — classified by Phillips Barry and others in *British Ballads from Maine* as secondary ballads — reproduce certain features found in "The Marriage of Sir Gawain." But Barry and the other editors do not claim that either "The Loathly Bride" or "The Half-Hitch" is a modernization of the enchanting medieval legend concerning King Arthur. In discussing these so-called secondary ballads, they comment on the rather unkingly attitude of the great King Arthur in his willingness to save himself from a fate worse than death by sacrificing the handsome, youthful, and devoted Gawain. There is no riddling in either "The Loathly Bride" or "The Half-Hitch," but there are decided similarities between these New England variants and the original ballad.

A man is rejected by his sweetheart and in desperation vows to marry the first woman he meets. His sweetheart, in order to try his sincerity, gets herself up as a repulsive old hag. True to his oath, though dejected at the prospects before him, he marries the hag, and then finds her transformed into the girl he originally hoped to marry.

The points of similarity between these two New England ballads and the original are the monstrous appetite of the hag, her ugliness, her uncleanliness, her demand for a public wedding, her husband's reluctance to embrace her, and her transformation on the wedding bed to a ravishingly beautiful young woman.

"The Loathly Bride" runs to 16 verses, plus some spoken lines, and "The Half-Hitch" has 18 verses also with spoken portions. No music is supplied in either case.

# Sir Gaunie and the Witch

## (Niles No. 18)

As a small child, I listened to the story of King Arthur and his troubles with the robber baron, read to me by an older member of the family. In my turn, I read a watered-down version of the same story to my son Tom. Probably most children who go in for the King Arthur and Robin Hood types of derring-do yarns have some knowledge of the robber-baron legend.

One is prompted to think of the endless chain of people who must have told the story of the marriage of Sir Gawain or sung the ballad based on the story as it is told in "The Weddynge of S$^r$ Gawen and Dame Ragnell," or in the tale of "The Wife of Bath" as reported by Geoffrey Chaucer, or as related by Gower in *Confessio amantis*. It was a long chain of storytellers, some of whom could read and write and some of whom (like my informant) could not.

In the case of "Sir Gaunie and the Witch," the 27 verses concerning King Arthur of merry Carlisle are condensed into 6 verses. The singer was one Bella Hawley, a cook and general houseworker who could neither read nor write. Her home was in Asheville, N. C., but at the time when I encountered her she was working as a cook near Swannanoa, N. C. She was fat and gay and rather noisy but delightful, and an excellent cook. She referred to her song as the "ballard" of Sir Gaunie and the Witch.

In the discussion following the singing of the ballad, she told me of the animal she had invented to amuse small children. It was called a "swamgona." I remarked that it sounded like Swannanoa. But she said the word came to her one day while singing "My Horses Ain't Hungry." There is a line in this folk song which goes: "So I'm goin' to hitch up my horses and drive right away." Bella Hawley had reduced the first four words to one word — swamgona — and then, as she explained it, it sounded so much like an animal name that she proceeded to make an animal out of it.

Bella told me that she had recently nursed two children belonging to a doctor's wife, and had even had to draw pictures of her trumped-up "swamgona" to keep the little ones amused. "I was hard put with them infants, because their mammy was such a flibbertygibberty. She was goin' to noontime lunches continual, with other female-persons she had known at school. Hit was a woman's club from some university or other. Both the children were drinlin* little things, and their daddy was a-passin' 'em all kinds of physic, but hit didn't do much good. I tied an asafetida bag on one of 'em, but the smell of it nigh on to turned their mammy's stomach, so I took it off . . .

"I believe," declared Bella, "that my singin' and rompin' with those little ones did more for 'em than all the pills and bottle-medicines. And what bothered me was that the doctor's wife was called to straw† before the summer was over, but I was gone when that third one was born."

Then we got down to the real reason for my visit, and we did some singing. I sang for Bella, and Bella sang for me. As if to explain away the magic in "The Marriage of Sir Gawain," Bella Hawley, who was surely on the plain side, said to me, "I've got this to tell you: many a man-person has bedded many a woman-person, and when he bedded her, she looked fat, had straggly hair and wasn't purty. But after a while, that woman-person don't look so fat, and her hair looks like it's been curled, and she gets to be almost purty." I marveled at Bella and her philosophy. Here is the ballad she sang:

* Puny, undersized.     † Childbed.

# Sir Gaunie and the Witch

## (Niles No. 18)

*(Minor mode on E)*

1. King Henry was a mighty man
   Who lived in Engeland.
   No harm e'er fell on honest folk
   From out of Henry's hand.

2. Sir Gaunie was a noble knight,
   Handsome for to see,
   And he's to marry with a witch
   To save King Henery.

3. The witch from out the deep green wood
   Told Henry what to say,
   She told him that a woman always
   Wanted for her way.

4. King Henry answered well and true,
   He spake so bright, so gay.
   The Baron sadly hung his head,
   And sadly rode away.

5. Sir Gaunie was a noble knight,
   And many a tear was shed
   The day he married with the witch
   And taken her to bed.

6. 'Twas then she turned a princess fair,
   And though they all did try,
   No fairer one was ever seen
   With sight of human eye.

# 19

# King John and the Bishop

(Child No. 45)

THIS MATTER of a king, prince, general, or other important official of high rank testing other persons with "hard questions" is as old as man. We discover in the Book of Judges that one Samson, born by divine intercession into a family named Danites, who lived in the community of Zorah, gave his Philistine in-laws such a riddle that they never did answer it in the seven-day period allotted. Only after Samson's wife wept (again, for seven days) did the biblical strongman relent a bit and give her a clue, which she passed on to her relatives and thus enabled them to come up with the answer.

Samson is not usually presented as a person with a sense of humor. Perhaps this is an error, in view of his answer to the Philistines after they had brought the solution to his riddles: "If ye had not plowed with my heifer, ye had not found out my riddle."

The Queen of Sheba, the legendary beauty of her period, was also given to the process of the hard question, for in the tenth chapter of 1st Kings we discover that

> . . . when the Queen of Sheba heard of the fame of Solomon concerning the name of Jehovah, she came to prove him with hard questions./And she came to Jerusalem with a very great train . . . and when she came to Solomon, she communed with him of all that was in her heart./ And Solomon told her all her questions: there

was not any thing hid from the king which he told her not.

Odin, the chief deity of Norse mythology, put forth many a hard question or riddle. English and Scottish broadsides of the 17th century present such interesting examples as: (1) "The King and the Bishop," (2) "The Old Abbot and King Olfrey," (3) "The Pleasant History of King Henry the Eighth and the Abbot of Reading," and (4) "King John and the Abbot."

From the Percy MS (Child No. 45 A) we discover that King John, branded as one who did much wrong and maintained little right, had developed a great jealousy toward the Bishop of Canterbury. This jealousy stemmed from the fact that the Bishop apparently lived in greater ease and comfort than the King. Thereupon, the King accused the Bishop of treason (a form of logic not unusual in those days) and sent him three hard questions. The questions were:

1. What is the King worth, to a penny?
2. How long would it take the King to ride around the earth?
3. What was the King thinking about (if at all)?

The time limit for achieving the answers was 20 days.

The Bishop fortunately had a half-brother, who was a very simple person, a shepherd, a wise man and a philosopher. This shepherd was dressed in the Bishop's clothes and sent up to London, where he confounded the King with the right answers:

1. 29 pence — one penny less than the price paid to Judas at the betrayal of Jesus Christ.
2. If the King would rise with the sun and ride with the same, he would circle the earth in 24 hours.
3. Here the shepherd proved himself master of the situation, as well as a man of humor, for he answered in words to this effect: "Sire, you think I am the Abbot of Canterbury, but I am not. I am only the Abbot's poor half-brother, who lives by tending sheep."

The King thereupon offered to make the shepherd a bishop, but the shepherd wisely declined, for he had discovered the rigors and uncertainties of a bishop's life. He was delighted, however, to carry back a pardon to his half-brother, the true Bishop of Canterbury. Here we have, for a change, a ballad with a happy ending.

# The King and the Bishop
## (Niles No. 19)

THIS BALLAD was sung by Rufe Ratliff, who at 85 years of age was living alone on a smallish farm in the southeastern end of Madison County, Ky. His farm produced a small tobacco crop, but for many years, his principal source of income came from the manufacture of hickory brooms. He knew quite a few ballads in fragmentary form. Being scornful of preachers, he took special delight in singing about the king who was going to hang a bishop. He said to me: "Preachers always get the best of everything. I've seen 'em get all the chicken breasts on the platter, but they be one who got what was a-comin' to him. He lived in olden times, and he was what they called a bishop."

The puncheon floor of Ratliff's cabin was swept, but the presence of hoes, axes, pitchforks, and cultivator shovels gave the room the air of a barn or toolshed. He must have realized that some form of explanation was in order.

"No," he said, "I hain't had a female person 'round me in a coon's age. 'Course, when I was a younglin', I was a dauncy boy, a-dressin' up in everythin' I could beg or borrow. Why, I even stuck my hair down with sweet-smellin' bear's grease. Naturally, the grease didn't come from no bear . . . twern't no bears in these hills to get grease from.

"Well, treckly I was waitin' on* a pretty little piece from across the valley, and we stepped off and got ourselves married up. I was so flummixed I didn't know the days of the week. But after the infare† was over, I discovered that married life was not for Ratliff."

I waited a long time for the rest of the story, and finally he said: "Hit's been lonesome in this cabin for the last thirty years. I can't even remember now which one of us hatched up the idea of leaving the other one. But one time, when I was right busy about the farm, she went up near Richmond to visit her sister. After a bit, I norated it around that I was a-hankerin' for her to come back, but she wouldn't come and I wouldn't fetch her, and I reckon as how that was the end of it. But I didn't miss much . . . she was such a doless‡ person."

After all this heartbreak, I feared Ratliff would never sing, but he did, and although he

* Courting. † Feast or entertainment at the reception of a bride in her new home.
‡ An unwilling worker or lazy dreamer.

# The King and the Bishop
## (Niles No. 19)

The King is gone to Can-ters town And loud-ly pulled the ring - o: "Lord Bish - op, my Bish - op, You are a pret-ty thing - o, You are a pret-ty thing - o."

(*Major mode on G*)

1. The King is gone to Canters town
   And loudly pulled the ring-o:
   "Lord Bishop, my Bishop,
   You are a pretty thing-o,
   You are a pretty thing-o.

2. "How do you live in such array
   And make me feel so small-o,
   With serving-men and draw-boys
   A-swarming through your hall-o?
   (*repeat last line of each verse*)

3. "Unless you answer well and true,
   Your neck will pay the bill-o,
   Or I will have you hanged
   On top of Malvery Hill-o."

\* Cowl.

4. The Bishop sought a shepherd out,
   Who was of wise renown-o,
   Who said that in the Bishop's coal,\*
   He'd go to Londers town-o.

5. And when the shepherd had supped and drank
   And answered all full good-o,
   King John did give him of his gold
   And thanked him where he stood-o.

6. "Go take this pardon quickly back
   And loudly pull the ring-o,
   And tell the Bishop he is free
   To preach and pray and sing-o."

was not consistent with his time values he was quite willing. The day was hot and the flies were bothersome. Finally, after many false starts, I was able to assemble some readable notes.

The tune is surely not distinguished; it is quite ordinary, in fact. The text, however, is revealing and interesting. One should note the use of "Canters town" for Canterbury and "Londers" for London. The second verse gives us a quaint yardstick for opulence: "serving-men and draw-boys" swarming through the hall. A draw-boy, one supposes, was a manservant who drew off liquors from large containers into mugs or pitchers. The details of the actual questions asked are entirely lost. This is what happens so often in the American survivals. Details are gone, but the bold outline of the ballad remains.

# 20

# The Twa Brothers

(Child No. 49)

## The Murdered Boy

(Niles No. 20)

IN DISCUSSING the possible origin of the legend behind the ballad of "The Twa Brothers," William Motherwell and Kirkpatrick Sharpe suggest that it might be related to an event that happened in 1589 near Edinburgh. It seems that a member of the prominent Somerville family was killed when his brother's firearm was discharged accidentally. Later Sharpe thought that it could be related to the case of a boy of thirteen who killed his brother for pulling his hair. Child brushes off both these suggestions as "unusually gratuitous surmises."

The ballad was widely known in England and Scotland, and perhaps even more widely known and sung in the United States. The American texts usually agree with the English-Scottish texts, and the actual reasons for the tragedy remain obscure. The motive of jealousy seems to be implied. The pathos of the situation of the dying brother who does not want his parents to learn the truth is not unusual and is found in ballads from Norway, Germany, France, and Sweden.

It is interesting to note that "The Twa Brothers" is one of the very few ballads Child indicates as having been sung in America.

## The Murdered Boy

(Niles No. 20)

MISS KATHERINE PETTIT of Lexington, Ky., long associated with Pine Mountain School, was widely known throughout the southeastern Kentucky mountains. We were together in Kingdom Come Valley, late in July of 1933, when Miss Pettit proposed that we go to Line Fork and visit some of her old-time friends, because there was a singer among them.

Kate (Mrs. Brown) Ramsey was the singer, and she sang one of the loveliest melodic lines I had heard in a long while. She knew only 2½ verses of her ballad, but she more than made up for the other half-dozen with a very wonderful tune.

# The Murdered Boy

## (Niles No. 20)

"Oh Broth-er, dear Broth-er, pray toss me a stone, Oh Broth-er, come play \_\_ at ball." "I \_\_ am \_\_ too lit - tle, I am \_\_ too young. Oh Broth - er, pray let me a - lone, \_\_\_\_\_ Oh Broth - er, pray let me a - lone."

*(Mixolydian mode on D)*

## The Murdered Boy (Niles No. 20)

1. "Oh Brother, dear Brother, pray toss me a stone,
   Oh Brother, come play at ball."
   "I am too little, I am too young.
   Oh Brother, pray let me alone,
   Oh Brother, pray let me alone."

2. "Oh Brother, dear Brother, your knife is so keen,
   Oh Brother, you've wounded me sore.

   . . . . . . . . . . . . . . .

3. "Oh bury me, Brother, oh bury me deep,
   My Bible-book place at my head.
   And when I am buried, please place me a rose,
   A rose that will bloom out red,
   A rose that will bloom out red."

# 21

# Lizie Wan

(Child No. 51)

## Lizzie May

(Niles No. 21)

ALTHOUGH the situation involved in this ballad is not unknown to the country people of the Southern Appalachians, the discussion of the subject matter would be avoided. Certainly the women would neither discuss it nor sing it. The only text Cecil Sharp encountered was sung by a man, Ben F. Finlay of Manchester, Ky. My informant was also a man. In all my years of collecting I have never heard a woman even refer to the ballad of "Lizie Wan." Attention should be called to the subject matter of "Sheath and Knife" (Child No. 16) and "The Bonny Hind" (Child No. 50): in each case, a situation somewhat similar to that in "Lizie Wan" exists.

## Lizzie May

(Niles No. 21)

CLUSTER WYATT was, on his statement, about 77 years of age when I knew him in 1933. He had been a schoolteacher in his early days, and was at this time living not far from McKee, Ky., on a small hillside farm that he rented. His house was really a lean-to shed, and it was full of newspapers and magazines, many of which had never been taken out of the original wrappers. "It puts a man in a strain to keep up with the printing presses," he said, when he saw me looking at the piles and piles of unopened and, I assumed, unread publications.

Wyatt lived alone. There were, however, three dogs and several large cats. There also were two small hinged sections, sawed out at the bottom of the door, and these — the cat door and the dog door — swung both ways, so that the animals could leave and enter at will.

I tried to establish the exact pronunciation of his name, thinking that it was really "Custer" and that he had been named after the general of Little Big Horn fame. But he steadfastly objected to my leaving out the L. His name was "Cluster," and nothing else would do.

As soon as I found a place where I could sit down (and it was not an easy thing to do in Wyatt's cluttered cabin), I went to singing. Wyatt sat on the floor, his eyes closed, a picture of delight.

"Music does two things for a feller," said he. "It pleasures him, and it saddens him. Now this

117

# Lizzie May
## (Niles No. 21)

*Sadly*

Now Liz - zie May sat in her bed - room door, She grieved and she wept ___ all day, ___ Till by ___ there came her fa - ther dear, Said: "What ails of ye, Liz - zie May?" ___

(*Dorian mode on G*)

ballad singin' of yours reminds me of a gal I was hankerin' for a great many years ago. I met her when I was lyin' out with the dry cattle.* I must have been eighteen or twenty. She was nothing for looks, but a winner for fun. She'd been a

pretty gal, but she was plagued with the buckest buck-teeth I most ever saw. They used to say she was so buck-toothed that she could eat vittles through a crack in a fence . . .

"Well, she married up with a railroad man.

* Going around with the young unmarried set.

Lived in Winchester, and didn't have anythin' but trouble. I warned her before she married him, but she flashed her buck teeth at me, and laughed loud and long . . . You know, nothin' on earth lasts forever but trouble, and if trouble gets a holt of you, it's like havin' a wildcat on your back: you can't shake it off. That girl I hoped to marry died in Winchester, not so very long after she left here, and I never did hone for any other woman. So I been readin' magazines and newspapers ever since, whenever the spirit moves me. I fox hunt at night with my neighbors, and a long while ago I used to join my voice with the Kentucky Harmony singers. But they're all dead. And I don't open my newspapers any more . . . Nope, never did have a woman-person around my cabin, not regular anyhow . . ."

His life's story was almost as sad as the ballad he sang. He said he had known "Barbary Ellen," "The Hangman's Tree," and "Lord Dondie," but that was too long ago for remembering. I concluded that he had made an effort to remember "Lizzie May" because it presented a girl in dire trouble, and, as he said, nothing on earth lasts forever but trouble. His wonderful melodic line was reminiscent of shape-note music.

## Lizzie May (Niles No. 21)

1. Now Lizzie May sat in her bedroom door,
   She grieved and she wept all day,
   Till by there came her father dear,
   Said: "What ails of ye, Lizzie May?"

2. "My ailing is a woman's ail.
   Dear Father, I'll tell ye why:
   I have a baby in my side
   All caused by my brother and I."

3. Now Lizzie May sat in her bedroom door,
   She grieved and she wept all day,
   Till by there came her mother dear,
   Said: "What ails of ye, Lizzie May?"

4. "My ailing is a woman's ail.
   Dear Mother, I'll tell ye why:
   I have a baby in my side
   All caused by my brother and I."

5. Now Lizzie May sat in her bedroom door,
   She grieved and she wept all day,
   Till by there came her brother,
   Said: "What ails of ye, Lizzie May?"

6. And when he found what the matter was,
   He showed her no mercy,
   But cut her body all so fair
   In pieces by one, two, and three.

7. Oh, he will sail the widest sea
   Beyond the farthest land-o,
   Because the blood of Lizzie May
   Was red upon his hand-o.

# 22

# Young Beichan

(Child No. 53)

## Lord Bateman

(Niles No. 22)

ALTHOUGH there is a great similarity between the events in the legend of Gilbert Becket, father of Thomas à Becket, and the ballad of "Young Beichan," it is safe to assume that the ballad does not derive from the legend. Ballads and legends following the general outlines of this ballad are found quite frequently. Parallel situations are encountered in ballads and legends coming from Spain, Italy, Norway, the Faroe Islands, Sweden, Iceland, and Denmark.

The legend of Gilbert Becket comes to us from the manuscript of a poetical narrative which must have been written down about a century after the death of Thomas à Becket in 1170. Gilbert takes up the cross and proceeds to the Holy Land, accompanied by one male servant, named Richard. Becket is ultimately taken prisoner by the "cruel" Saracens, and from this point onward the similarity between the legend and the ballad is quite remarkable.

In the ballad the conclusion is a happy one —

assuming that one is on the side of the Turkish lady, whom Young Beichan marries, rather than on the side of the "forenoon bridelet," whom he discards. In the legend, Gilbert Becket likewise marries the Turkish lady, but only after she has agreed to accept Christianity.

There is no evidence, incidentally, that the real Gilbert Becket took up the cross, crusaded, or married a Middle Eastern woman.

Though the ballad of "Young Beichan" probably did not derive from the legend of Gilbert Becket, it is interesting to note that it was surely affected by it, if only in the names involved. Note the similarity between the name of Becket and those found in variants of the ballad — for example, Young Beckie, Lord Bateman, Lord Bakeman, Lord Bacon, Young Beechman, Young Beichie, Young Bengie, etc.

Variants and fragments of the ballad of "Young Beichan" are widely spread over the North American continent.

## Lord Bateman

(Niles No. 22)

IT IS unusual for anyone to remember 25 verses. This memory problem is one reason why more of the shorter ballads have remained in oral tradi-

tion. But Granny Cilla Baker, who lived on Red Bird Creek near Manchester, Ky., was a remarkable woman. In spite of her 82 years, she never

# Lord Bateman

## (Niles No. 22)

*(Mixolydian on E, strongly pentatonic)*

1. In London town was Bateman dwelling,
   He was a man of high degree.
   His father wore a noble bearing,
   His father and his family.

2. Now he was born like it was Monday,
   And he was christened Tuesday e'en,
   King Henry and his court attended
   Because hit was a royal scene.

3. Now Bateman traveled many cities,
   He sailed through all the Northern Sea,
   The mighty King of France he holpen,
   They give him shelter and some fee.

4. He sailed in the Middle Ocean
   Right up into the Turkish shore,
   And in the harbor he made an anchor,
   And then his sailin' days were o'er.

any months he lay lamenting,
    ner to the Turkish king.
      not see the light of summer,
        not hear the songbirds sing.

6. A u.. grow inside that prison,
   To hit Lord Bateman he was tied.
   He pulled beside a span of oxen,
   He pulled untwil he all but died.

7. The Turkish king, he had one daughter,
   And she was of a high degree.
   She stole the keys of her father's prison,
   Said: "They be a prisoner I must see."

8. "Have you got lands, have you got living,
   Have you got any houses free?
   What would you give to the fair lady
   Who out of prison set you free?"

9. "Yes, I've got lands and I've got living,
   Umberland town belongs to me.
   I'll give hit all to the fair lady
   Who out of prison sets me free."

10. She took him to her father's castle,
    She bad him drink the strongest wine,
    "I do not want Lord Bateman's siller,*
    I only wish that he were mine."

11. They made a vow, they made a promise,
    They made hit free, so hit would stand.
    He vowed he'd marry ne'er another,
    She vowed she'd have no other man.

12. She took him down unto the sea sad,†
    She left him sailin' o'er the main,
    Said: "Fare ye well, my own, my true love,
    I fear I'll ne'er see you again."

13. Now several years have come and gonèd,
    And fourteen days, by one, two, three.
    She clothed herself in gay apparel,
    Said: " 'Tis Sir Bateman I must see."

14. When she did come to Bateman's castle,
    How boldly tingled on the ring.
    "Who's there, who's there?" cried the proud young
        porter,
    "Who's there, who's there that would come in?"

15. "Is this, is this Lord Bateman's castle,
    Or is the noble lord within?"
    "Oh yes, oh yes," cried the proud young porter,
    "This is the day of his weddin'."

16. "Has Bateman wedded to another,
    Has Bateman clean forgotten me?"
    And with a sigh said the Turkish lady,
    "I wish I were in my own country!"

17. "Go tell Sir Bateman for to remember
    And for to send some bread and wine,
    And not forget the fair young lady
    Who let him out of close confine."

18. "What news, what news, what news, my porter?
    What news, what news bring you to me?"
    "There is a gay and handsome lady,
    The fairest ever eye‡ did see.

19. "The gold she wears upon her fingers
    Would buy one-half of this country.
    Some bread, some wine was all she cravèd,
    In memory of your settin' free.

20. "Sir Bateman, I have been your porter
    Some thirty years and more by three,
    There at your portals stands the fairest
    Ever the eye of man did see."

21. Up spake the bride's old mother,
    "Shame on this house, and shame on ye,
    If he excepted not my daughter,
    He should remember my great beauty."

22. Sir Bateman flew into a passion,
    He kicked a table to a side,
    "I will forsake both lands and dwelling,
    Suzanna now will be my bride."

23. "Take back, take back, take back your daughter,
    I'm sure she's none the worse for me,
    She came here by a horse and saddle,
    I'll send her back in a coacheree."

24. Then angry spoke the forenoon bridelet:
    "Your love is cold to me so soon?
    Is this the custom of your country,
    To choose again ere it be noon?"

25. He took Suzanna's hand so tender,
    He stood before the nobles all,
    "Now I will wed my own, my true love,
    And welcome her to my bower and hall."

---

* Silver.    † Side.    ‡ Perhaps "I."

faltered a bit, or had to sing back over a verse in order to pick up the next one.

Her people had been engaged in certain family wars, and some of the best men had been lost. It was a long series of troubles, and had gone on for nearly 20 years, according to Granny Baker. Said she: "There's no peace left in all this country, and I'm a-goin' west. I stayed around in the neighborhood of Manchester till the old folks was dead and buried. I'm pleasured to say that some of 'em died in bed."

The date was July 12, 1907, and the melodic material was very fine. She sang with a convincing voice, but she gave the impression of great sadness. She said that in her youth she knew and sang enough "old-timey" music to keep a body listening all afternoon. But now she was 82. Her birthday was October 12.

# The Cherry-Tree Carol

(Child No. 54)

## The Cherry Tree

(Niles No. 23)

**A**LTHOUGH Francis J. Child referred to "The Cherry-Tree" as a carol, he grouped it, numbered it, and published it as one of *The English and Scottish Popular Ballads.* The story told in this carol is not part of Holy Writ, but comes from several apocryphal sources, namely: the Pseudo-Matthew Gospel, Chapter 20; Thilo, "Historia de Nativitate Mariae et de Infantia Salvatoris," in *Codex apocryphus Novi Testamenti,* page 395; and Tischendorf's *Evangelia apocrypha,* page 82.

According to these sources, we are led to believe that Mary's and Joseph's flight into Egypt was made before the birth of Christ. On this journey, the unborn Christ Child performed several important miracles, one being the bending down of the fruit tree and another, the miraculous harvest. This last event is the basis for the American carol "The Miraculous Harvest," which is not included in this volume because it has no counterpart in Child.

In "The Cherry-Tree Carol" we find that the fruit varies from country to country. As Child said, "The truly popular carol would be sure to adapt the fruit to its own soil." In Spain and in southern France the fruit is the apple. In England it is invariably the cherry. Elsewhere, we find the fruit to be the coconut, the fig, and the date. In the 15th-century mystery plays given at Coventry, we discover that the cherry-tree

blossoms and fruits out of season, because Mary happens to desire cherries in midwinter. (It might be added that the cherry-tree legend in the Coventry play is not in the form of a carol intended for singing, but is rather a dramatic episode expressed in dialogue.)

In both play and carol, Joseph is usually presented as an ill-natured fellow who seems to be out of sorts over the matter of parenthood. In several of the English and American texts, Joseph is covered with remorse and prays forgiveness when he discovers the miraculous power of Jesus and hears the prophecy of His birth.

Some idea of the antiquity of the cherry-tree legend may be gained from the fact that, in somewhat localized form, it is part of the Finnish national epic, the *Kalevala: The Land of Heroes.* In the 50th runo, or canto, a young virgin eats a cranberry* (not unlike a cherry in size and color, and a well-known fruit in Finland) and discovers herself with child. She is rejected by her family and seeks shelter among the local peasantry. But, before she leaves home, she makes a prophecy that she will bear a noble offspring, a mighty conqueror, as great as the hero of the *Kalevala,* Väinämöinen. Her prayer for aid and comfort before her child is born is a thrilling piece of poetry. The boy-child is born on the straw of a horse's stall, and is wrapped in

* In her prose translation of the *Kalevala,* Aili Kolehmainen Johnson refers to the cranberry as a cowberry. It is interesting to observe that the word for cranberry in Finnish, *puolukka,* is sometimes used as a pet name for a cow.

swaddling clothes. Finally, after many adventures, he becomes King of Karelia and Lord of All the Mighty.

On hearing the news concerning the new king of Karelia, the mighty Väinämöinen, leaving his sacred harp, Kantele, behind, sails away in his copper boat, sails away to loftier regions, "to the land beneath the heavens."

# The Cherry Tree
## (Niles No. 23)

When Jo-seph was an old-en man, Had lived full man-y a year, a year, He court-ed and wed-ded the Queen of Heav'n, And call-ed her his dear.

(Minor mode on B)

# The Cherry Tree

## (Niles No. 23)

AUNT BECKY SIZEMORE (singer of "The Cherry Tree") was of unknown age. She was convinced that she had lived so long and so comfortably because she had tried to stay out of trouble. She had never contended with a single man- or woman-person. She had gone to church when there was church to go to, and she had never voted. A distant female relative of hers had once been involved in a shooting-war at a voting place. This relative had missed being killed by a very small margin, and there were those who said that the four men who were killed in the fracas might have survived if this female-person had not tried to vote. Aunt Becky was over 75 years of age at the time of this voting-place shooting, and she vowed that day she would never become involved in politics.

Another relative of hers, a member of the Combs family, fled the law in 1894, and holed up in a cave some miles from the Kentucky River in Breathitt County. Now this man lived in his cave quite comfortably for a matter of years. His people brought him supplies, powder and ball, tobacco, food, and other necessities. He was 40 years of age when he became a cave dweller. By the turn of the century, the law had forgotten all about him, but he had discovered the delights of cave dwelling and just went right on living in his cave, free of his debts, his family responsibilities, the law, and his enemies.

## The Cherry Tree

1. When Joseph was an olden man,
   Had lived full many a year, a year,
   He courted and wedded the Queen of Heav'n,
   And callèd her his dear.

2. Then Joseph was a carpenter,
   And Mary baked and spun, and spun,
   And when 'twas ripe-cherry time again
   A family was begun.

3. Then Mary in her meekness,
   Then Mary what was mild, so mild,
   Said: "Cherries is the bestest thing,
   For women bearin' child."

4. Then up spake Joseph to Mary —
   He was a man unkind, unkind —
   "Oh, it's who has sired your baby
   That's a-botherin' my mind.

5. "Go tell this one, and straightway,
   That cherries hain't nothin' to me, to me;
   If he's e'er a man to sire a child,
   He's a man to climb a tree."

6. Then Mary's Son, our Saviour,
   He spake from Mary's heart, her heart;
   "I'll make this tree bow low, low down,
   I'll take my mammy's part."

7. Then the cherry tree hit bowed low down,
   Hit bowed down to the ground, the ground,
   And gentle Mary helped herself
   To cherries without a sound.

8. Then Joseph said in terror:
   "I see my wrong is great, is great,
   Pray come, my gentle Queen of Heav'n,
   The secret do relate."

9. Then said the Virgin Mary,
   "The secret I will share, will share:
   On Christmas Eve, in a ox's stall,
   The Christ Child I will bear."

By 1934, when I knew Aunt Becky, he was 80 years of age, and had spent 40 years as a cave man, living the life of Riley. It was reported that he had the most beautiful white beard in all those parts. I never discovered how he spent his days, but I did discover that he was greatly envied by many of the men I encountered in that part of Kentucky.

Aunt Becky Sizemore told me that as a young woman she went to all the play-parties and sang and danced till the rafters and the floor joists shook. She yearned for those great times, saying, "Young folks don't know how to enjoy their- selves no more. All they think of is drinkin', shootin', and votin' . . . yes," she added, sum- ming up her argument, "this politics business is a caution to the jaybirds!"

# 24

# Dives and Lazarus

(Child No. 56)

## Dives and Lazarus
(Niles No. 24)

IN THE last thirteen verses of the 16th chapter of the Gospel according to St. Luke we discover the dramatic story of Dives and Lazarus. As early as 1557 this subject matter was woven into a ballad. At least the *Register* of the Company of Stationers in London indicates that a license was issued for such a ballad about July 19, 1557. This early work had been co-authored by a gentleman named Master John Wallye and a female person named Mistress Toye. We do not have the text of this 1557 ballad, but of the versions so far discovered, either in this country or in England, not a one approaches the power of the original story as it is found in the Bible.

The ballad of "Dives and Lazarus" was no doubt known in the literary circles of Elizabethan England. John Fletcher (1579–1625), of Beaumont and Fletcher fame, mentions the ballad in his play entitled *Monsieur Thomas,* having a fiddler declare that he can sing "the merry ballad of Diverus and Lazarus." This would place the ballad as part of a London theatrical production of about 1610.

Ballads on this subject have been found in many of the countries of continental Europe as well as in the British Isles and the United States.

## Dives and Lazarus
(Niles No. 24)

IN HARLAN, Ky., it had rained early on the morning of June 3, 1934, and the remainder of the day was overcast. Late in the afternoon I wrote down the text and tune of "Dives and Lazarus" from the singing of a very obliging old lady named Grandmother Lottie Higgins. (She objected to being called "Granny" but approved of "Grandmother.") She had been a schoolteacher in her early days, and had spent some of her middle years in the neighborhood of Atlanta, Ga. She had been a regular member of a shape-note singing group and owned a copy of *The Sacred Harp.* Her copy had been published in Haleyville, Ala., and was not an early edition. The melodic line employed in Grandmother Higgins's singing of "Dives and Lazarus" was not unlike the shape-note tunes in structure and feeling.

129

# Dives and Lazarus

## (Niles No. 24)

*In the manner of a hymn*

There lived a man in an - cient times, The Bi - ble doth __ in - form us, His sins a - gin the __ word __ of God Were __ great, and they __ were nu - m'rous, Were __ great and they __ were __ nu - m'rous.

(*Major mode on F*)

Grandmother Higgins was a Mother Hubbard type — fat, roly-poly, and very gay. She was in Harlan for the purpose of "holpin'" her sister's children. The father of this numerous brood was recovering from a mine accident, and Grandmother Higgins was looking after a newborn baby and spreading good cheer wherever she could. She said that if she were bothered enough, she would "hightail it out of Harlan and go right on back to Atlanta." One of the older girls said: "Now, Grandmother, don't get yourself into a pure hissy!"*

"You stop advisin' me," the old lady retorted,

* A fit of anger.

"and go out yonder and move that hat-rack cow of your father's."

The cow, staked out on a short link chain, was eating the weeds on the side of the road. She was indeed a hat-rack: you could have hung your hat on either of her hipbones.

"If somebody in this valley don't go to minin' some more coal pretty soon," said Grandmother Higgins, "we'll all be eatin' hoppin' john — you know, cornmeal and cow-peas . . ." Everyone laughed. I have never seen such a happy group of people, to have so little of the world's goods.

They sang, and I sang. It was "The Seven Joys of Mary," "Jesus Born in Beth'ny," "The Old Lord by the Northern Sea." Finally, two of the younger girls sang a very creditable performance of "Barbary Ellen." But it was Grandmother Higgins who brought out my notebook with her accurately sung version of "Dives and Lazarus":

## Dives and Lazarus (Niles No. 24)

1. There lived a man in ancient times,
The Bible doth inform us,
His sins agin the word of God
Were great, and they were num'rous,
Were great, and they were num'rous.

2. This rich man fared very well
And dressed himself in linen.
He lived a life away from God
And spent his time in sinnin'.
   (*repeat last line of each verse*)

3. As it fell out upon a day,
Small rain from sky did fall,
Rich Dives set a mighty feast
Before his neighbors all.

4. Poor Lazarus at the rich man's gate
To raise his hands unable,
He waited in humility
For crumbs from Dives's table.

5. Rich Dives sent his hungry dogs
That they would set upon him.
The dogs in pity licked his sores,
And thus they did befriend him.

6. "Be gone, be gone," rich Dives cried.
"Thou art no friend, no brother.
I will not give thee food nor drink
In the name of Christ the Saviour."

7. As it fell out upon a day,
Poor Lazarus sicked and died,
And from God's heaven angels came
His soul to heavenward guide.

8. Rich Dives died upon a day,
But see his dreadful station:
From heaven Lazarus viewed down,
Saw Dives in damnation.

9. Rich Dives cried, "In heaven's name,
Send Lazarus with cold water.
My thirst is great, my pain is sore
With hell's tormenting tortures.

10. "Oh, had I yet an hour again
On earth among the living,
I'd spend my time in prayer and song
And help the poor with giving!"

# 25

# Sir Patrick Spens

(Child No. 58)

## Patrick Spenser

(Niles No. 25)

**M**Y INVESTIGATION into the background of the ballad of "Sir Patrick Spens" has caused me to look into the writings of 25 world authorities in the field of ballad literature, not to mention the encyclopedia and the dictionary. Most of these authorities agree and disagree with one another in a quiet, gentlemanly manner until they reach the subject of the ballad's historical background: here they begin to sound acrimonious. As a rule, the American authorities are inclined to believe that a fine ballad is a thing of beauty, so let us be thankful for it, whatever its historical background may be. With direct reference to the ballad in question the incomparable Francis Child said that "a strict accordance with history should not be expected, and indeed would be almost a ground of suspicion."

As far as I can tell at this writing, the attitude of the American authorities on the background of "Sir Patrick Spens" is entirely sound, with one exception: not enough has been said about the possible penetration of the legend of Tristan and Isolde. I shall develop this idea later. But first let us set down the gist of the American scholars' conclusions:

1. We are not compelled to regard the ballad as historical.
2. The ballad did not come into existence until the close of the 16th century.
3. The version that first appeared in print, by

way of Thomas Percy in 1765, is by far the most perfect poetic whole.

4. The so-called "complete version" produced by Sir Walter Scott is a rather unfortunate patch-work.

5. The authenticity of the grave of Sir Patrick Spens on the lonely island of Papa Stronsay (half-way between Scotland and Norway) is open to doubt.

6. Attributing the writing of the ballad to one Lady Wardlaw is not sound.

The debate about "Sir Patrick Spens" — whether it is fact or whether it is fiction — has been complicated by the existence of historical happenings suggestive of those in the ballad. There's an attempted voyage to Denmark in the time of James VI (late 16th century). Then, going still further back, there's the matter of Alexander III of Scotland, who died in 1285 and secured the throne to his granddaughter, known as the Maid of Norway, daughter of Eric, King of Norway, and Margaret, daughter of Alexander III. Edward I of England thought up the idea of marrying his son, Edward, then Prince of Wales, to the Maid of Norway, who was soon to become the Queen of Scotland. But the young lady died, and the scheme fell through. Sir Patrick Spens, if he lived at all, may have lost his ship, the Scottish lords, and his own life in an attempt to bring the Maid of Norway back to

England, but the only evidence we have is the ballad tradition. Finally, let us remember that the legend of a king sending either a reliable sea captain, a courtly representative, or a delegation of knights to bring back a princess who was to become his wife and queen had been in circulation since the distant past.

When Gottfried von Strassburg put down his pen and died in about 1215, he had finished 19,552 lines of the romance of *Tristan and Isolde*. Critics have said that next to the *Canterbury Tales* and the *Divine Comedy* the *Tristan and Isolde* of Gottfried von Strassburg is the greatest poem of the Middle Ages. But Gottfried and his two continuators, Ulrich von Türheim (about 1240) and Heinrich von Freiburg (about 1290), were not working with original materials. They dealt with a legend inherited from Thomas, the Anglo-Norman poet, who wrote sometime between 1155 and 1185. We are inclined to believe that this Anglo-Norman poet Thomas crossed the channel in the train of Eleanor of Aquitaine, wife of Henry II Plantagenet, and in England wrote under the influence of the Queen.

But neither did the Anglo-Norman Thomas work with entirely new and original materials. There was a Celtic tale of the 11th century concerning a Pictish knight from Scotland, and his name was Tristan, and the crude story of his long-ago love is full of love potions and ancient bearded kings and sea voyages to bring back princesses with white hands and of unbelievable beauty. We could go still further back and declare that there was a King Mark in legend as early as 850.

Indeed, the triangle of Tristan, King Mark, and Isolde has cast its shadow on poetry, drama, folk legend, and world-wide lore for nearly a thousand years. And on the basis of all this evidence, perhaps we may conclude that the ballad of "Sir Patrick Spens" may well have sprung from a fragment of ancient lore built around the desire of a mythical king to warm his bed and glamorize his life by way of an imported princess rather than from a historical situation.

# Patrick Spenser

## (Niles No. 25)

AT PITMAN CENTER, Tenn., not far from Gatlinburg, on a bright, hot summer morning of 1934, I backed* a letter for a crippled old man, and thereupon made the acquaintance of one of the most colorful ballad singers of my entire experience. His name was Christopher Bell. On his own statement, he had no regular home. Occasionally, he slept in houses, "like God-fearin' people do." At other times, he slept in barns or farm buildings, and when these failed, as they often did, he slept out.

"Hit ain't very comfortable in wet weather," said Christopher with a laugh, "and in flytime, you have to wake at dayrise, unless you have

* Addressed.

some person handy who'll kindly swing a flybresh and drive the flies and the dirt-daubers† offen your face."

Everything seemed to amuse Christopher Bell. He laughed at his own misfortunes, and at my white linen cap, saying it made me look like the left end-man in a minstrel show.

He was born in 1849, and when he was 15 years of age, he was taken into the Confederate Army. I never discovered his military rank or assignment, but I pictured him as one of those indefatigable drummer boys known to painters and poets. His only battle was one known as Buzzard's Roost; the historians have renamed it

† Wasps.

# Patrick Spenser

## (Niles No. 25)

Oh, the King stood with his fighting men, The King sat with his court. A sailor man he sore did need, And one of good report, report, A sailor man he sore did need, And one of good report.

*(Major mode on F)*

# Patrick Spenser (Niles No. 25)

1. Oh, the King stood with his fighting men,
The King sat with his court.
A sailor man he sore did need,
And one of good report, report,
    A sailor man he sore did need,
    And one of good report.

2. Then went the King to Dunfertown
To burble the wine so red,
"Are all my sailing captains gone?
Mayhap they all be dead."
    (*repeat last 2 lines of each verse*)

3. "The season's off," an old knight said.
" 'Tis winter," cried a youth.
"Your cargo and your ship will drown
In the Northern Sea, forsooth."

4. Oh, strong was Patrick Spenser's arm
And sharp his seaman's eye,
And sharper still the sense of him
To ken a sullen sea.

5. The King spoke to his footy page,
"Ye must not stop nor stay
Until Pat Spenser well doth know
The royal will today."

6. "What man hath done me all this ill,
What man hath done me sore,
To send me forth agin the sea
When I should not sail more?

7. "Oh, hasten ships and sailor men,
Oh, hasten sandlers,* too,
Oh, hasten down the endless sea
The King's wild will to do.

8. "For two days past I saw the sun
And yester eve'ing the moon,
Tonight I saw a blood-red star
And know my end is soon."

9. When Patrick Spenser sailed away,
A laugh did light his eye.
When Patrick Spenser came to rest,
Hit was his time to die.

10. Oh, some sit in the chimney book,†
And some walk on the strand,
And some do watch the whole day out
For Spenser's ship to land.

11. But Patrick Spenser's long since home
Where sailors all must haven.
The Scottish lords and all their crew
Are in the sailors' heaven.

12. Oh, at his feet the Scottish lords
Lay mid the ocean's wailing,
And at his head, in letters red,
The orders for his sailing.

---

the Battle of Dalton (Ga.). After the battle (May 9, 1864), the Union Army retreated, and Christopher Bell lay on the battlefield sorely wounded. It was quite a while before the harassed medics got around to him, and when they did, the treatment was hurried and not overly effective. He never regained the use of his left arm. But the Confederates carried the day, and that seemed to make up for more than 70 years of crippled living. Yes, this little man was gay and full of song and laughter. It was hot and muggy that day, and I remember Bell's saying, "Mister, I'm as hot as the devil windin' water‡ in hell."

At a very early age Christopher Bell became interested in shape-note music. His book was *The Sacred Harp*. He had attended singing conventions all over northern Georgia and eastern

* Chandlers?     † Nook.     ‡ Drawing water, as with a windlass.

Tennessee as a singing teacher. In recent years this source of income had dried up. Music was being taught everywhere, even in the grade schools. But Christopher Bell was still light-hearted. On this particular hot June morning he was on his way to Gatlinburg, where he hoped to attend a celebration of Old-Timers' Day. I believe there was a prize of some sort at stake; he would be one of the singing competitors.

He had never worked at any kind of trade, and neither did he farm. "Hit takes two hands," said he. But he did work from time to time in a cow-pound, or cattle yard, near Rossville, Ga. — probably, he thought, around the turn of the century. He was not overly sure of his dates, and to rationalize this failing, he said: "Mister John, when a fellow lives as many years as I have, they all run together. It's somethin' like a muddy freshet runnin' out into a clear stream."

To get Bell started, I sang first; but when he went to singing he could hardly be stopped. First it was a lovely carol concerning the birth of Christ. This was followed by a ballad he called "Patrick Spenser" — in reality "Sir Patrick Spens," and a very rare ballad indeed. He could not remember how he had learned it, but he surmised it must have been from his grandparents, who moved to Georgia from eastern North Carolina at the end of the 18th century. He also sang several delightful play-party songs, and promised the singing of as many ballads as I could write down.

His singing was clear and accurate, although his voice was no longer strong. However, for an 85-year-old man his was a remarkable performance. We planned to meet at the Old-Timers' Day celebration, but when the rifle shoot was silent and the horseshoes were all pitched, when the coverlids had been admired, the shape-note hymns all sung, and the bountiful evening meal eaten, I could not find the delightful little Christopher Bell. He had disappeared, and the place knew him no more.

The warm weather had brought on a light rain. It was a wonderful night for sleeping. My room at the Mountain View Hotel was lined with red-cedar panels, and I wondered where Christopher Bell might be spending the night. I worked a while trying to unscramble my notes. Out of it all came a fun-loving old man with a limp left arm, a wonderful sense of humor, and a poetic understanding of song.

# 26

# Lady Maisry

(Child No. 65)

## Sweet Maisry
(Niles No. 26 A)
## Lord Dillard and Lady Flora
(Niles No. 26 B)

**B**ALLADS containing the story-line of "Lady Maisry" have been encountered in Norway, Sweden, Finland, Denmark, Iceland, the Baltic States, the Germanic countries, France, Spain, Portugal, and, of course, England, Scotland, and on the North American continent. In almost every case, there is agreement on the important points. The heroine rejects all the local suitors. An employee on her father's estate, a kitchen worker, or a rejected suitor reports that the heroine is about to give birth to an illegitimate child. She loses her life at the stake or in some

equally violent manner, her true lover arriving too late to save her but in time to avenge her death with sword and fire.

Child ballad No. 64, entitled "Fair Janet," tells a story with striking similarities to "Lady Maisry." In the Scandinavian and Germanic countries ballads not unlike "Fair Janet" involve not only a tragic ending but also an execution brought about by senseless torture. In our country, the ballad of "Lady Maisry" has been found only a few times.

## Sweet Maisry

(Niles No. 26 A)

IN JULY 1934 a woman who lived on the side of one of the highest of the Southern Appalachian mountains sang a 20-verse version of a very rare ballad called "Lady Maisry." She knew other ballads, too, but they were ones with which I had filled my notebooks. "Lady Maisry," or "Sweet Maisry," was a find of the first order.

It was noonday, and the sun was as brilliantly

bright as I had ever seen it. There was not a cloud in the entire vault of the sky, but the wind swept by, sharp and cool, for we were more than a mile above sea level.

My informant was willing to sing under one condition: that I never use her family name nor give her exact address. All this because the singing of the ballad involved the repeated use

# Sweet Maisry

## (Niles No. 26 A)

*(Dorian mode on C)*

1. Oh, they courted her with watches,
   And they courted her with rings,
   They courted her with honeyed words
   And other pretty things,
   And other pretty things.

\* Lord.

2. "Oh, it's get ye gone, you nobles,
   You men of high degree,
   For I've give my love to an English lorl\*
   And I hope he marries me."
   *(repeat last line of each verse)*

...ie," cried her brother,
...meat and fee,
...agin my name,
...you shall be."

...me high and hang me well
If I've spoke false-ry
But Lady Maisry's growin' great
With an English lorl's baby."

5. He went into her chamber,
Strode heavy on the floor,
"They're tellin' me, my Sister dear,
That you've become a whore."

6. "A whore, a whore, dear Brother,
Ah, that could never be!
But I have a babe by an English lord
And I hope he'll marry me."

7. In steppèd her old father,
Steppèd heavy on the floor,
"Oh, it's how do you do, Lady Maisry,
Since you've become a whore?"

8. "A whore, a whore, dear Father,
Ah, that could never be!
But I have a babe by an English lord
And I hope he marries me."

9. In steppèd her old mother,
Stepped sadly on the floor,
"They're tellin' me, Lady Maisry,
That you've become a whore."

10. "A whore, a whore, dear Mother,
Ah, that could never be!
But I have a babe by an English lord
And I hope he marries me."

11. In steppèd her young sister,
Stepped lightly o'er the floor,
"Oh, how do you do, Lady Maisry,
Since you've become a whore?"

12. "Very bad, very bad, dear Sister,
As you can plainly see,
For Father and Mother are gatherin' wood
To burn my poor body.

13. "Go down, go down, little runner,
To where Lord William be.
Give him this token of my love,
Ere they burn my poor body."

14. Oh, he ran the prince's highway,
He ran the meadow wide,
Oh, he bowed his breast and he swam across
A many a ragin' tide.

15. "Oh, is my castle burned,
Or is my still o'errun?
Or has my lady brought to me
A daughter or a son?"

16. Lord William took the token,
He kissed it tenderly.
"Your lady's folks are a-gatherin' wood
To burn her poor body."

17. "Go saddle up my speedest horse,
Go bridle up my brown,
Go girdle up the fastest horse
That ever ran the ground."

18. He took his horn and bugle,
His sword dragged to the ground,
And as he rode the King's highway,
He made his bugle sound.

19. "Oh Mother and oh Father,
I fear you not a straw,
For yonder comes Lord William,
His merry men and all."

20. He lifted down her body,
He lifted up her head,
He kissed her lips, he kissed her chin,
Sweet Maisry was dead.

of the word "whore." My informant suggested that I might use her name if I substituted "loose woman" or "loose one" for "whore." This compromise would not only destroy the rhyming scheme, but would turn a powerful ballad text into something rather ridiculous. So we agreed that I would write down her verses as she sang them but would always omit her family name and address. After all, her name and address were not nearly as important as a good clear version of "Lady Maisry."

Fortunately, my informant said I might mention her first name — fortunately because it is a rare name, and should be spelled "Telighthul." At least, that was her pronunciation of it so far as I could make out. She had once been married, but had lost her husband to a family war. At the time when I knew her, she was living with her father and her brother. Both men were tie-hackers. That is, they chopped out crossties with either broadaxes or just plain hand axes.

like hoggin' down a corn crop. But strawberries are safe from geese and ganders."

After a while Telighthul went out and rang a dinner bell. Presently, her menfolk appeared from the tie-yard. Both seemed pleased with a visitor from the outside world. "Telighthul has been expectin' you," said her father, and explained that a woman employed by the county had told them I would be visiting them sometime during the first half of July.

The noonday meal was delicious, and the cabin was as clean as a pin. Telighthul's father was full of laughter and good cheer. Her brother was as silent as a stone post. The old man said he might be encouraged to sing after dinner.

"I'm a little like a bagpipe," he said. "I never make no sound or song until my belly's full."

And his son added without a smile, "Full o' wind."

"Hit takes wind to sing," rejoined the father almost sharply.

Telighthul's cabin was surrounded by a profusion of flowers and flowering trees and shrubs. Flowering bobby-bush, bamma-gilly (Balm of Gilead), and cow-cumber were everywhere. Following a method employed by every garden clubber in the known world, she went to telling me that her flowers and shrubs were just past their prime. Now if I had only come a couple of weeks sooner . . . It was almost as good as a Ruth Draper reading.

Just beyond the cabin was a well-matted strawberry patch, where a bunch of violent-looking hooded geese were "goosin' down the weeds."

"Them geese-birds don't care nothing for strawberry leaves," laughed Telighthul. "Now if they had a hankerin' for 'em, hit would be most

After dinner I sang and Telighthul sang, but the old man seemed to have changed his mind about singing with us.

"Of course, most boastin' is ninety per cent lyin', but when I was a young feller, I could sing old-timey music as long as a body would listen."

A noisy hound-dog joined the two men. The old man turned to me and said: "A little barkin' saves a lot o' bitin'." Then he and his silent son strode off toward the tie-yard.

Telighthul very clearly said "lorl" for lord until after the 4th verse of "Sweet Maisry." From there on, she said "lord" with equal clarity. Her use of the Dorian scale was a marvel of accuracy. She started out in the key of what seemed to be E minor. Her C-sharp was as clear as if it had been struck by an expert string player.

# Lord Dillard and Lady Flora

## (Niles No. 26 B)

FROM THE SINGING of Anna Wilmer, who admitted to 50 years and was most likely closer to 60. She was gay and full of fun. She lived in the southwest end of Rockcastle County, Ky., and made what living she had by collecting and selling herbs. When she was young, and wild ginseng was in demand, she had made a very nice income, walking the forests about five months each year. Her father, who lived with her, said she had an eye for ginseng and also for men.

"Not every woman-person can spot a tiny 'sang' plant in the gloom of a forest," she said rather proudly. And said her father, "Not every woman-person can spot a likable man at a county fair, either."

I refrained from asking any questions about the whereabouts of a possible husband. There were no young people in sight, and no mention of any children was made by Miss Annie Wilmer.

The old father said: "Hit's a shame how tastes do change. Time was when the heathen Chinee used up a power of sang root, tryin' to restore their manhood, their power. Nowadays, the Chinee has got so triflin', they don't mind bein' weak and low in manhood."

He said they found a little sang from time to time, and as their product was the wild kind, it brought a better price than the cultivated variety. Cultivated ginseng, raised in beds partially covered with slats to keep out sunshine and simulate forest conditions, was less valuable.

"A two-rooted stem of sang, one that looks a lot like a man's body, that's what the buyers want, and that's what they will pay for," said Miss Wilmer. Her father smiled and nodded, "Sister, don't talk like that."

"Now, Pappy," said Anna, "you know hit's gospel!"

"Yes, Sister," said the old man, "but the crossroads is a poor place to tell your secrets."

"Like as if this singin' man is goin' in the sang business!"

"Well, mister," continued the father, "I suppose we'll be movin' out of these parts. I'm a-sufferin' from a stone,* and the land's run out, and Annie here ain't gettin' any younger. I've about sold this land of ours to a rich feller who wants to make it in a game preserve. So we'll be a-goin'. I always did say that a good fast run is better than a bad stand."

"The man who wants to buy our land is powerful rich," said Anna. "There's no road in here, and only a few folks know anything about this end of the county. But I guess shootin' birds and pheasants pleases those rich folk mightily." She paused, then added, "Beggars breed babies, but rich men tend money-trees."

When at last we got around to singing, Miss Annie told me she knew a song named "Lord Dillard and Lady Flora." But she was reluctant to sing, so I sang first — all 17 verses of "Barb'ry Ellen," "The Seven Joys," and several love songs. Finally, old Mr. Wilmer encouraged his daughter to sing for me. They had boiled up a pot of sassafras tea, and between cupfuls of that wonderful pink concoction Miss Annie did her singing.

She had told me her ballad was named "Lord Dillard and Lady Flora," but I soon discovered that she was singing a shortened version of "Lady Maisry." Even in the scant 5 verses she sang, the outlines of the tragedy could be detected. One might almost say that Anna Wilmer's 5 verses are as concentrated a tragedy as one can find in English ballad poetry.

My notes show May 1934 as the time of my meeting with the Wilmers. The spring flowers were blooming, and it had rained the night before.

* Kidney stone.

# Lord Dillard and Lady Flora
## (Niles No. 26 B)

*(Minor mode on A)*

1. "Oh little boy, oh pretty boy,
   I'll give you meat and fee,
   If you will to Lord Dillard go
   And fetch him quick to me."

2. "Go saddle up my bestest horse,
   The one that foaled last spring,
   And let me have my bugle horn,
   And I'll make the bridle ring."

3. "Oh Mother, Father, Brother,
   How hateful are you all!
   I soon will die a-burning,
   And be beyond recall."

4. Lord Dillard and his merry men
   For help they came too late.
   And how they'll swing their trusty swords
   Because of all this hate.

5. Lord Dillard went into the blaze
   And lifted up her head,
   But nevermore a word said she,
   'Cause she and her son were dead.

# 27

# Young Hunting

(Child No. 68)

## Lady Margot and Love Henry

### (Niles No. 27)

T<small>HE TRAGIC BALLAD</small> of "Young Hunting" is based on a practical joke, or it may even have been mere teasing. A young man tells his sweetheart that he is giving her up for a much more beautiful girl, who lives nearby. The young lady believes him, and to keep her rival from gaining the man of her choice, she murders him on the spot. Later a bird, in some cases a parrot or a poppinjay, comes and tells her that her lover loved no one but her, that he came to marry her.

But once the man is killed, the problem of disposing of the body remains. In some cases the girl keeps the body awhile. In others, she keeps it until she is involved in a complicated bit of bribery. In the American version offered herewith she even tries to bribe a "fine pretty bird" who threatens to "fly the King's highway and tell this mean story."

## Lady Margot and Love Henry

### (Niles No. 27)

I<small>N THE MONTH</small> of August 1933, a folk festival was held on White Top Mountain, about 25 miles from Marion, Va. Getting up to the top of this mountain was a feat of driving, and getting down was even more so. The road was littered with automobiles of all kinds and makes. Even so, the festival was well attended. There was a direct wire to the outside world, so that the festival promoters could keep the press and radio informed, hour by hour. There also were political overtones. However, quite a few local characters arrived, and there was some interesting folk music sung.

Pete Johnson, a small hunchbacked man of undetermined age, held the stage at the folk festival for quite a while. I heard him sing "Barbary Ellen" and decided to follow him around until he could find time to sing something for my notebook. It was rumored that he knew the ballad "Judas"; he never sang it, however. He did sing some fragmentary bits of Robin Hood ballads, and finally started to sing what he called "The Sisters" (this was "The Twa Sisters," or "The Old Lord by the Northern Sea"). The master of ceremonies asked him how many verses were in "The Sisters." Pete said there were more

# Lady Margot and Love Henry

## (Niles No. 27)

*With foreboding*

Lady Mar - got sat in her bow - ing room A - fore she went____ to bed.____ Oh, she heard the sound of a mu - si - cal horn, And hit made her bod - y sad,____ Hit made her bod - y sad.____

(*Minor mode on G*)

verses than enough. The master of ceremonies, thinking in terms of show-business values, quietly led Pete Johnson offstage, and thereupon missed something of real importance.

Almost at once Pete Johnson started walking home. He was in a huff; it was hard work walk-ing to the top of a mountain, and now they had almost run him off. He had planned to stop overnight in Konnaroch, Washington County, Va. I offered to drive him that far, and he accepted. I also suggested we stop for food and drink long enough for him to sing one of the songs he had ed to sing at the festival. He then it was that I took down the "Love Henry." It was not easy. xt, and he varied the tune, and

only after many repeats did he arrive at what he thought was "the right and proper way."

Before he began to sing, Pete said: "There's a pretty idea in this old-timey song — a talkin'

## Lady Margot and Love Henry (Niles No. 27)

1. Lady ot sat in her bowing room
   Afore she went to bed.
   Oh, she heard the sound of a musical horn,
   And hit made her body sad,
       Hit made her body sad.

2. Lady Margot stood in her bowing door,
   In her bowing door stood she,
   And when she heard his bridle ring,
   Hit made her full merry.
       (*repeat last line of each verse, omitting 1st
       syllable when not needed*)

3. "Light down, light down, Love Henry,
   And spend the night with me,
   For I have a bed, and a very fine bed,
   And I'll share it up with thee."

4. "I can't not light, I will not light,
   And pass the night with thee,
   For they be a gal in the merry, merry lea,
   And I love her full many times more."

5. He bended over the garden wall,
   He gave her kisses three,
   But with the penknife she held in her hand
   She stabbed him heartily.

6. "Woe be, woe be, my love," cried he,
   "To all your family,
   For don't you see my own heart's blood
   Come twinklin' down at my knee?

7. "I'll have to ride east, I'll have to ride west,
   I'll ride o'er land and sea,
   To find some curin' doctor,
   To come and cure me."

8. "You needn't ride east, you needn't ride west,
   You dasn't ride under the sun,
   For there's ne'er a doctor in all Scotland
   To cure what Margot's done."

9. She called her tender maidens,
   She bade them for her stand,
   Said: "All the gowns I ever wear
   Shall be at your command."

10. One taken him by the golden hair,
    One taken him by the feet,
    One taken him by the lily-white hand,
    And she by the middle so neat.

11. They drugged him to that doleful well,
    They drapped him with a sound,
    "Lie there, lie there, Love Henry,
    Where you will ne'er be found."

12. Up spake a bird and a very fine bird,
    With a nest in the green valley,
    "Ah, woe betide thee, cruel girl,
    He loved no one but thee."

13. "Light down, light down, my fine pretty bird,
    And peck wheat off my knee,
    And your cage shall be made of beaten gold
    Instead of the willow tree."

14. "I can't not light, I will not light,
    And peck wheat off your knee,
    For you could kill a bird as well
    As you killed Love Henry."

15. "I wish I had my little bow,
    My dart and tuneful string,
    I'd shoot you through your lyin' heart
    As you do sit and sing."

16. "But you hain't got your little bow
    To shoot me from this tree.
    So I will fly the King's highway
    And tell this mean story."

bird. I always did think birds and other critters could talk, and were a-talkin' all the while. One bird says 'teacher, teacher, teacher' over and over, all day long. And another says 'willie little, willie little, willie little.' And horses and mules — they talk continual. I used to know a mule-critter who preached a short sermon every Christmas Eve, regular."

When the singing was over, Pete said he honed* for my white cap, but I gave him a dollar and a twist of chewing-tobacco instead, and he beamed with pleasure. A short time after he left my car at Konnaroch, I developed a flat tire, and four of the noisiest swashbucklers came along and helped me change it. They, too, were singers, and had been refused an audience at the White Top festival. One of them sang, and three of them prompted, but that will develop later, when we come to "Fair John and the Seven Foresters" (Niles No. 41). It took quite some time to get that tire changed. The moon came up, and the night was iridescent.

It was a pity that the good folks up on White Top could not have been more patient with this pathetic little hunchback Pete Johnson. He and I made an appointment to meet the next morning in Marion, Va. But Pete did not keep the appointment, and I never saw him again.

* Yearned.

# 28

# Lord Thomas and Fair Annet

(Child No. 73)

Lord Thomas and Fair Ellender
(Niles No. 28 A)

Lord Thomas and Fair Ellen
(Niles No. 28 B)

Lord Thomas and Fair Ellen
(Niles No. 28 C)

Thomas and Ellen
(Niles No. 28 D)

In "Lord Thomas and Fair Annet" we find a crass, fortune-hunting nobleman who, on his mother's advice, marries the wrong girl. Fair Annet is beautiful but poor, while the "brown girl" is unusually dark, unlovely, and very rich. Lord Thomas's mother makes the decision, based no doubt on the dwindling family fortunes. Fair Annet is the one he really loves, and he admits it in the presence of his new wife, the brown girl, saying to Annet in the 12th stanza (Niles 28 A):

*"Dispraise her not, Fair Ellender mine,*
*Dispraise her not unto me,*
*For I think more of your tiny finger*
*Than I do of her whole body."*

This is too much for the brown girl, who stabs Fair Annet (Fair Ellender) on the spot. As soon as Lord Thomas discovers what has happened, he cuts off the brown girl's head, kicks it against the wall, and commits suicide.

"Lord Thomas and Fair Annet" is almost as widespread in North America as "Barbary Ellen." It is one of a trilogy of ballads telling somewhat the same story, the other two being "Fair Margaret and Sweet William" (Child No. 74; Niles No. 29) and "Lord Lovel" (Child No. 75; Niles No. 30).

## Lord Thomas and Fair Ellender

(Niles No. 28 A)

On February 26, 1936, a grand old white-haired lady sang me the 18 verses offered herewith. Her name was Hannah Smith, and everyone referred to her as Granny Smith. She lived at a place called Willscott Mountain in Cherokee County, N. C.

147

# Lord Thomas and Fair Ellender

## (Niles No. 28 A)

*(Pentatonic scales on D and G)*

According to my notes, it was a warm, rainy afternoon, and I had never seen such muddy roads and lanes. But, the notes continue, "spring is coming. There's laurel and ivy about to bud out. It was almost dark as I walked down the mountain, and I thought I heard a whippoorwill.

My mind went back to four lines of a sonnet by Edmund Spenser,

*Fresh Spring, the herald of love's mighty king,*
*In whose cote-armour richly are displayd*
*All sorts of flowers the which on earth do spring,*
*In goodly colours gloriously arrayd . . ."*

# Lord Thomas and Fair Ellender (Niles No. 28 A)

1. "The brown girl she hath house and lands,
     Fair Ellender she hath none;
   The best advice I can give to you:
     Go bring me the brown girl home."

2. He dressed himself in scarlet red
     And his servants all in green,
   And every town that he rode through
     They thought 'twas a royal scene.

3. He rode till he come to Fair Ellender's gate
     And he dingled so loud on the ring,
   There's none so handy as Fair Ellender
     To run and welcome him in.

4. "What news, what news, Lord Thomas?"
     said she,
     "What news have you brought to me?"
   "I've come to ask you to see me wed,
     The brown girl's the bride to be."

5. "Oh Mother, oh Mother, come read me a
     riddle,
     Come riddle hit both in one:
   Shall I today see Lord Thomas wed,
     Or tarry this day to home?"

6. "Oh, many a body may be your friend
     And many your foe might be,
   But I should advise you this day to stay
     And tarry to home with me."

7. "Oh, many a body may be my friend
     And many a one my foe,
   I'll venture, I'll venture my own heart's blood,
     To Thomas's wedding I'll go."

8. She dressed herself in satin white
     And her servants all in green,
   And every town she passèd through
     They took her to be some queen.

9. She rode up to Lord Thomas's gate
     And she dingled so loud on the ring,
   There's no one so handy as Thomas himself
     To run and welcome her in.

10. He took her by the lily-white hand,
      He led her through the hall,
    He seated her at the table's head
      Among the nobles all.

11. "Be this your bride, be this your wife
      That looks so wondrous brown,
    When you could have married a woman as
      fair
      As ever the sun shone on?"

12. "Dispraise her not, Fair Ellender mine,
      Dispraise her not unto me,
    For I think more of your tiny finger
      Than I do of her whole body."

13. The brown girl hath a tiny penknife,
      Hit was both long and sharp,
    Betwixt the long ribs and the short
      She speared Fair Ellender's heart.

14. "What matter, what matter, Fair Ellender
      dear?
      You look so pale and wan!
    You used to have a color as fair
      As ever the sun shone on?"

15. "Oh, be you blind, Lord Thomas?" said she,
      "Or can't you very well see?
    For yonder is my very heart's blood
      Come a-twinklin' down to my knee."

16. He took the brown girl by the hand,
      He led her through the hall,
    And with his sword he cut off her head
      And threw it agin the wall.

17. He put the handle 'gainst the wall
      And the p'int against his breast.
    Goodbye, goodbye, three lovers dear,
      God send them all their rest.

18. They dug a grave both large and wide,
      They dug hit long and deep.
    They buried Fair Ellender in his arms
      And the brown girl at his feet.

# Lord Thomas and Fair Ellen

## (Niles No. 28 B)

WHEN General John Bell Hood went forward at about 8:30 on the morning of September 20, 1863, the Battle of Chickamauga hung in balance. It was General Longstreet's intention that Hood's five units would drive a wedge between the Union forces of Brannan on the right and Van Cleve on the left, now that Wood's forces had been pulled out of the front line.

By noontime the breakthrough was of such magnitude that it could not be equaled in any major battle of the war. Only the Union left held out. Along the Dry Valley road, leading three miles to McFarland's Gap, there was a clutter of abandoned caissons, wrecked gun carriages, demolished baggage wagons, and fleeing Union soldiers. The dead of both armies lay in windrows, and among those dead were two brothers from Charleston, S. C. — Edward and John F. Maypother — who had made a modest fortune in indigo and rice. Their graves were, of course, unmarked. They fell in windrows, like their comrades, and they were buried the same way.

But Chickamauga was an empty victory. The senior generals in the Confederate high command concluded that General Bragg had thrown away "the fruits of victory," won at such great cost in the cedar thickets and the tangle surrounding Chickamauga Creek.

It fell my lot to explain these and many other details to a frail white-haired woman of great dignity and great sorrow. In her early youth Miss Bertha Maypother worked diligently as a needleworker and hatmaker. Born in Charleston, S. C., in 1852, she was 81 years of age when I knew her in 1933. She was a little more than 8 years old when her uncles, Edward and John F. Maypother, closed up their factors'* shop in Charleston and joined the colors. Bertha Maypother never saw them alive again.

When she was young her needlework and hatmaking were profitable, and she could have afforded the trip to Georgia and the Chickamauga battlefield, traveling like a lady. But time crept away, and left the ghosts of the almost forgotten years behind. She never made the trip until 1933, and then slowly and uncomfortably, sitting up in day coaches and eating badly cooked meals in railroad stations. Finally, she arrived in the Chattanooga vicinity, and decided to stay a while at Ringgold, Ga., where she found employment tufting spreads for a woman who operated a candlewick-spread enterprise in near-by Dalton. The spreads and the candlewick were brought to Miss Maypother on Monday, and the finished product was collected on Friday. Meanwhile, she found time to go over to the Chickamauga battlefield and look at the cemetery and wonder and weep.

The man who collected the spreads told me that Miss Maypother was an expert seamstress, and also that in spite of her years she was a fine singer of old-timey music. But, he said, "she yearns mostly to know all about the Battle of Chickamauga. That's where she lost the remaining menfolk in her family."

I talked with her all one very hot afternoon in July 1933, and with the aid of a hastily drawn map and some newly acquired information, I did the best I could to explain General Polk and General Rosecrans, General Longstreet and General John Bell Hood (who, while leading the victorious attack, lost his right leg to a Minié ball). It was noon then, noon of September 20, 1863, and by that time Miss Maypother's uncles, Edward and John F., lay dead among the other dead.

The map I had drawn is found in my notebook and is quite clear, even after all these years. I find the following notes: "Long evening, translucent sky. Bertha Maypother a most tragic figure. Never have I been so sad and so depressed over anyone's lot . . . alone, alone, alone. I tried to explain the battle in an historical manner, but

---

* A factor is a moneylending sort of banker. He lends money on crops, etc.

my history was too quickly learned. My map was a poor thing, and all I can say is that it was the best I had at the time . . . Her singing was fabulous."

When it was my turn to explain myself and my occupation, I did this by singing several of the longer ballads. Finally, Miss Maypother put down her needlework and sang for me, sang in

and shook hands with me in a rather preoccupied manner. Finally, she said: "You've been a great benefit to me. I found out many things today I never knew before. I'll forget them, of course, but it was pleasant to know them once."

I said goodnight, but she said goodbye, and we left it there. I don't believe she ever got back to Charleston.

a light, age-dimmed voice the tragic ballad of "Lord Thomas and Fair Ellen." She had already seen my notebook, as I sketched the battle map. When I went to writing down her text and tune, she never asked a single question. Then I sang again, and she went back to her candlewick. She was stitching white candlewick in a geometric pattern stamped on lavender cotton.

In my notebook there is a hastily drawn staff and a G clef with nothing under it save these words: "I hoped to get her to sing her version of 'Jackie Randal' (no doubt 'Lord Randal'), but she simply shook her head and wept. The tears fell on her tufting."

Her performance of "Lord Thomas and Fair Ellen" was so charming and so accurate, the melodic line was so thrilling, that I felt under great obligation. That evening, during the long twilight, I drove her down to the Dry Valley road, the road leading over to McFarland's Gap, and tried to explain a battle I only half understood. After a bit, she said: "It's all right — I can see it better without the explanation. General Bedford Forrest and his cavalry operated out of Ringgold, General Hood came up out of the creekbed, and my two uncles died on the side of this very road . . ."

It was growing dark. I turned around, and we drove silently back to Ringgold. When at last we came to the shambling little house in which she had one room, she stepped out of the car

On the way back to my hotel in Dalton, I took a side road to the left and drove over to the Chickamauga road, which is an important road running to La Fayette. A few miles down this road, I turned off again to the left, onto an almost unused dirt lane, a "dim road" indeed. Here I got out and walked about. Never had I seen so dark a night. The stars seemed to be ever so close. A sonnet began to formulate itself, and later that night I wrote it down in my notebook. It was rewritten in 1937, and then the rewriting was discarded. Here it is, as it appeared originally:

*The bundled sheaves of stars are splashed across*
*The endless, unbrushed threshing floor of night,*
*From Northern Star to brilliant Southern Cross,*
*Eking out their tiny shafts of light.*
*How many times these kindly stars looked down*
*And wept with those who thought they wept alone,*
*Or cried the joy of village, farm and town*
*When celebration called the night its own!*
   *Ah, galaxy of stars, your years of light*
   *Sift like fallen feathers to the earth,*
   *Where in pitchforked windrows they do wait*
   *The tick of earthly time to tell your height,*
   *The written word of God, your very birth,*
   *Your span of life, and then your final fate.*

Here are the verses and the music of Bertha Maypother's version of "Lord Thomas and Fair Ellen":

# Lord Thomas and Fair Ellen
## (Niles No. 28 B)

*(Minor mode on E)*

1. "Oh riddle me, Mother, riddle me,
   And sing it all in one:
   It's shall I marry sweet Ellen the fair,
   Or bring the brown girl home?
   Or bring the brown girl home?"

2. "You know that the brown girl has farms
   and lands,
   You know fair Ellen hath none.
   That's why I say, my own dear son,
   Go bring the brown girl home."
   *(repeat last line of each verse)*

3. He dressed himself in scarlet red,
   And he wore a golden ring,
   And every village he passèd through,
   They took him for some king.

4. He rode up to fair Ellen's gate,
   And tingled on her ring,
   And none was so handy as Ellen herself
   To rise and let him in.

5. "What news, what news, what news?" cried
     she.
   "You've come so far away."
   "Oh, it's I've come to invite you
   To guest my wedding day."

6. She dressed herself in scarlet red,
   And she wore a bodice of green,
   And every village she passèd through,
   They thought she was some queen.

7. She proudly rode to Thomas's gate
   And loudly tingled the ring,
   And none was so spry as Thomas himself
   To run and let her in.

8. He led her by the lily hand,
   He led her through room and hall,
   And sat her down in a canopy chair,
   Well placed against the wall.

9. "Is this the bride?" fair Ellen cried,
   "She is so wondrous brown.
   You might have wed the fairest girl
   Who ever walked the ground."

10. Then up spake the nut-brown maiden,
    She spake in bitter spite,
    "Where got you the water of roses, fair Ellen,
    That washes your skin so white?"

11. "Oh, you could wash in melted snow,
    You could wash in the sea,
    You could wash till the clap of doom
    And ne'er be as white as me."

12. Oh, the brown girl pluckèd a bodkin
    From out the hair of her head,
    And plunged it into fair Ellen's heart,
    And Ellen lay cold and dead.

13. Lord Thomas's sword was in his hand,
    He slashed both right and left.
    The brown girl cried, the brown girl died,
    Her life, it was bereft.

14. He put his sword against the wall
    And drove it through his heart.
    And there three true loves all lay dead,
    And never more did part.

# Lord Thomas and Fair Ellen

## (Niles No. 28 C)

CONTRIBUTED by Miss Christine Brown (now Mrs. Forrest Pogue), who in the late 1930's taught art in Lexington, Ky. Miss Brown told me that her grandmother sang these verses, but the music was never taken down, and now it is too late.

## Lord Thomas and Fair Ellen (Niles No. 28 C)

1. "Oh Mother, oh Mother, go read this riddle,
   Go read it one, two, three,
   And say whether I shall go to Lord Thomas's
       wedding
   Or stay at home with thee."

2. She dressed herself in scarlet white,*
   Her waist it was of green,
   And every city that she passed through,
   She was taken to be some queen.

3. She rode till she came to Lord Thomas's yard,
   She jingled at the gate,
   No one so ready as Lord Thomas himself
   To rise and let her in.

4. He took her by her lily-white hand,
   He led her through the hall,
   And placed her at the head of the table
   Among those ladies all.

5. "Lord Thomas, Lord Thomas, is that your
       bride
   That looks so very brown,
   When you could have married as fair a one
   As ever the sun shone on."

6. The brown girl she had knife in hand,
   Both keen and very sharp,
   Between a long and the end of a short†
   She pierced fair Ellen's heart.

# Thomas and Ellen

## (Niles No. 28 D)

THIS CURIOUS Negro version of the Child ballad was sung to me in Sylva, N. C., by Clara Turner, a cook in a restaurant. She was a large, handsome woman with a commanding voice. She said she knew most of the hymns in the Baptist hymnal by heart, and announced herself as a "singing preacher." I never quite understood what a "singing preacher" was, and I could not stay over and attend her service on the following Sunday.

She told me she had once had the ballad of "Thomas and Ellen" "on a long narrow sheet of paper," obviously a broadside, which she had purchased in Atlanta, Ga., while attending a church convention. Once she learned the verses, she threw the slip of paper away. Her tune, though odd in places, was very effective. Clara said her church did not encourage the singing of "love ballads" because they usually were full of men running off with other men's women. But she did sing several delightful nursery rhymes, including an excellent version of the Tottenham Toad. I asked her whether the reference to the Red Girl, or Indian, was in the original set of verses she had purchased in Atlanta. She said it was not; it must have "crept in" as she sang the ballad, because of the many Indian girls at the nearby Indian reservation.

* *Sic!*    † Ribs, of course.

# Thomas and Ellen

## (Niles No. 28 D)

*(Minor mode on E)*

1. "Oh Thomas, my Thomas,
   Listen what I said,
   Don't marry no white girl,
   Don't marry no red."

2. "Oh Mama, oh Mama,
   I will tell you what,
   White girls got lots of things
   Those brown girls ain't got.

3. "Ellen she got horses,
   She got house and gear,
   She got cabin, she got lands,
   I love her so dear."

4. "Oh Thomas, my boy Thomas,
   You best hear what I say,
   Marry up with Annie Brown,
   Send Ellen away."

5. Now the Brown girl stabbed fair Ellen,
   Ellen lay like dead,
   And Thomas flung that Brown girl
   Dead across that bed.

6. Please go dig a grave,
   Bury one, two, and three.
   And dig that grave in a quiet place
   'Neath a weep-willow tree.

7. Rose growed up from Ellen,
   Briar from the Brown.
   Hear how those folks are sorry,
   Weepin' in the town.

8. Thomas was a-weepin' too,
   Down in the cold, cold ground.
   But grave for three so wide, so deep,
   No one heard him sound.

# 29

# Fair Margaret and Sweet William

(Child No. 74)

## Lady Margot and Sweet Willie
(Niles No. 29 A)
## Lady Margot and Sweet Willie
(Niles No. 29 B)

THIS IS the second in the trilogy of tragic ballads to which I referred in connection with "Lord Thomas and Fair Annet." In "Fair Margaret and Sweet William," we have what seems to be a lovers' quarrel, resulting in the death of two of the three people involved. There is no question of house and lands, oxen, horses, and cows; the restoration of a family's fortune has nothing to do with the case. It is simply a case of the young man deciding to marry the other girl — one might say, the wrong girl.

The ballad "Fair Margaret and Sweet William" must have been known at the turn of the 17th century, because it is twice quoted in Beaumont and Fletcher's *Knight of the Burning Pestle*, produced in London in 1611. The ballad is very widely known in America; it has been reported more than a score of times in Virginia alone.

It is interesting to observe that neither in the original English and Scottish versions nor in the American survivals is there an absolutely clear explanation of Sweet William's conduct. It is indeed a betrayal, but the reasons for it are obscure.

# Lady Margot and Sweet Willie
## (Niles No. 29 A)

ONE MORNING in July 1932, I took down 15 verses and the lovely tune of "Lady Margot and Sweet Willie" from the singing of a very willing old lady known as Granny Holcolm. She had already sung "The Cruel Brother" ("Brother's Revenge"), and from a younger member of her family I had obtained a version of "The Maid and the Palmer." All in all, it was a very fruitful morning.

As I mentioned earlier, driving the road into Kingdom Come Valley in 1932 was a hazardous enterprise. All morning the sky had been full of sound, and it was still thundering and it was raining lightly when I reached the Holcolm cabin.

157

# Lady Margot and Sweet Willie
## (Niles No. 29 A)

*Moving along*

Sweet Wil - lie rose up in the month of May, And he decked him - self in red, Say - in', "How, oh how, can a man find out If La - dy Mar - got's love is dead?"

*(Dorian mode on E)*

Once Granny Holcolm looked up at the sky and said, "Old Devil is a-arguin' with his mother-in-law."

When I closed my notebook after taking down "Brother's Revenge" (Niles No. 8), I did not expect that a person as old as Granny Holcolm would be willing or able to sing another long ballad. But she was both willing and able — and her singing was clear and concise. She did change key occasionally, but it is not unusual for elderly people to vary their pitch when singing for an extended period of time. A young grandson prompted her with her text occasionally. Otherwise, she never faltered.

# Lady Margot and Sweet Willie (Niles No. 29 A)

1. Sweet Willie rose up in the month of May,
   And he decked himself in red,
   Sayin', "How, oh how, can a man find out
   If Lady Margot's love is dead?

2. "Oh, I've never done my true love harm,
   And she never harmèd me,
   But ere the sun draps to yon high hill,
   Lady Margot my bride will see."

3. As Margot sat in her tower room,
   A-combin' her hair of gold,
   Then up did ride Sweet Will and his bride
   As the church bells gaily tolled.

4. Oh, it's down, down, down went that ivory
        comb,
   And wild her hair did toss,
   For none did know as well as Margot
   How much she suffered loss.

5. 'Twas late, late, late in the middle of the
        dark,
   When honest men did sleep.
   Something white did fright that fair young
        pair
   By standing at their feet,

6. Sayin', "How do you like your soft weddin'
        bed,
   And how like ye them pillows and sheets,
   And the soft yellow hair of that young
        woman fair,
   What lies in your arms asleep?"

7. "'Tis well I like my weddin' bed,
   And my wife's fair golden hair,
   But the ghost of one I used to love,
   Hit makes my blood run cold.

8. "Such dreams ain't fitten for honest men,
   They bring the sleeper no good,
   For why, I see my fair young bride
   A-covered up with blood."

9. Next morn said Willie to his mounted men,
   "Go ye by two, by three,
   And ask the leave of my fine new wife
   If Lady Margot I might go see."

10. He rode up to Lady Margot's powder chest,
    And quickly knocked ting-a-ling,
    And none was so spry as the prince, her
        brother,
    To run and let Willie in.

11. "Lady Margot's not with her merry maids,
    Lady Margot's not in the hall,
    Lady Margot's in that long white coffie*
    That lies twixt the altar and yon wall."

12. Her father budged the coffie lid,
    Her brother unwound the sheet,
    And after sweet Willie kissed her many times,
    He died there at her feet.

13. Lady Margot died like hit might be at night,
    Sweet Willie, he died of the morrow.
    Lady Margot, she died of a pure heart,
    Sweet Willie, he died of his sorrow.

14. Oh, it's bury them out in the quiet church-
        yard,
    Where praying folk retire,
    And see how it growed from her heart a rose,
    And up from his heart a briar.

15. And it's let them grow up to the church's
        peak,
    Till they can't not grow no higher,
    And there they'll tie a true-lovers' knot,
    The red rose and the briar.

* Coffin.

# Lady Margot and Sweet Willie

## (Niles No. 29 B)

*(Minor mode on F)*

1. Sweet Willie rose up in the month of May,
   And he dressed in green and gold,
   Said, "I can't quite forget the love of fair
   Margot
   That never, never grows cold.

2. "I have no harm for fair Margot,
   And she has no harm for me.
   But some fine morning at eight o'clock,
   My bride she shall surely see."

3. Fair Margot was in her dowel* room,
   A-combing her wonderful hair,
   When she saw Willie and his new-wedded
   wife
   That made such a handsome pair.

4. Oh, down she flung her ivory comb,
   In silk she tied her hair,
   And out of her dowel room she ran,
   And was never again seen there.

5. When day was gone and night had come,
   And honest men did sleep,
   Something appeared to Willie and wife
   And stood at their bed feet,

6. Sayin', "And how do you like the way of
   your bed,
   And how do you like your sheets?
   And how do you like your new-wedded wife
   That lies in your arms and sleeps?"

7. "Oh, it's very well I like my bed,
   And better I like my sheets,
   But best of all is the lady gay
   That stands at my bed feet."

8. He called up his mounting men,
   By one, by two, by three,
   Said, "I'll quickly away to fair Margot's
   bower
   And leave my new lady."

9. He rode up to Margot's dowling door
   And quickly kicked the ring,
   And none was so handy as her brothers tall
   To run and let him in.

10. Fair Margot was not in her dowling room,
    Fair Margot was not in the hall,
    Lady Margot was in her coffin so long,
    Lyin' pale agin the wall.

11. Her father budged the coffin lid,
    Her brothers unwound the sheet,
    Sweet Willie kissed her clay-cold lips
    And died at her dear feet.

12. Fair Margot died like it was today,
    Sweet Willie died of a morrow.
    Fair Margot died of pure true love,
    Sweet Willie died of his sorrow.

13. Fair Margot was buried in the lower grave,
    Sweet Willie in the higher.
    Her heart did sprout a red, red rose,
    His heart did sprout a briar.

14. The rose and briar grew and grew
    Till they could grow no higher,
    And then they looped and tied a knot,
    The red rose and the briar.

# Lady Margot and Sweet Willie
## (Niles No. 29 B)

IN THE SUMMERTIME of 1933 I spent a night near the Hindman Settlement School in Knott County, Ky. While there I took down a clear version of a ballad called "Green Beds" (not in Child), and also found out about Carson ("Tombstone") Mullens.

Mullens, originally from North Carolina, was said to know all the verses of a ballad about a man who married one woman while in love with another. Several people in the ballad died, I was told, and the song was slow and sad. I made a mental note of this information, thinking the

\* Perhaps "bower."

ballad might be "Lady Margot and Sweet Willie." On paper I took down a map to guide me in finding Mullens, and the next day, in a light rain, I took off in the direction of Dwarf (pronounced "Deewarf"), Perry County, Ky.

There was much backing and filling, and retracing of footsteps. Finally I gave up my car and took to a swinging bridge over Troublesome Creek. By noontime, I was sitting in the doorway of the tombstone shop, watching Mullens chip out the upper and lower stones of a quern.* As a small boy, I had helped operate a quern (it takes two people to turn it). The center hole in the top stone is filled with corn, wheat, or other grain, and after a bit of turning a wonderfully coarse kind of meal sifts out of the lower stone through the "ventings," which are skillfully cut openings in the lower stone. The two stones are housed up in a wooden frame, which is placed over a box intended to catch and contain the ground grain.

Carson Mullens's brother, known as Silent Hillard, was chopping out a headstone with a short-handled broadaxe. "Hit's for an old critter over the hill," said Carson. "He can't last long, and if we hain't got the stone ready for the family on the day of the buryin', they'd be sure to forget all about it in a week, and then we'd lose a sale."

For dinner that day Mrs. Mullens served a large loaf of delicious home-baked bread, made of a mixed hand-ground flour. According to my notes, it contained wheat, barley, and cornmeal. "She's forever lending women-persons starters of yeast," said Carson proudly. "And when she runs out of yeast mother, she can make some more. Just cooks up a small batch of cornmeal and potatoes and adds a little mildew offen the sides of the old yeast crock."

"You forgot the short sweetnin'," † said Mrs. Mullens slyly.

Finally we got around to the singing. But only after I had observed and admired querns and tombstones, and sung my heart out, to boot. But, here again, my rewards were great.

The tombstone for the old critter dying slowly just over the hill was finished, and the quern was incased in a wonderfully fitted wooden frame, and then Carson Mullens — who was 72 years of age, had once lived in North Carolina and yearned to return — said to me: "I only know a few ballards, but there's one I know powerful well. I used to have the ballat of it [meaning the text], but . . ." He paused, as if to remember some forgotten lines, and then he began, softly at first. Picking up in sound and motion he moved on into the tragedy of "Lady Margot and Sweet Willie."

What with querns and tombstones and homemade yeast, I forgot to mention that Carson Mullens and his brother Hillard had been regular members of a shape-note singing group when they lived in North Carolina. When I returned to the neighborhood of Dwarf in 1936, I inquired about Carson Mullens and discovered that he had indeed returned to North Carolina, bag, baggage, and short-handled tombstone broadaxe.

---

* From an Old Saxon word. It is a grain-grinder made of two stones. The bottom stone is stationary, the top one is turned by hand. The grain is introduced through a hole in the top stone.

† Short sweetnin' is sugar (white); long sweetnin' is molasses or sorghum.

# 30

# Lord Lovel

(Child No. 75)

## Lord Lovel
(Niles No. 30)

THE BALLAD of "Lord Lovel," the third in the tragic trilogy, presents the legend of a weakling member of the nobility who suffered from an Englishman's usual desire to see far places. Lord Lovel was continually traveling. Indeed in text C of Child's collection, Lord Lovel becomes Lord Travell. His sweetheart, named Lady Ouncebell, Fair Nancybelle, Lady Ounceville, Lady Oonzabel, or just plain Isabell, really dies of what seems to be boredom. Child refers to her as one who died "not of affection betrayed, but of hope too long deferred."

We may safely say that Lord Lovel died a laggard's death. In my family, the ballad of "Lord Lovel" was thought to be slightly ridiculous, and was sung for humor's sake, if at all.

Versions of this ballad are widely known in Scandinavia, the Baltic States, and all across continental Europe, as far west as Spain. The melodic material offered herewith is not distinguished, but it is the tune I sang as a child, and I never went to the trouble to seek out a better one, in view of the equally unimpressive story line.

## Lord Lovel
(Niles No. 30)

It should be noted that the extent of Lord Lovel's wanderlust cannot be gauged from the following version. By contrast, in one of the Child originals he stays away seven years. The humorous touch about the sexton is an American addition, not found in Child originals. It does ap-

pear, however, in several American variants besides my own.

Lord Lovel has been printed more often in American songbooks and broadsides than any other Anglo-American ballad.

# Lord Lovel

## (Niles No. 30)

*In a swinging manner*

Lord Lov - el he stood in his sta - ble door, A -
comb - ing his milk - white steed, _____ When down came La - dy
Doun - ce - bell, A - wish - ing her lov - er good -
speed, _____ A wish - ing her lov - er good - speed. _____

*(Major mode on E♭)*

# Lord Lovel (Niles No. 30)

1. Lord Lovel he stood in his stable door,
   A-combing his milk-white steed,
   When down came Lady Douncebell,
   A-wishing her lover goodspeed,
   A-wishing her lover goodspeed.

2. "Oh, it's where be ye going, Lord Lovel?" she cried.
   "I pray ye, do tell me."
   "I'm a-going to ride my milk-white steed
   And look at some far country."
   *(repeat last line of each verse)*

3. He had not been in that far country
   Above a year and a day,
   When he thought and he thought of Douncebell,
   And the thought won't go away.

4. He mounted up his milk-white steed,
   And he rode to London town.
   And there the bells in the high chapel rang,
   And the people sat mourning around.

5. "Who's dead, who's dead, who's dead?" cried he.
   "Is it someone dear to me?"
   " 'Tis Douncebell, who loved you well,
   And called herself your Nancy.

6. "Go open her coffin, open it wide,
   And turn the winding sheet down,
   And let him kiss her cold, cold lips,
   And see the tears twinkling down."

7. Lord Lovel was buried in the chancel church,
   Douncebell lay in the choir,
   And out of her grave grew a sweet, sweet rose,
   And out of his grave a briar.

8. The rose and briar grew and grew,
   And was known in village and town,
   And would be growing unto this day,
   But the sexton come cut them down.

# 31

# The Lass of Roch Royal

(Child No. 76)

## Who's Goin' to Shoe Your Pretty Little Foot
(Niles No. 31 A)

## Who's Goin' to Shoe Your Pretty Little Foot
(Niles No. 31 B)

VERSES containing the phrases "shoe my foot" or "glove my hand" have been encountered in scores of American ballads and love songs. Their presence alone does not identify the ballad in question as "The Lass of Roch Royal." In its more or less complete form, this ballad tells the story of a distraught young woman, about to become a mother, who has traveled a considerable distance in a quickly built ship in search of her lover. She does find his home, but is denied admission by the young man's protective mother.

The lass turns away, loses her life in the sea, and the young man, discovering the awful facts, denounces his mother and takes his own life.

Up to this writing no one has reported a ballad from the North American continent containing all the elements of the legend. An interesting study of the plot material in this ballad is found in an article by David C. Fowler, in the *Journal of American Folklore,* Vol. 71 (1958), No. 282. The article is entitled "An Accused Queen in 'The Lass of Roch Royal.'"

## Who's Goin' to Shoe Your Pretty Little Foot
### (Niles No. 31 A)

ON THE GEORGIA ROAD south of Murphy, N. C., I encountered a singing truck driver named Phil Stater. I asked him if his full name was Philip. He asked me if I was a member of the Georgia state police, writing everything down in a little black book. I showed him my dulcimers and assured him I was just a wandering singer, and no policeman. Thereupon he told me that his full name was Philbrick Stater, and that he lived near

enough to Atlanta to get in on the fun and far enough away to miss the police and the taxes. He was driving a truckload of fruit and vegetables, and was quite gay about everything.

Stater was between 50 and 55 years of age, red-faced and noisy. After some discussion about a cowboy song concerning "little dogies," I sang some verses of "Barb'ry Ellen." That started him off, and before he had done and started his truck

167

# Who's Goin' to Shoe Your Pretty Little Foot

## (Niles No. 31 A)

*(Minor mode on C)*

in a northerly direction, he had sung fragments of shape-note hymns, ballads, and a garbled version of "The Seven Joys of Mary." He said he was "a pistol with the girls," promising that when he got to Asheville he would "go to a dance on the roof of the City building and hug all the girls on the dance floor." He said that in his early youth (before he got to be such a pistol with the women) he had been a singer in a foot-washing Baptist church choir. "Learned a lot of singin' from them Baptists, but they hampered me too much. Had to give 'em up."

Here are the text and tune of "Who's Goin' to
Shoe." It was the only thing Stater sang clearly
and accurately.

### Who's Going to Shoe Your Pretty Little Foot (Niles No. 31 A)

1. Oh, who's goin' to shoe your pretty little foot,
   Oh, who's goin' to glove your hand,
   Oh, who's goin' to kiss your red-rosy cheeks,
   When I'm in that far-off land?
   Ah ——

2. The pretty little birds did choose sad notes,
   And they sang a roundelay,
   They sang a sad little goodbye song,
   'Cause they knew I was goin' away.
   Ah ——

3. Oh, when my eyes are smilin',
   My heart is full of pain,
   'Cause I know when they put me in that cold, cold ground,
   I'll never see you again.
   Ah ——

# Who's Goin' to Shoe Your Pretty Little Foot
## (Niles No. 31 B)

IN AUGUST 1933, while interviewing a dulcimer maker near Marion, Va., I made friends with an herb- and skin-collector named Pres Wilcox. Pres called himself a "yarb man." According to my notes, he was a white-bearded old fellow who had come upon hard times because there was so little demand for his products. Very few "yarbs" were bought, and the skin business was nonexistent. (The skin business involved the trapping of wild animals and the tanning and preparation of their hides.) I spent the entire morning with the dulcimer maker and his friend Pres, and I learned a lot about the great hunting and trapping days at the turn of the century.

Pres said sadly: "There ain't no yarb business, and there ain't no skin business, and I ain't no business either . . . I am too old to need anythin' much save buryin'." The dulcimer maker sang some carols, I sang a long ballad, and Pres Wilcox sang 5 verses of "Who's Goin' to Shoe Your Pretty Little Foot." In fact, his 5 verses told some of the original "Lass of Roch Royal" legend.

# Who's Goin' to Shoe Your Pretty Little Foot

## (Niles No. 31 B)

*(Six-note recitation formula, minor mode on C)*

1. Oh, who's goin' to shoe your pretty little foot,
   Oh, who's goin' to glove your hand-ee-o,
   Oh, who's goin' to kiss your red-rosy lips,
   When I'm in that furrin land-ee-o?

2. Oh, it's call in a fine carpenter,
   It's make a ship for me-o,
   For I must seek out Lovin' George
   Wherever he can be-o.

3. How far, how far, she sailèd east,
   She sailèd many a mile-o,
   Until her boat was just fornenst*
   The castle and the pile-o.

4. "Be you the lass of Royal Run,
   Or give me a token true-o,
   That I will know you be no witch
   With hair wet of the dew-o."

5. Love George he kissed her red-rosy lips,
   And swore he'd glove her hand-ee-o,
   And died beside her as she lay
   Cold on the salt-sea sand-ee-o.

* Opposite.

# 32

# The Unquiet Grave

(Child No. 78)

### The Wind Blew Up, the Wind Blew Down
(Niles No. 32 A)

### The Resurrected Sweetheart
(Niles No. 32 B)

### The Green Grave, or The Restless Dead
(Niles No. 32 C)

THE GREEKS, the Romans, the Persians, the Germans, the Scandinavians, the Scottish Highlanders, the English, and even the realistic Americans had, and in some cases still have, a common notion that obstinate, excessive weeping for a departed loved one is an error and might even be a sin. This concept is the basis for a vast folk tradition, resulting in ballads, tales, and sagas.

Three American variants of "The Unquiet Grave" will be found in this collection. The ballad concerns a young man who sits on his sweetheart's grave and laments her death in continuous weeping until the long buried young woman comes out of the grave and warns her lover against his unreasonable grief and further tells him that if he should try to kiss her, he would surely die.

The ballad is still sung in England and has been encountered, up to this date, 10 times in the United States. The similarity between the variants offered herewith and in other American collections might indicate that somewhere along the line there was a broadside printed. Although the ballad might have been extant from very early times, the Child versions all come from the 19th century.

# The Wind Blew Up, the Wind Blew Down
(Niles No. 32 A)

"EARLY SPRING of 1934. Rain-washed roads . . . spring plowing is about over, and planting soon to begin. Bright days, cool nights . . ." These are the notes I find in my field notebook, and this line is added: "Corie was the singer."

The reference is to a young woman named Corie Netter, who lived with her husband Philip Netter, a disabled coal miner. They lived in a slab house on the side of a hill about two miles from Flat Lick, in Knox County, Ky. The day I

173

# The Wind Blew Up, the Wind Blew Down
## (Niles No. 32 A)

*(Minor mode on E)*

visited the Netter household, Corie was toting a baby on her hip and tending the pots on the stove, and she continued with both these chores as she sang me her ballad. She was quite gay about everything, in spite of her hard way of life — and in spite of the fact that her husband,

in the opinion of the neighborhood, was a "triflin' no-count," more lazy than disabled.

"Mr. Netter is a silent one," said Corie. "Yes, he's as silent as a bird of prey."

But later a neighbor-woman took me aside and told me of Netter's unwillingness to provide. "If he was my man," said this bustling type, "I'd put him in harness. I'd say, Netter, you either dig or hold the lantern."

Corie had a large garden planted, and she proudly displayed a belled sow with a litter of seven brand-new piglets. She sang very willingly. Her melodic line was clear, and her pitch was accurate to the end. This is the way she sang "The Unquiet Grave"; she called it "The Wind Blew Up, the Wind Blew Down":

### The Wind Blew Up, the Wind Blew Down (Niles No. 32 A)

1. The wind blew up, the wind blew down,
   It brought some drops of rain;
   My own true love is only one,
   And she in the grave has lain,
   And she in the grave has lain.

2. Ah, weep your tear and make a moan,
   As many a gay youth may,
   And sit and grieve upon her grave,
   For a season and a day.
   (*repeat last line of each verse*)

3. And when the season's past and gone,
   The fair young maid did say,
   "What man is weeping on my grave,
   The night and most the day?"

4. " 'Tis I, 'tis I, my fair young love,
   Who can no longer sleep,
   For want of a kiss of your darling lips,
   The day and the night I seek."

5. "Cold clay I am, my lips cold clay,
   To kiss them would be wrong,
   For if you go against God's law,
   Your time will not be long.

6. "See there, see there, the sun has set,
   The day has passed fore'er,
   You cannot bring it back again,
   By foul means or by fair.

7. "See there, alas, the garden green,
   Where often we did walk,
   The fairest flower that e'er was seen
   Is withered at the stalk.

8. "Our own hearts, too, will die, my love,
   And like the stalk decay,
   So all that you can do, my love,
   Is to wait your dyin' day."

# The Resurrected Sweetheart

## (Niles No. 32 B)

CISSLIE GRAVES, wife of Henry Graves, unemployed lumber-snaker who lived between Pineville and Arjay in Bell County, Ky., was a brow-beaten, world-weary matron who admitted to 56 years and looked as if she had been around much longer. Her mother, Granny Cottrell, who was proud of her 80 years and snow-white hair, was a different type. She had once been quite

# The Resurrected Sweetheart

## (Niles No. 32 B)

**Moderately slow, tenderly**

The wind blew east, the__ wind blew__ west, Hit__ rained small drops__ of__ rain,_____ I had one love and__ on - ly one, And she in the grave was__ lain,_____ And she in the grave__ was lain.

*(Dorian mode on G)*

well off in the way of the world's goods. Her husband had been in the lumber business and had prospered, but when he died, relatives and business partners fought over the estate, and Granny Cottrell came out with a very small part of what she had expected.

Somehow I was led to believe that she would have accepted her straitened circumstances with more grace if her married life had been more rewarding while it lasted. Said she: "When my husband was young, he was rich. We used to go all the way up to Louisville and stay at the

Galt House . . . He'd be out selling lumber. But he carried everything he had in his pocket. What love and affection he had for me and the girls he carried the same way . . . Love and affection fit the heart better than the pocket."

There was a long pause. Then she said: "Now take my daughter Cisslie. Her man married her thinking she was rich. He got hold of what little she had and wastreled it away. And now he snakes logs a little, and then he sits on the front porch and whittles all the other times."

Henry Graves, husband to Cisslie, was bitter, too. Said he: "I've been livin' with two naggin' females too long. I'm headin' out — Cincinnati maybe."

I tried to clear the air by doing some singing. Henry had sauntered off in the direction of some men who were chopping out railroad crossties. It may have been the sound of my tuning that brought Henry Graves back to the cabin, because before I knew it there he was, bending over me with a bit of conversation.

In subdued tones, he made a great statement, and one that explained his own problems quite accurately. "Mister," said Henry, "hit's a poor barnyard where the hens crow louder and oftener than the roosters."

Not feeling that it was up to me to solve their domestic difficulties, I said yes and no, and went on with the job of tuning as quickly as possible. When I had sung for them, Granny Cottrell shook her head. "I don't see what you're doin', wastin' your time with us. Why, people in cities might hire you to sing for 'em."

I didn't feel I could explain myself, so I laughed it off, and went on encouraging Cisslie Graves and Granny Cottrell to sing for me. I had been told by a roadworker that they knew some wonderful ballads. At long last, they did sing a delightful version of "The Unquiet Grave."

## The Resurrected Sweetheart (Niles No. 32 B)

1. The wind blew east, the wind blew west,
Hit rained small drops of rain,
I had one love and only one,
And she in the grave was lain,
And she in the grave was lain.

2. I'll do as much for any love
As she will do for me.
I'll sit upon her lonesome grave
And mourn in misery.
      (*repeat last line of each verse*)

3. I'll do as much for my true love
As any lover may.
I'll sit and grieve upon her grave
A season and a day.

4. The season's past, the season's gone,
And then the dead did speak:
"What man is weeping on my grave,
So loud I cannot sleep?"

5. " 'Tis I, 'tis I, 'tis I, my love,
Who can no longer sleep
For want of the kiss you did not give,
The kiss that I do seek."

6. "Cold clay, cold clay, my lips cold clay,
My breath of earth is strong.
If you should kiss my clay-cold lips,
Your time would not be long.

7. "See yonders way the garden green,
Where we were used to walk,
The finest flower that e'er was seen
Is withered to the stalk.

8. "The stalk is withered dry, my love,
The flower is in decay.
Our hearts will wither, too, my love,
When God calls us away."

As I was taking my leave, Granny Cottrell took me aside and said, "We're a-leavin' this place. I've got it sold already. Henry wants to go to Cincinnati. He can go, and glory go with him. Cisslie and I will go to Corbin. We got kinfolk there . . . hit's a good place to die. And remember what I said about love and affection. Hit don't fit in any man's pocket."

# The Green Grave, or The Restless Dead
## ( Niles No. 32 C )

*(Dorian mode on A)*

# The Green Grave, or The Restless Dead

## (Niles No. 32 C)

I CANNOT REMEMBER what took me to Science Hill in Pulaski County, Ky., one May night in 1913, but out of my notes emerge a delightful group of people who entertained me and for whom I did a performance of music. They were young people, about my own age then, and there was fun and dancing and laughter, and as I had some limited experience in the "great outside world" I was plied with all manner of questions.

The train I came on arrived late in the afternoon, almost at suppertime, and I seem to remember that the group who had come to meet me were reluctant to wait while I interviewed a pair of elderly people who caught my eye as I stepped off the train. They said their names were William Isaac Nolan and Belinda Nolan. The man was selling pencils and shoestrings, and the woman was singing from a much thumbed Baptist hymnbook. The pencil salesman was no surprise, but his singing companion, I thought, might well prove to be a singer of ballads. She did — and so did he. Their "Barbary Ellen" was not distinguished, and I did not bother to take it down, for I was already singing a "Barb'ry Ellen" that pleased me and seemed to please my audience, and in those days, I could see no reason for taking down another.

## The Green Grave, or The Restless Dead

1. The wind across the graveyard blew
   With tiny drops of rain,
   "I never had but one true love,
   And she in the grave one year hath lain,
   And she in the grave hath lain."

2. He sat and grieved upon her grave
   As many lovers may,
   He sat and grieved and made a moan
   A twelvemonth and a day,
   A twelvemonth and a day.

3. And when the grieving time was past,
   The maiden's ghost did say,
   "Who sits a-weeping on my grave
   A twelvemonth and a day,
   A twelvemonth and a day?

4. "My lips are cold as coldest clay,
   My breath is earthy strong,
   Now you have kissed me once again,
   Your days will not be long,
   Your days will not be long."

My diary has a note that explains quite a lot about the Nolans. It reads as follows: "The Nolans said they sang about the grave because they were near the grave." It was indeed "The Green Grave" about which they sang, subtitled "The Restless Dead." At first their music did not appear to be very interesting, but suddenly the tune turned Dorian for a brief moment, and I took it down in grateful haste. In my notes I see that, at first the unique turn of their tune must have been doubtful to me, for there is a separate pair of measures with the raised 6th prominently indicated. How fortunate it is that I resisted the impatience of the friends who had come to welcome me long enough to listen to the Nolans. I am pleased to discover, too, from the same notebook, that I bought a dozen pair of shoelaces at two pairs for five cents and gave them back to Mr. Nolan. Thirty cents was quite a lot of money in 1913.

The Nolans' voices were thin and faint and wispy, but quite accurate. The woman, Belinda, who did most of the singing, was the older of the two; the man, William Isaac, was partially blind.

Nothing I could write at this late date would serve to recapture that night in Science Hill quite so well as the faded, penciled notes of my notebook. They are as follows:

(Back at the hotel, later the same night.) "I did some music, and it was not overly good. I sang B. E. ["Barb'ry Ellen"] and some carols. There was dancing . . . of course, they had an organ, and there was a rather hopeless piano. One girl, a dark girl, slim, lovely, with the most yearning eyes I had ever seen . . . she sat leaning against the organ and watched me with a kind of hypnotic gaze . . . she says she will go out in the great world in the fall, up to Lexington to the State College or to the Normal School at Richmond [Ky.] . . ."

I have no record of the girl's name, but on the same page in my notebook I find a sonnet brimming with romantic love. I know that I was just past 21 years of age, and classifiable as a very callow youth. I knew the sonnet form, could recognize and write down the medieval modes, and had experienced the delight of looking long into the yearning eyes of a girl as she sat on the floor and watched me stumble through the verses of the great ballads to the uncertain accompaniment of a wheezy pump-organ.

The final result of all this is the fact that the Nolans sang a most delightful, shortened version of a rare ballad to a tune Pythagoras might have envied. I never saw the Nolans again. In fact, I have never returned to Science Hill from that day to this. Thus, I have never had a chance to see the pleasant people who entertained me or the slim, dark reed of a girl with the provocative eyes, the one who must have been "the dark lady" of my sonnet.

I can still return, though, to "The Green Grave, or The Restless Dead," as I took it down from the Nolans' singing, just beside the Southern Railway station at Science Hill in May of 1913.

# The Wife of Usher's Well

(Child No. 79)

### The Little Dead Boys
(Niles No. 33 A)
### The Wife of the Free
(Niles No. 33 B)
### The Fine Lady Gay
(Niles No. 33 C)
### The Cartin Wife
(Niles No. 33 D)

THE WIFE of Usher's Well, whom we may assume to be a person of wealth and position, sends her three sons off to gain what passes for an education. A plague falls upon the land, and the three sons die. The mother wearies the heavens with her prayers, and at long last the children return as ghosts. But the lads will accept neither food nor drink, and being ghosts they must depart — according to legend — before the

cock crows at daybreak. Before leaving, they give their mother a veiled warning against unreasonable grief.

As late as the 1930's the ballad was widely sung in the Southern Appalachian mountains. The melodic line in one variant (No. 33 A) is unusually beautiful, and the poetry is of the very finest.

# The Little Dead Boys

## (Niles No. 33 A)

THIS VERY interesting version of "The Wife of Usher's Well" was sung to me by two young women, Mrs. Anner Ledford and Mrs. Maggie

Henson, who lived at a place called Hot House, in Clay County, N. C. The time was April 1936.

# The Little Dead Boys

## (Niles No. 33 A)

There was a wom-an, she __ lived __ a - lone, Some ba - bies she had three; She sent them off to the North Co - ma - ree To learn __ their __ gram - mar - ee.

*(Pentatonic scale on E)*

1. There was a woman, she lived alone,
   Some babies she had three;
   She sent them off to the North Comaree
   To learn their grammaree.

2. They hadn't been gone but about three weeks,
   'Bout three weeks and a day,
   Cold death, cold death spread abroad in the land,
   And swept her babes away.

3. She prayed to the God who was in Heaven,
   A-wearin' a starry crown,
   "Oh, send me back my three little babes,
   Tonight or in the mornin' soon."

4. It was so near to the Christmas time,
   The nights be long and cold;
   Her three little babes come a-runnin' up,
   All into their mother's arms.

5. She fixed a table for them to eat,
   On it put bread and wine:
   "Come eat, come drink, my three little babes,
   Come eat, come drink of mine."

6. "Dear Mother, I neither want your bread,
   Nor will I drink your wine,
   For just before the break of day,
   Our Saviour must we jine."

7. She fixed them a bed in the back side room,
   On it she put a clean sheet.
   On the top she spread a golden cloth,
   And fixed her babes to sleep.

8. "Rised up, rised up," said the oldest one.
   "Rised up, rised up," said all three,
   "Our Saviour smiles and bids us come,
   And follow him, hit must be."

9. "Cold clods of clay rolls over my head,
   Green grass grows at my feet,
   And the tears you shed, sweet Mother dear,
   Would wet our winding sheet."

# The Wife of the Free

## (Niles No. 33 B)

IN JULY of 1933, a shy, middle-aged man and his wife, Mr. and Mrs. Carston Geer, sang the only version of "The Wife of Usher's Well" involving magic, and, interestingly enough, the place where the magic was to be learned was New York.

Mr. and Mrs. Geer sang for me on the porch of the Dickey Hotel in Murphy, N. C. In those days, dinner at a small-town hotel was an enormous operation that took place at noontime, during the hottest part of the day. The food may not always have been of the first order, but there was a lot of it. In the case of the Dickey Hotel, there were dishes and dishes of food and they were excellent. Of course, one needed a young digestion to manage it — I mean, the food.

Mr. and Mrs. Geer used a strange term in the very first line of their ballad: they referred to the wife of Usher's Well as "the wife of the free." I tried diligently to discover the meaning of this expression, but I never succeeded. Mrs. Geer said she had learned it that way from a schoolmate many years ago, and had been singing it as she had learned it, even though it did not make sense. Said she: "It's not easy to teach an old bear to dance a do-si-do."

Carston Geer and his wife were a pair of truly delightful people. In our conversation I discovered that they were east Tennessee people, and that both of them had been schoolteachers in their earlier days. They were very proud of the part which the Tennessee Volunteers had

# The Wife of the Free

## (Niles No. 33 B)

Wife, wife, wife of the free, It's she had bright boys three, _____ And she sent ____ them off to New York-a - ree To see what the world __ would be, _____ To see what the world __ would be. _____

*(Minor mode on A)*

played in winning the Revolutionary war.

"The Battle of King's Mountain turned the tide," said Carston Geer proudly. "After October 10, 1780, Lord Cornwallis didn't have anything to fight with . . ." There was so much talk about John Sevier and his young son, James Sevier, and Isaac Shelby, and Robert Young (who shot the English commander with a rifle called "Sweet Lips") that we almost lost sight of the tragic wife of Usher's Well, who sent her young sons away to learn magic, and to die, and to return once more as ghosts.

Here are the verses and the tune of "The Wife of Usher's Well," known to Mr. and Mrs. Geer as "The Wife of the Free":

## The Wife of the Free (Niles No. 33 B)

1. Wife, wife, wife of the free,
   It's she had bright boys three,
   And she sent them off to New York-a-ree
   To see what the world would be,
   To see what the world would be.

2. They hain't been gone some very long time,
   A month by days one, two, and three,
   "I hope they learn their magic well
   And come straight back to me."
   (*repeat last line of each verse*)

3. It was about the Christmas time,
   Three months had passed and a day,
   When all three boys dièd cold and dead,
   Yes, all three passed away.

4. Then back they came to Umberland,
   Back they came, one, two, and three,
   And when their mother saw them well,
   She rejoiced with joy-a-ree.

5. "Oh come, oh come, my little ones,
   Here is your bed so fine,
   And here is a meal of vittles all cooked
   For the three of you to dine."

6. "Oh Mother dear, we cannot sleep,
   Nor can we ever eat-a-ree,
   For Christ, our Saviour, called us home,
   And we must pray at his feet-a-ree.

7. "Cold clods of clay is all we need
   To cover us head to feet,
   But the tears you will forever shed
   Will wet our winding sheet."

# The Fine Lady Gay

## (Niles No. 33 C)

IT WAS July 1932, the Democrats were fixing to choose a presidential candidate, and, according to my notes, the banks in Whitesburg, Ky., were in great trouble. Many people were "on the

# The Fine Lady Gay

## (Niles No. 33 C)

*In an even, flowing manner*

*There was a fine la-dy, a la-dy gay, Who had wee ba-bies one, two, and three,____ But she sent them off to a North Coun-try priest To learn their gram-mar-ee.____*

*(Major mode on A and minor mode on F♯)*

1. There was a fine lady, a lady gay,
   Who had wee babies one, two, and three,
   But she sent them off to a North Country priest
   To learn their grammaree.

2. They hadn't been there but a moon and a day
   When sickness did cause them to grieve,
   They hadn't been there but a moon and two days
   When death had taken his leave.

3. "If they be a God who lives in the sky,
   Who used to wear a fine crown,
   Pray do send me back my wee babes
   Tonight or in the morn."

4. One morning, one morning, the winter was near,
   Then the lady gay stood at the door,
   And who should she see but her wee tiny babes,
   Come hastening home once more.

5. She sot them a table both long and wide,
   And she spread it, oh, very fine,
   Sayin', "Come now and sit, my wee tiny babes,
   Come eat some bread and some wine."

6. "Oh Mother, oh Mother, we can't eat your bread,
   Oh Mother, we can't drink your wine,
   For yonder now stands our Saviour dear,
   We must to him resign."

7. She spread out a bed in backward room,
   She spread out a white, white sheet,
   She spread out on top a coverlid
   To make them sleep so sweet.

8. "Take off, take off," says the boldest one,
   "Take off this sheet I say!
   For pride is the cause of your little dead ones
   Now lyin' in cold clay."

9. "Rised up, rised up," says another one,
   "For the cock is a crowin' the day.
   And yonder stands the sweet Saviour of all,
   To bear our soul* away."

10. "Green grass, green grass will grow 'round our head,
    Cold clay, cold clay, at our feet,
    But the tears you shed over us last night
    Have wet our winding sheet."

county." I had a standing offer of free gasoline if I would drive back from wherever I happened to be in the eastern counties and spend the night at the Daniel Boone Hotel in Whitesburg — hotel guests were that scarce.

It was July 1932, and the air was full of radio

* It is "soul" in my notes, not "souls."

broadcast concerning a political convention in Chicago. A local politician told me of a middle-aged maiden lady who was said to be a singer of old-timey music, and I lost interest in the convention almost at once. Her name was Tillie Cornett, and she, too, was only mildly interested in the statements spewing out of the loudspeakers. I noticed, however, that she sniffed the odor of coffee coming out of the hotel kitchens. It was a wonderful smell, she said. She loved good strong coffee.

Tillie had spent her early days in Letcher County, and as a young woman she had migrated to Dayton, Ohio, where she lived in what she called slow starvation — "like cow-beasts, hat-rackin' it out on brown lespedeza hay." In 1930 she had moved back to Knott County, Ky., and at the time I met her, she was nursemaiding some relatives' children in Whitesburg. Tillie Cornett's own private depression had begun long before the 1930's. Never having had much of the world's goods, she had little to lose.

No, Tillie Cornett was not much interested in conventions. On the advice of a friend, I invited her to join me in the hotel dining room for a "handsome meal of vittles," as she called it. Tillie Cornett loved good food, and especially good strong coffee. As we talked, she told me of another convention she had once heard, by way of radio broadcast, in which 24 persons were voting for a man named Underwood. "They kept a-sayin' twenty-four for Underwood," she re-called. "Then they'd say it again, twenty-four for Underwood, and again twenty-four more for Underwood. It's no wonder he never did get elected. Twenty-four votes ain't enough votes to elect a jaybird!"

Out in the lobby a radio continued to pour out the news of the convention then going on. A motley group of men, most of them rough, unshaven, hung on to every word. Tillie watched them awhile and shook her head. "Yes," she said, "it's like my granny used to say: where there's a dead critter, there's where you'll find the buzzards."

And then we talked about her granny, and some of her other folks, in Letcher County, and then she began to sing. She called her song "The Fine Lady Gay," and it was, of course, another version of "The Wife of Usher's Well."

When the singing was over, we went to the grocery store nearest the hotel and I bought Tillie Cornett a five-pound bag of coffee. She almost wept for joy. "This," she said, hugging her bag of coffee, "this will sure take the place of them roasted acorns we've been a-bilin'."

She was a very willing singer. Here are the verses and the tune of Tillie Cornett's version of "The Wife of Usher's Well":

On the same page of my notebook with the text of Tillie Cornett's wonderful ballad, I find the following:

Sonnet in Whitesburg same night [it must have

been July 7, 1932, although the date is not actually indicated]:

*Breathe not too deep, lest you shall break our dream,*
*For all the sturdy fabric of our love*
*Might be unraveled strand by strand and seem*
*As formless as a snow-shower from above.*
*And surely I would never have it so,*

*For I have wooed thee, woman, with such pains,*
*Have taught my heart the way you'd have it go*
*And satisfied my senses with what gains*
*Your slightest whim has sent my humble way.*
*Ah, touch the bubble gently if at all,*
*For what appears to me a paradise*
*Is made of such ethereal stuff and may*
*Evaporate before our eyes and fall*
*Like tears into the ocean, in a trice.*

# The Cartin Wife

## (Niles No. 33 D)

FRED POTHER, whose home was in Georgia but who was living at the time (June 1934) near Cashiers, N. C., assembled his grandchildren, boys and girls, and we had a great singing afternoon. They were primarily interested in shape-note hymns. I sang some carols. They responded with a version of "The Seven Joys of Mary" (only they had 13 joys), "Barbary Ellen," "The Carrion Crow," and, finally, "The Cartin Wife."

Although they were in the habit of singing with a group of shape-note singers, using *The Sacred Harp,* the Pothers were as variable a group as I've ever encountered. They changed time, rhythm, and pitch whenever the idea oc-

curred to them. After much effort, I did get a fairly clear manuscript.

Here we have, of course, a shortened version of "The Wife of Usher's Well." I believe the word "cartin" was an attempt to say "carlin." The glossaries tell us that a carlin, or carline, is an old woman, a wealthy woman, a low-born woman, or a peasant woman.

In the case of "The Cartin Wife," the text is much superior to the music. The melodic line leaves so much to be desired, I have tried to arrange the music in such a way as to heighten the sense of tragedy.

# The Cartin Wife

## (Niles No. 33 D)

(Minor mode on A)

1. "Old woman, old woman, come tell of us true,
   You once had boys of one, two, three,
   But now you cry far more than enough
   To get them back to thee, to thee."

2. "I wish the wind would never blow,
   And the flood would never tide,
   For my three boys are gone from me
   Over the ocean so wide, so wide.

3. "I am no very cartin wife,
    I do no man a harm,
    But my three boys are dead of the ague,
    When they were once live and warm, and warm."

4. She's made a bed, and a very fine bed,
    And she set out bread and wine,
    But neither would ever a one of them eat
    For fear they had not time, not time.

5. Then crowed the cock, and a very red cock,
    Then up and crowed the gray,
    When the three of all the little boys
    Said, "Christ bids us away, away."

6. "Oh Mother dear, you sent us off
    When we shoulda stayed near by,
    And now our Saviour calls us on
    To our home beyond the sky, the sky."

# Little Musgrave and Lady Barnard

(Child No. 81)

## Little Mattie Groves
(Niles No. 34 A)
## Little Matthey Groves
(Niles No. 34 B)

So FAR AS public performance is concerned, the three most popular ballads I know are, in the order named, "Barb'ry Ellen" ("Bonny Barbara Allan"), "Little Mattie Groves" ("Little Musgrave and Lady Barnard"), and "The Hangman" ("The Maid Freed from the Gallows"). It is safe to say that I've sung "Little Mattie Groves" a thousand times in the past 25 years. These performances were spread all over the U.S. and Canada, Great Britain, Holland, Belgium, Finland, and Estonia.

At one time in my life I knew only 7 verses. As years ground by, I learned additional verses from native singers, usually one or two at a time, until I knew a dozen verses; and then, in 1934, I took down 27 verses from one singer. Thereupon I discarded my previous text and learned what I consider the classic version. However, in all my 27 verses there is one situation I have missed. It can be found in the 13th verse of text A, "Little Mosie Grove and Lord Burnett's Wife," on page 291 of *Traditional Ballads of Virginia,* edited by Arthur Kyle Davis, Jr. In this 13th verse we have actually the makings of a play within a play. The background for what happens is this: among Lord Burnett's men is one who admires his daughter. The daughter's admirer hears Lord Burnett promise this girl to the "little foot-boy" who has just brought him

the news of his wife's faithlessness — provided, of course, that the news is true. If it is false, the page boy will be hanged without further ado. To make the page boy out a liar and secure Lord Burnett's daughter for himself, the merry man in Lord Burnett's entourage blows his horn, we learn in the 13th verse, hoping that little Mosie Grove upon hearing it will be warned and take to his heels before Lord Burnett returns.

In my text A, one of the merry men likewise blows his horn — but he is described as "one who wished no ill," rather than as one who wanted something for himself. In either case, the result is the same: Mosie Grove (or Mattie Groves) hears the horn, but is so captivated with Lady Burnett's (or Lady Arling's) charms that he is readily persuaded it is only a shepherd's horn, and accedes to the lady's suggestion that he lie down again and keep her back from the drafts that must have plagued the drafty English castles. When they wake, death at the hand of the irate husband is staring them in the face.

Audience reaction to this part of the performance is always revealing. I shall not soon forget a Chicago performance, at which the first row was largely taken up by some clerical-collared clergymen. They roared with laughter and slapped one another on the back with what their superiors might have thought unbecoming enthusiasm.

I usually try to avoid singing "Mattie Groves" for the good ladies of the music clubs. Once, however, when I made the mistake of singing it to such a group in Wisconsin, I was told later that the ladies didn't mind too much, "because evil got its just desserts when Mattie Groves was executed by Lord Arling."

In the early 17th century the ballad was quoted in part in seven different plays presented on the London stage. Broadsides appeared in the latter part of the 17th century, and it is from these, no doubt, that the American versions derive. The 20th century has found this ballad more widely known and sung in America than in the land of its origin. In the late 1930's RCA Victor issued a 78 r.p.m. recording of my performance of "Mattie Groves," and from that day onward, the folk-music nightclubs from New York to Los Angeles had a field day of it, with all sorts of garbled and "improved" texts appearing. I believe it was not sung in public performance before I began singing it in 1934.

In the discussion under "Lord Randal" preceding Niles No. 9 A and B, one will find 20 titles under which that great ballad has existed. Some are simple misunderstandings of the original name; others seem to be pure invention. The ballad of "Little Musgrave and Lady Barnard," being widely distributed geographically, has also enjoyed great variation in title. Here are a few of the renamings I have encountered in my investigation: Young Grover and Lady Banner; Young Musgrave and Lady Barnet; Little Mattie Grove and Lord Donald's Wife; Little Matthy and Lord Arnold's Wife; Young McGrover and Lord Banner's Wife; Young Musgrove and Lord Banner; Little Massy Grove and Lord Arnold's Wife; Young Red Rover and Lord Banner; Little Musgrove and Lady Barnswell; Little Matthew Groves and Lord Daniel's Wife; Little Marthy Grove and Lord Arnold's Wife; Little Mathy and Lady Vanner; Little Mathey Grones and Lord Arnald's Wife; Little Mathigrew and Lord Daniel's Wife; Young Magrove and Lady Vanner.

# Little Mattie Groves

## (Niles No. 34 A)

ON AUGUST 4, 1934, I met a young man named Sam Gentry, who said he had been born near Hot Springs, N. C., and was at that time living in Asheville. He was a road worker, and when I met him, he was visiting a family of relatives living near the Higgins farm on Turkey Mountain. I had been up to "the top of Turkey," and on the way down I helped push Gentry's car out of the ditch. He saw my instruments in the back of my car, and asked about them. This led us into a discussion of ballad singing. At length, Gentry told me that he knew a "ballard" about a fellow named Mattie Groves, and would be pleased to meet me the following Tuesday at the Battery Park Hotel in Asheville and sing it for me.

That was an important day for me as a singer of American folk ballads. As soon as I learned Sam Gentry's 27 verses, I discarded my 12-stanza version and went to singing the heartbreaking tale of Mattie Groves to audiences wherever I went. This is the text which RCA Victor recorded, as previously mentioned.

I had great difficulty with Sam Gentry, because he changed pitch from verse to verse and his diction was so slurred that it took hours to make a clear copy. I heard from Sam Gentry occasionally until the middle years of World War II. Then I stopped hearing from him altogether.

# Little Mattie Groves
## (Niles No. 34 A)

*In a declamatory manner*

Oh hol - i - day, high ho - ly day, The best day of the year, ___ Lit - tle Mat - tie Groves ___ to ___ church did go Some ho - ly words to hear, ___ Some ho - ly words ___ to hear.

*(Minor minor mode on C)*

1. Oh holiday, high holy day,
   The best day of the year,
   Little Mattie Groves to church did go
   Some holy words to hear,
   Some holy words to hear.

2. He spied some ladies wearing black
   As they come into view,
   But Arling's wife was gaily clad,
   The flower of the few.
   *(repeat last line of each verse)*

3. She trippèd up to Mattie Groves,
Her eyes so low cast down,
Said: "Pray do stop the night with me
As you pass through the town.

4. "Oh pray, oh pray, with me come stay,
I'll hide thee out of sight,
And serve you there beyond compare
And sleep with you the night."

5. "I can't not go, I dare not go,
I fear 'twill cost my life,
For I know you by your middle ring
To be Lord Arling's wife."

6. "This may be false, this may be true,
I can't deny it all,
But Arling's gone to consecrate
King Henry of Whitehall."

7. Her footy page did listen well
To all that they did say,
And ere the sun did set again,
He quickly sped away.

8. Now he did run the King's highway,
And he did swim the tide.
He ne'er did stop untwil he come
Unto Lord Arling's side.

9. "What news, what news, my bodey boy,
What news bring you to me?
My castles burned, my tenants wronged,
My lady with baby?"

10. "No wrong has fell your house and lands
Whilst you have been away,
But Mattie Groves is bedded up
With your fair lady gay."

11. "If this be false," Lord Arling cried,
"As I take hit to be,
I'll raise a scaffold tower high
And hangèd you shall be."

12. "Sir Arling, if what I have said
Is false as false can be,
You needn't raise a scaffold up
But hang me to a tree."

13. Lord Arling called his merry men,
And bade them with him go,
But bound them ne'er a word to speak
And ne'er a horn to blow.

14. Among Lord Arling's merry men
Be those who wished no ill,
And the bravest one he blew his horn,
A blast so loud, so shrill.

15. "What's this, what's this?" cried Mattie Groves.
"A horn so loud, so clear!
'Tis nothing more than Arling's men,
The ones that I do fear!"

16. "Lie down, lie down," cried Arling's wife,
"And keep my back from cold.
'Tis nothing but my father's horn
That calls the sheep to fold."

17. Now Mattie Groves he did lie down,
He took a nap of sleep,
But when he woke, Lord Arling was
A-standing at his feet.

18. "How now, how now," Lord Arling cried,
"How do you like my sheets?
How do you like my new-wedded wife
That lies in your arms asleep?"

19. "Oh, it's very well I like your bed,
It's well I like your sheets,
But best I like your lady gay
What lies but hain't asleep."

20. "Put on, put on, put on man's clothes,
As quick as e'er you can,
In England hit shall ne'er be said
I slewed a naked man."

21. "I can't not rise, I dare not rise,
I fear 'twould cost my life,
For you have got two bitter swords,
And I hain't got a knife."

22. "I know I've got two bitter swords,
They cost me deep in my purse,
But you shall have the bestest one,
And I will take the worst."

23. The firstest stroke Little Mattie struck,
Hit hurt Lord Arling sore.
The nextest stroke Lord Arling struck,
Little Mattie struck no more.

24. "Rised up, rised up, my gay young wife,
Draw on your pretty clothes,
And tell me, do you like me best
Or like you Mattie Groves?"

25. Oh, she lifted Mattie's dying face,
She kissed from cheek to chin,
"It's Mattie Groves I'd rather have
Than Arling and all his kin!"

26. Oh, he took his wife by the lily-white hand,
And he led her through the hall,
And he cut off her head with his bitter sword,
And he stove hit agin the wall.

27. "Oh woe is me, my merry men,
Why stayed you not my hand?
For here I've slewed the fairest folk
In all of Engeland."

# Little Matthey Groves

## (Niles No. 34 B)

THIS TEXT came to me from a woman who was cooking for a preacher's wife in Asheville, N. C. Neither the preacher's wife nor the cook wished to have her name used, and so they must both remain anonymous. The cook whispered her text, and made me promise faithfully I would keep her secret, for fear her Baptist friends would have her churched. There was no singing, the text being spoken. It is interesting to see how the typical ballad stanza has been lost in the transition from the sung to the spoken word. Indeed, released from the formal restraint of melodic line, the text itself loses form.

The date was July 28, 1934 — just a few days before the recording of 34 A with its far superior text.

1. Oh holiday, oh holiday,
   The very first day of the year,
   Little Matthey Groves went to church
   The Holy Word to hear.

2. The very first one that he saw there
   Was Lord Arling's wife.
   She stepped up to him and said:
   "Little Matthey Groves, you must go home
   With me tonight."

3. "I cannot, I dare not, for my life,
   For I perceive by the gold rings you wear
   That you are Lord Arling's wife."

4. "And if I be Lord Arling's wife
   As you presume me to be,
   Lord Arling's away with all his merry men
   At the New Cassea.
   And he won't be home today
   And he won't be home tonight."

5. Her little foot page was standing by,
   Heard all the words that Matthey said.
   He ran to carry Lord Arling the word,
   He ran till he came to the deep blue sea,
   He doubled his breast and he swam
   Until he came to dry land.
   He buckled his shoes and he ran
   Until he came to where Lord Arling was
   With all his merry men.

6. "News I bring thee, Lord Arling,
   News I bring to thee.
   Little Matthey Groves is in bed
   With your gay lady."

7. "If this be a lie, as I presume it to be,
   Little foot page, you shall be hanged
   To the highest tree.
   But if it be the truth, as you presume it to be,
   It's a married man you shall be.
   I have but one little daughter in this world,
   And marry her you shall."

8. Lord Arling called together
   All his merry men.
   He ordered them all to march
   And not a horn be blown.

9. The foremost man in the lot,
   He knew Little Matthey well.
   He raised his horn all to his lips
   And blew a note all loud and shrill:
   "Little Matthey Groves, rise up and go."

10. It woke Little Matthey all from his sleep.
    He said to the lady: "I must go,
    For I hear Lord Arling's horn."
    She said to him, "Little Matthey,
    Lie still and keep me warm.
    It's only my father's new shepherd
    A-driving the sheep home."

11. The very next thing Little Matthey knew,
    Lord Arling was standing at his bed-feet.
    "How do you like my fine featherbed
    And how do you like my sheets,
    And how do you like my gay lady
    That lies in your arms asleep?

12. "Rise you up, Little Matthey,
    Rise you up and put on some clothes,
    For it shall never be said in an English land
    That I slayed a naked man."

13. "I cannot, I dare not, for my life,
    For you have two bright swords
    And I have not so much as a knife."

14. "It's true that I have two bright swords,
    They cost me long and deep.
    But the best one I will give to you
    And the worst one I will keep."

15. The very first lick Little Matthey struck
    He knocked Lord Arling to the floor.
    The very first lick Lord Arling struck,
    Little Matthey Groves could strike no more.

16. He took his gay lady,
    And seated her on his knee,
    Saying: "Pray tell to me which you like best,
    Little Matthey Groves or me."

17. "Very well I like your cheek,
    Much better I like your chin,
    But I wouldn't give Matthey Groves' little
        finger
    For you and all your kin."

18. Lord Arling took his sword
    And cut his own wife's head off
    And dashed it against the wall,
    Saying: "Lie there, lie there,
    For you will never fool me any more."

# The Bonny Birdy

(Child No. 82)

## The Tattletale Birdy

(Niles No. 35)

"THE BONNY BIRDY" is a ballad in which betrayal plays the major part. In fact, it is the only part played at all. In place of the page boy of "Little Mattie Groves," in "The Bonny Birdy" we have a feathered friend who carries the doleful news.

## The Tattletale Birdy

(Niles No. 35)

THE ONLY TIME I encountered this ballad was in the summer of 1934, at a tiny place called Gum Log Gap about seven miles from Boone, N. C. It came to me from the singing of three members of the same family. I could never establish their exact relationships to one another, but they were called Red Dock Dockery, Florine Dockery, and Aunt Fanny Dockery. Then there was a fourth (male) member of the family, called Black Dock Dockery. He never spoke a word all the while I was in the cabin, but sat in stony silence watching every move I made, with what I thought was a sinister smile on his face.

The three singing Dockerys sang one quite lovely tune to the syllable "Ah," steadfastly claiming it was "a ballad without words." Then they went into the singing of the song they called "The Tattletale Birdy." There was the usual amount of arguing and squabbling among them — an almost inevitable situation when a ballad is performed by more than one person.

The 2nd verse of their ballad did not appear until after the third singing. After that, it was in the performance every time.

199

# The Tattletale Birdy
## (Niles No. 35)

*(Minor mode on E)*

1. "Little birdy, little birdy,
   Oh where was you hatched?"
   "Away down in a swamp
   In a little holly bush."
       *Oh ginn-a-day and ginn-a-way,*
       *No time to stay, oh diddle-aye.*

2. "Little birdy, little birdy,
   What do you eat?"
   "White bread and cow's milk
   And a little sweet meat."
       *(repeat refrain after each verse)*

3. "Little birdy, little birdy,
   What did you then?"
   "I was give to a lady
   What lives in the glen."

4. "Little birdy, little birdy,
   What did you there?"
   "I watched my mistress,
   Your own lady fair."

5. "Little birdy, little birdy,
   What did you see?"
   "Your mistress making free
   With men one, two, and three."

6. "Little birdy, little birdy,
   You lie and you lie!"
   "I couldn't lie more than
   You lie if I try."

7. "Little birdy, little birdy,
   Where shall I go?"
   "Home to shoot your mistress
   For doing you so low!"

# Bonny Barbara Allan

(Child No. 84)

## Barb'ry Ellen
(Niles No. 36 A)

## Barbara Allen
(Niles No. 36 B)

IT WOULD SEEM that an endless foreword might be written about the most popular ballad in the Anglo-American tradition, but this, I regret, does not follow. As performance material, however, "Barbara Allan" (known to my family as "Barb'ry Ellen") is positively foolproof. I have sung this ballad for nigh on to 60 years, and I have never found it to fail to hold the listeners. The most severe critics have said that "in the ballad of 'Barbara Allan' the singer seemed to hold the audience in the hollow of his hand." In all the thousands of performances I have done of this ballad, I have never seen it fail, and I am sure that the performance — that is, the actual singing — had very little to do with it.

If the legend of Barbara Allan were part of the historical structure of Plantagenet or Tudor, the chroniclers would have named it. But they did not. It is simply boy meets girl, boy falls in love with girl, girl rejects boy, boy dies of love, girl follows, dying of sorrow, both are buried close to one another, and, in the fullness of time, a love knot is tied by a rose and a briar. No Plantagenets here. Hardly even a Tudor.

If the number of public performances and the love and affection of people world-wide prove anything at all, then we can say that our case is won — to wit, that all the dark and bloody intrigues of the great kings and princes and men of high degree cannot prevail against the legend of the love of a man for a woman, if it is written in simple, direct quatrains and sung to deathless, though simple, music.

"Barbara Allan" found its way into print in the 18th century. It was mentioned, however, by the indomitable Samuel Pepys,* and the date of his diary entry was January 2, 1666. Pepys said: "In perfect pleasure I was to hear her [Mrs. Knipp, the actress] sing, and especially her little Scotch song of 'Barbary Allen.'"

This statement by Pepys has led some folk to conclude that "Barbara Allan" was a theatrical device from the very beginning, and that Mrs. Knipp might have been singing the ballad currently in some London theatrical production.

None of this seemed to matter at all to my audiences — whether in the Baltic States, the Scandinavian countries, the British Isles, Canada,

* Born 1633, was graduated from Cambridge University, and married a 15-year-old daughter of a Huguenot refugee in 1655. Served in several governmental posts, and finally became the Clerk of the Acts of the Navy Office in 1660. Failing eyesight caused him to give up this post, and thereupon he became the most important of naval officials. Pepys was an eloquent public speaker. In his diary he takes the reader with him everywhere — "to the play, to church, to the office, by water to Chatham and Sheerness, to the King's Court and to the mean plague-stricken City."

or the United States. The same look of deep emotional concern and satisfaction came into the faces of the listeners. I was in a position to see it.

If I had wanted to clutter my already over-stuffed notebooks, I might have gained this doubtful benefit by putting down every "Barbara Allan" I encountered. But I avoided this entirely. Meanwhile, as I moved around in the Southern mountains, I listened to this ballad morning, noon, come night — in cabins, in schools, in railroad stations, in churches, once in a cave, and many times out under God's own blue sky. As a young lad I learned a few verses from my father, sang them, and was fairly well satisfied, because I was too young to understand the con-notations of this tragic love story. But as years passed, a verse came from one source, and two verses were added from another, and as late as 1932 I was singing the ballad of "Barb'ry Ellen"

in a text of 10 quatrains. But in the fall of 1933 I encountered a young man who sang what seemed to me to be a completely integrated text. I learned his version and have adhered to it ever since.

This has been widely accepted and is now looked upon in most places as the standard working text and tune. In the next few pages the reader will discover this text and tune as Niles No. 36 A. No. 36 B is a transcription of a version of "Barbara Allan" from the hand-writing of a 12-year-old girl. Only the text is given. She said there was no music to it, because it was too sad for singing.

Other evidences of this ballad from English printed sources are "Bonny Barbara Allan" in *The Tea-Table Miscellany* (Vol. IV, p. 46), 1740 and 1763 editions; "Sir John Grehme and Barbara Allan" in Percy's *Reliques* (Vol. III, p. 131), 1765.

# Barb'ry Ellen

## (Niles No. 36 A)

ON PUNCHEON CAMP CREEK in Breathitt County, Ky., in the autumn of 1933, I encountered a young man named Carter Sizemore. His clothes were faded and tattered, but they were washed clean and bright. He had a guitar tied on his back, and he carried a small poke, which con-tained all his other worldly goods. He was "headin' out."

He had worked in a sawmill, and he had mined some coal, and although he had never been farther away from home than the county seat of Breathitt (Jackson), he was headin' out. He had been caught by the lure of far places.

I unlimbered my dulcimer, and he untied his guitar, and there, in the warm sun of an Indian summer afternoon, we sang for one another. He was fascinated with me, and I was fascinated with him. He had never seen a man-person

wearing city clothes who could sing in a country way, and I had never seen so unspoiled a type as Carter Sizemore. He said he was going to join the army at the very first recruiting station.

He said he had once planned to stay right where he was born — farm a little, mine a little coal, drink a little, fight a little, and marry the girl he had been "talkin' to" since his earliest days. But the girl went off to take nurse's train-ing, and when she left she took the makings of Carter Sizemore's happiness with her. She had been gone for some months, and he had never heard from her. That's why he was joining the army.

I wrote down two of his carols, and I admired his "Barb'ry Ellen" enormously, and before he left, he offered me the "loan" of six verses I needed so sorely. With his additional verses, my

# Barb'ry Ellen

## (Niles No. 36 A)

*(Pentatonic scale on E)*

"Barb'ry Ellen" was a complete tragedy in 16 verses.

We shook hands. I put my dulcimer back into its oilcloth bag, and he tied his guitar onto his back.

"Hit's a long way to Lexington, Kentucky," said Carter.

"It's a long walk," I agreed.

"But I've got ridin' money, and I'm goin' to ride all the way up to Lexington. That's where I'm a-goin' to enlist, and that's where my doanie is workin', in some hospital or other . . . Take care of yourself. I always says, bend a bit and break later."

...nds again, and he went on down ...e I turned and went on in the direction of the headwaters. We were both heading for uncertain destinations.

## Barb'ry Ellen (Niles No. 36 A)

...wn where I was born,
There was a fair maid dwelling,
Made ev'ry youth cry "Well-a-day,"
Her name was Barb'ry Ellen.

2. 'Twas in the merry month of May,
    When the green buds they were swelling,
Sweet William on his deathbed lay,
    For the love of Barb'ry Ellen.

3. He sent his servant to the town,
    To the place where she was dwelling,
Said, "Master bids you come to him,
    If your name be Barb'ry Ellen."

4. Then slowly, slowly got she up,
    And slowly went she nigh him.
And as she drew the curtains back,
    "Young man, I think you're dying."

5. "Oh yes, I'm sick, I'm very sick,
    And I never will be better,
Untwil I have the love of one,
    The love of Barb'ry Ellen."

6. "Oh ken ye not in yonders town,
    In the place where you were dwelling,
You gave a health to the ladies all,
    But you slighted Barb'ry Ellen."

7. "Oh yes, I ken, I ken it well,
    In the place where I was dwelling,
I gave a health to the ladies all,
    But my love to Barb'ry Ellen."

8. Then lightly tripped she down the stair,
    He trembled like an aspen.
" 'Tis vain, 'tis vain, my dear young man,
    To hone for Barb'ry Ellen."

9. He turned his pale face to the wall,
    For death was in him dwelling.
"Goodbye, kind friends and kinfolk all,
    Be kind to Barb'ry Ellen."

10. As she did pass the wooded fields,
    She heard his death bell knelling,
And every stroke hit spoke her name,
    "Hardhearted Barb'ry Ellen."

11. Her eyes looked east, her eyes looked west,
    She saw his pale corpse coming,
"Oh bearers, bearers, put him down,
    That I may look upon him."

12. The more she looked, the more she grieved,
    Until she burst out crying,
"Oh bearers, bearers, take him off,
    For I am now a-dying."

13. "Oh Mother dear, go make my bed,
    Go make it soft and narrow;
Sweet William died for me today,
    I will die for him tomorrow.

14. "Oh Father dear, go dig my grave,
    Go dig it deep and narrow;
Sweet William died for love of me,
    And I will die for sorrow."

15. They buried her in the old churchyard,
    Sweet William's grave was nigh her,
And from his heart grew a red, red rose,
    And from her heart a briar.

16. They grew themselves to the old church wall,
    Twill they couldn't grow no higher;
They grew twill they tied a true-lovers' knot,
    The red rose round the briar.

# Barbara Allen

## (Niles No. 36 B)

THIS TEXT (without tune) was written in my notebook by Miss Florie Medars, aged 12 years; the place was in Caldwell County, N. C., somewhere between Rhodhiss and Granite Falls, and the date was July 1934. As I have said earlier, she would not sing the ballad, because she said it was too sad for singing.

## Barbara Allen

1. Early, early in the spring
   The spring buds they were swelling.
   Sweet William Gay on his deathbed lay
   For the love of Barbara Allen.

2. He sent his servant to her tower,
   He sent him there a-dwelling,
   Said, "Young maiden there's a call for you
   If your name be Barbara Allen."

3. Slowly, slowly she got up
   And slowly she went to him.
   And all she said when she got there was,
   "Young man I think you're dying."

4. "Oh yes, I'm sick and I'm very sick
   And death is with me dwelling,
   And never no better shall ever I be
   Till I get Barbara Allen."

5. "Oh yes, you're very sick and you're very
   sick
   And death is with you dwelling,
   And never no better shall ever you be
   For you can't get Barbara Allen."

6. Slowly, slowly she got up
   And slowly she went from him.
   She had not got a mile in town
   When she heard the death bells tolling.

7. She looked to the east, she looked to the west,
   She saw his cold corpse coming.
   "Hand down, hand down that corpse of clay
   That I may gaze upon him."

8. First she wept and then she mourn
   And then she burst out crying.
   "I might have saved that young man's life
   If I had done my duty."

9. "Oh Mama, oh Mama, go make my bed,
   Go make it long and narrow.
   Sweet William Gay died for me today,
   I die for him tomorrow."

10. "Oh Papa, oh Papa, go dig my grave,
    Go dig it long and narrow.
    Sweet William died in love for me,
    I'll die for him in sorrow."

11. Sweet William died on Saturday,
    Barbara died on Sunday.
    Their mothers died for the love of both,
    They died the following Monday.

12. They buried Sweet William in one church
    yard
    And Barbara in the other.
    From William's grave sprang a red, red rose,
    From Barbara's grave a briar.

13. They grew and they grew up the old church's tower,
    Till they could not grow no higher.
    And they looped and they tied a true love's knot,
    The rose around the briar.

# 37

# Lady Alice

(Child No. 85)

## Earl Colvin
(Niles No. 37 A)

## Young Collins
(Niles No. 37 B)

THIS BALLAD was not overly valued by Child. In fact, he presents only two rather incomplete texts. In the United States, however, it has flourished, and, no doubt by way of the Irish migration to Pennsylvania and West Virginia, some new and intriguing situations have been added to it.

Although the poetry in the first version given by Child is very fine — and particularly in the 4th verse:

> "And bury me in Saint Mary's church,
> All for my love so true,
> And make me a garland of marjoram,
> And of lemon-thyme and rue."

we must admit that the more sturdy form of the text found in the southeastern part of the United States is more arresting.

It is among these texts that we discover the presence of the mermaids and also of the five or six pretty girls from Dublin. Earl Colvin (or Young Collins, Giles Collins, George Collins, Miles Collins, or whatever he may be called) becomes a ladies' man of unshakable persuasion. In the English texts this galavanting tendency is not found, but in our country the hero seems to have moved in a wide circle — so wide, in fact, that when the news of his death reaches Dublin, six pretty girls die on the same day and, in one case, three mermaids join them.

## Earl Colvin

(Niles No. 37 A)

ON AUGUST 1, 1934, Mr. Carson Shook and his wife sang a ballad they called "Earl Colvin" or "The Man Who Loved a Lot of Girls." The first verse was not sung; it amounted to a kind of spoken prologue. In the next 10 verses the story evolved quite naturally. Mrs. Shook then offered

a 4-line epilogue, which, she said, came from a man she had known as a child. The epilogue contains two lines of a well-known Ohio River valley love song and two revealing lines concerning Earl Colvin. Like the prologue, it was spoken rather than sung.

# Earl Colvin

## (Niles No. 37 A)

Earl Col - vin rode home from the wa - ter - side, He rode through wind — and rain, — And then he lay down on his straight lit - tle bed — And died, all a - wrack — of pain, — And died, all a - wrack — of pain. —

(Melodic minor mode on E)

I took down the ballad of "Earl Colvin" in one of the warehouses belonging to a co-operative in Asheville. We sat on burlap bags full of barley seed. The Shooks, man and wife, were accurate in their singing and obliging in their attitude. They started out with a 4-line recitation by Mrs. Shook:

*Oh, you who ride and you who walk,*
*And you who tarry and stay,*
*Come listen a while and I will tell*
*Of Earl Colvin's passing away.*

Then they began to sing, timidly at first, but gathering confidence as they moved along with one of the finest tunes in all my collection.

## Earl Colvin (Niles No. 37 A)

1. Earl Colvin rode home from the waterside,
He rode through wind and rain,
And then he lay down on his straight little
  bed
And died, all a-wrack of pain,
And died, all a-wrack of pain.

2. Oh, they gave him water, they gave him wine,
They gave him gruel with a spoon,
But when he turned his face to the wall,
The bell in the tower struck noon.
     (*repeat last line of each verse*)

3. Now Alice May sat in her father's hall,
She sat and rested her head.
She did not know Earl Colvin was sick,
She did not know he was dead.

4. Alice May sat in her mother's bower,
She sewed at her mother's side,
When in come a runner with foam on his
  horse,
Said: "Earl Colvin, your lover, has died."

5. "Oh daughter, oh daughter, what makes you
     weep?
Oh daughter, what makes you cry?"
"Oh Mother, oh Mother, my lover is dead,
Oh Mother, I fear I must die."

6. At first she looked out of the window wide,
And then she looked out of the door,
And then she spied as fair a corpse
As ever shoulders bore.

7. "Whose coffin, whose coffin, whose coffin?"
     cried she,
"Whose coffin so stark and so new?"
"It is one that holds Earl Colvin's clay,
Who once did love of you."

8. "Sit down, sit down the coffin box,
Lay off the coffin lid."
And the bearers put him down on the grass
And did as they were bid.

9. Oh, it's long she looked into his face,
Oh, it's deep she grieved and sore,
Oh, it's hard she pressed his clay-cold lips,
As she did oft before.

10. "See yonders dove, hit mourns its love
And flies from pine to pine.
Today you will weep at Earl Colvin's grave,
Tomorrow you'll weep at mine."

Then Mrs. Shook recited this 4-line epilogue:

*Look down, look down that lonesome road,*
*Hang down your head and cry.*
*Earl Colvin loved a many a maid,*
*And that's why he did die.*

As they were singing, I could not keep from thinking how I might turn this fine melodic line into oboe music, sometime in the far future. After the singing, we broke open a watermelon, and I sang "Jimmy Randal" and "The Old Lord by the Northern Sea," and it was considered a right pretty afternoon.

# Young Collins

## (Niles No. 37 B)

It was old Charlie Walsh who recited what he called "Young Collins." He positively refused to sing. He said he had left his voice in Hickory, N. C., where he had been a potter for quite a few years. He was bent over, and one of his legs was slightly drawn up. He had turned pottery on an old-style potter's wheel, long before the day of the labor-saving electric motor. He "kicked the wheel," using footpower. I did not ask his age. He declared that preachers stopped folks from singing old-timey music and ballads.

He said his ballad of "Young Collins" was well known to many people in the time of his youth. He told me that if I had come along 30 years sooner, I would have heard many people singing "Young Collins" and other ballads. He had once known "Barbary Ellen" and "The Hangman's Rope" and "Little Mack Groves" and "The Croodlin Doo," but he had left them, with his voice, in Hickory. He said he had a little money, and his relatives were glad enough to house him up. He was "interested mostly in fishin'."

It was July 1934, and my notes tell us it was a bright, clear day between Oteen and Swannanoa, N. C. Charlie Walsh recited a version of "Lady Alice" (Child No. 85) referred to by Belden and Hudson in *Folk Songs from North Carolina,* Vol. 2 of *The Frank C. Brown Collec-* tion of *North Carolina Folklore,* as type 3, because of the presence of mermaids or sea-elves. The 3rd line of his 5th verse contained the term "dabblin' girls." In other American versions they turn out to be "Dublin girls," and there are six of them. But Charlie Walsh was steadfast in his use of the word "dabblin'," and there were only five of them. I said, "What is a dabblin' girl?" "Why," said he, smiling in surprise at my naïveté, "a dabblin' girl is a girl what dabbles with menfolk."

I then asked him about the sea-maids, and he said they were rather large fishes with girls' bodies. "I hain't never been lucky enough to hook one in all my fishin'," said he. A pretty girl, sitting on the porch above us, said, "Uncle Charlie, how you do talk!" and went right on thumbing through a mail-order catalogue. Charlie Walsh never used the word "mermaid."

The serious student of balladry might enjoy reading Child ballad No. 42 and Grundtvig No. 47, and also the carefully prepared notes on the ballad of "Lady Alice" (Child No. 85) on pages 131–33 of *Folk Songs from North Carolina.* A further investigation of the 5 variants recovered in West Virginia by John Harrington Cox and included in his book, *Folk-Songs of the South,* will be greatly rewarding.

Here follow Charlie Walsh's verses.

# Young Collins

1. One morning, one morning, one morning in May
   The fields were all a-flower.
   Young Collins come ridin' down out of the north
   A-seekin' sweet Mattie Belle's bower.

2. They walked across the flower fields,
   They walked close side by side,
   They sat and talked as lovers will,
   All on the salt sea side.

3. Young Collins snatched Mattie about the waist,
   He kissed from cheek to chin,
   'Twas then the sea-maids come up the bank
   And pulled Young Collins in.

4. Now Collins swam and Collins ran,
   And Collins tinkled the bell.
   His mother gave him gruel and wine,
   He died ere he got well.

5. Young Collins died like it was today,
   Mattie Belle died of a morrow.
   Five dabblin' girls and three maids of the sea
   Died of purest sorrow.

6. Oh, see yon lonesome little dove,
   How it will weep and pine.
   Today they mourn o'er Collins so young,
   Tomorrow o'er ladies nine.

# 38

# Lamkin

(Child No. 93)

## Lamfin

(Niles No. 38)

THERE WAS a time when some parents and many nurses used the most terrorizing devices on small children. This is possibly the reason why the ballad of "Lamkin" had such wide distribution. As a bedtime story it was told and retold, and made over to fit local situations, to become, as Child put it, "the terror of countless nurseries."

I have seen a version of this ballad, from Caroline County, Va., indicating a strange complication — namely, a trip by the lord of the newly built manor to London, to purchase the nursemaid a ring. If this were a fact, then the nursemaid, carrying on an affair with the lord of the manor, might easily have developed a hatred for her ladyship, and a willingness to co-operate with Lamkin in his plot.

The almost satanic hatred and demand for revenge on the part of the stonemason Lamkin might be explained as part of the resentment built up out of the many iniquities from which the laboring classes once suffered. Motherwell, who must have had a bitter sense of humor, wrote in his *Minstrelsy:* "Indeed, it seems questionable how some Scottish lairds could well afford to get themselves seated in the large castles they once occupied unless they occasionally treated the mason after the fashion adopted in this ballad."

A version of "Lamkin" was once sung in the public schools of Louisville. I do not remember what text was employed, but it did not seem to be quite so sadistic as the earlier English and Scottish versions.

## Lamfin

### (Niles No. 38)

THE FACT that all 11 verses of "Lamfin" are crowded onto a single small page of my notebook may account for the fact that little additional information was collected at the time except a short conversation I had with the singer, Aunt

Annie Shelton, who lived near Cleveland, Ga.

I said, "Aunt Annie, where did this fellow Lamfin come from?"

She answered, with complete assurance, "Philadelphia."

# Lamfin

## (Niles No. 38)

*(Major mode on G and minor mode on E)*

I said, "That's a long way off, Philadelphia . . ."
"Why, you just don't know how them brick-layers and stonemasons will travel." She paused a moment, then added, "Just like potters." There was a pottery in the village of Cleveland, where a very high grade of so-called "stoneware" was made.

Here, then, is Aunt Annie's ballad, and across the page are the verses. The tune smacks of the shape-note hymn: in her youth, Annie Shelton had been a member of a *Sacred Harp* singing group. She was alone in the world when I encountered her, living with some distant relatives. In spite of all this, she was rather gay.

It was quite early in the morning when I got to Cleveland, and I asked Aunt Annie if she had had her breakfast.

"Why, of course I have," said she, almost offended. "I wouldn't sing afore breakfast, and for two reasons: first, without something in the stomach, a body hain't got no notes, and then, the old folks always said, 'Sing before breakfast and cry before supper.' "

## Lamfin (Niles No. 38)

1. Young Lamfin laid a many a stone,
   He laid a many a brick,
   But when he asked for his bricklaying pay,
   All he got was a kick,
   All he got was a kick.

2. The landlord started to London,
   To buy rings one, two, three.
   "Beware if Lamfin knocks the door
   And makes you think it's me."
   (*repeat last line of each verse*)

3. The tower bell, hit struck a twelve,
   Young Lamfin he did come,
   And none was so gay as the false nurse herself
   To run and let him in.

4. "How can we get her down the stair,
   So cold and dark the night?"
   "We'll stick her baby full of pins,
   And he'll cry with pain and fright."

5. "Go feed my child with breast-milk,
   Feed him a little pap.
   Rock him in his cradle
   Or rock him in your lap."

6. The landlady came running down the stair,
   Not thinking any harm,
   When Lamfin struck upon her
   And held her in his arm.

7. "I'll give you of my daughter,
   I'll give you all your pay,
   And you shall have all the gold
   Your horse can haul away."

8. He would not have her daughter,
   He would not have the fee.
   The false maid and young Lamfin
   Has killed the landlady.

9. Oh, bonny was the blackbird's voice
   With many a tune and trill,
   And high was Lamfin's scaffold
   That stood upon the hill.

10. Oh, sweetly sang the wild birds
    As music they did make,
    And see the false maid dyin',
    Burnèd at the stake.

# The Maid Freed from the Gallows

(Child No. 95)

## The Hangman
(Niles No. 39 A)
## Granny and the Golden Ball
(Niles No. 39 B)

THE MAID FREED FROM THE GALLOWS" has been discussed by almost everyone seriously concerned with ballad study. These discussions have taken the form of classroom lectures, scholarly papers, and articles set up for publication. In all of these learned items, there is a considerable measure of repetition, because there are only a few things to be said. These few things have been said so eloquently in *South Carolina Ballads* by Reed Smith in his chapter entitled "Five Hundred Years of 'The Maid Freed from the Gallows,'" that I should like to summarize Smith as follows: The ballad was composed before Chaucer's time; sung in England and Scotland during the reign of Elizabeth I; recorded by Bishop Thomas Percy; brought to America by the early settlers; is still lingering in out-of-the-way places here and abroad; and, finally, the ballad has become (a) a rustic English tale, (b) a Negro *cante-fable* in the Bahamas and West Indies, (c) a playlet used at a Negro school commencement, and (d) a children's game in the slums of New York City.

Smith concludes by saying, "A long life and a varied one!"

When Reed Smith's book was published in 1928, I had not yet collected or popularized my North Carolina version of "The Maid Freed from the Gallows." Had he written 10 or 15 years later, he might not have said that this ballad can be heard today only in remote, out-of-the-way places. It ranks third in popularity in my concert programs, and my recording of it has found its way into many a home.

If we admit, as I think we must, that "The Maid Freed from the Gallows" and the legend of the Golden Ball are parts of the same fabric, then the ideas offered by Dorothy Scarborough on this legend serve to illuminate some of the problems associated with "The Maid Freed from the Gallows." Miss Scarborough declares that the legend is an allegory, with the golden ball (a thing of great price) being a maiden's honor, which when lost can be restored to her (?) only by her lover. Rationally this suggestion does not hold much water, but poetically it might pass.

Indeed, a version of "The Golden Ball" found in my collection and published here as No. 39 B contains certain suggestions that bear out Miss Scarborough's conclusions. The lover arrives after the grandmother refuses assistance and declares that he has brought gold and fee to ransom the girl from the scaffold. By way of explanation, he concludes:

*"We lost that pretty golden ball,*
*And we have never found it at all.*
*But I can't see you hangèd high,*

*And everybody knows right well why.*
*And everybody knows right well why."*

Note that the lover does not say, "*You* lost," but "*We* lost."

All this pettyfogging may simply lead to greater confusion, however. After all, the great men of ballad study have wearied the heavens with this investigation, only to conclude, as Child did, that all the English versions of "The Maid Freed from the Gallows" are defective and distorted.

In northern and southern Europe the situation is different. In Sicily, Spain, the Faroe Islands, Iceland, Denmark, Germany, Estonia, Russia, Little Russia, Finland, and the Slavonic states, the legend of "The Maid Freed from the Gallows" is really the legend of a maid freed from pirates, brigands, oppressive noblemen, or venal jailers, and in most cases it is fully told.

To all this I might add that as a small boy, under the age of 8, I used to play a game with other children wherein one of us had lost a fancy golden hatpin. If the loser could not restore the lost article, he or she might be destroyed by hanging. After a while, we quit playing this game. As I remember, our parents grew apprehensive.

I remember turning the pages of a seemingly endless collection of Swedish-Finnish folklore once in Helsinki and coming upon two items: one concerning a maiden freed from a boatload of sea brigands by a lover who, after the usual routine of family refusals, ransoms the girl with pots of gold; and another — involving what I took to be an echo of the *Kalevala* — about one of the lesser gods, traveling about in a bronze boat, who rescues a maiden from a sea-spirit by giving up one of his oars as payment (after this, the little god rowed on one side with the remaining oar and on the other side with his hand, thereby growing webbed fingers).

Once long ago in London I attended the meeting of a learned society (England is full of such delightful enterprises). On this occasion a paper was read concerning the persistence of myths and superstitions. In the discussion that followed, a gentleman with a white beard and gold-rimmed spectacles — I believe it was Professor George Saintsbury — told a wonderful Irish folk tale concerning "The Maid Freed from the Gallows." Actually, his story was perhaps even closer to the legend of the Golden Ball. As I recall, the story proceeded in this manner:

It seems that an eminent Irish scholar once had a jewel of great price, which he gave for safekeeping to a maidservant employed in his castle. Now according to legend, this maidservant was more than usually beautiful; indeed, she was truly a ravishing beauty. The scholar had a wife, as most scholars do, but the wife was a poor thing — poor in looks and low in spirit.

The maidservant kept the jewel carefully, and reported its whereabouts to the scholar at regular intervals. One fine day the scholar asked the maid to return the jewel, and she could not. It was gone.

An investigation followed and a trial was held, and the law of the land being what it was, the beautiful maidservant was condemned to hanging as a thief. On the scaffold the maid pleaded for help from any kind passer-by, so she might have gold to pay off the judge and the scholar and thus save her life.

While all this was going on, a fish in the Irish Sea swam up on the beach and regurgitated the jewel, which, happily, a fisherman found. Thereupon the fisherman rushed into the city, delivered the jewel to the judge and the scholar, while the girl was freed amid cries of delight. On the testimony of the fish, relayed by the fisherman, it was discovered that the scholar's wife had thrown the jewel into the sea, hoping to discredit the maidservant and get rid of her. Thereupon the scholar cast his wife into outer darkness and took the beautiful maidservant to his bosom as his wife, and everything turned out happily for everybody, except wife No. 1, who was so poor in looks and so low in spirit.

The only new idea I have encountered in the investigation of this ballad is the rumor of a study being made by a graduate student at Harvard University who believes he has evidence pointing to a relationship between "The Maid Freed from the Gallows" and certain ancient druidic rites. Meanwhile, we may take comfort in a great piece of dramatic material, and be thankful that good fortune tipped the cornucopia our way and spilled out text and tune of "The Maid Freed from the Gallows" for our entertainment, enlivenment, and edification.

# The Hangman

## (Niles No. 39 A)

ELLA WILSON, colored, was positive that she was 10 years old when the War Between the States concluded. That would have made her 89 years of age when I first knew her in 1934. Her mind was fairly clear, and though she suffered from arthritis and dropsy, she managed to move around her cabin pretty well. She was living alone, doing all her own cooking and what housekeeping she needed.

She lived at a place called Texana, not far from Murphy, N. C. The community had a poor reputation, and I had been warned to stay away. But, nothing daunted, I drove up the rutted road and discovered that the Indian-Negro half-breeds, the so-called escapees from the road gangs, and the half-naked children were accommodating, harmless, and entertaining. I never lost the smallest article while in Texana, and no one offered to cut my throat. Of course, I came armed with a great basket of provender — rising powder, soda, salt, sugar, flour, cornmeal, pepper, fat back, lard, grits, cotton gloves, string, thread, needles, chewing gum, chewing tobacco, snuff, cigars, cigarettes, liniment, aspirin, and, when available, corn whiskey. I became known as "that singin' man what gives gifts."

It is a great pity that I could not make a broader study of Ella Wilson and her folk music. In her youth she had worked as a cook for various families in the neighborhood, and so she was steeped in the folk music of both races. She said that in her earlier days she could "sing a half a day and not repeat very often." Someone should have worked with her at the turn of the century.

It was in the early summer of 1936 that she sang what she called "The Hangman." I took it down feverishly, and then sang it back to her. Little Negro children sat on the ground outside Ella Wilson's open cabin door, fascinated by Aunt Ella and the man who could "sing off a piece of paper." Ella Wilson stood up and acted out the drama of the ballad as well as her infirmities would permit. Since that day, I too have sung "The Hangman" standing up and acting out the story behind the text. Here, then, are the verses of "The Hangman" as Ella Wilson sang them to me in Texana.

# The Hangman
## (Niles No. 39 A)

*(Minor mode on D)*

1. "Hangman, hangman, slack your line,
   Slack it just a while,
   'Cause I think I see my papa comin',
   Traveling many a mile,
   Traveling many a mile.

2. "Papa, Papa, has you brought gold,
   For to pay this hangman's fee?
   Or did you come to see me swingin'
   High from this hangman's tree?"
   *(repeat last line of each verse)*

3. "Daughter, daughter, I brought you no gold
   For to pay this hangman's fee,
   But I come to see you swingin', swingin'
   High from this hangman's tree."

4. "Hangman, hangman, slack your line,
   Slack it just a while,
   'Cause I think I see my mama comin',
   Traveling many a mile.

5. "Mama, Mama, did you bring gold
   For to pay this hangman's fee?
   Or did you come to see me swingin'
   High from this hangman's tree?"

6. "Daughter, daughter, I brought you no gold,
   For to pay this hangman's fee,
   But I come to see you swingin', swingin'
   High from this hangman's tree."

7. "Hangman, hangman, slack your line,
   Slack it just a while,
   'Cause I think I see my lover comin',
   Traveling many a mile.

8. "Sweetheart, sweetheart, did you bring gold
   For to pay this hangman's fee,
   Or did you come to see me swingin'
   High from this hangman's tree?"

9. "Darling, darling, I brought you that gold,
   For to pay this hangman's fee,
   'Cause I don't want to see you swingin',
   swingin'
   High from no hangman's tree."

# Granny and the Golden Ball

## (Niles No. 39 B)

SHE SAID her name was Augusta Singleton, and she was fishing off the stern of a smallish houseboat, the kind river people use to live on while floating down the Ohio River with the current. She said her name was Augusta Singleton, and in my notes I have the one word "elderly." As I remember her, she was neither old nor young, but in her youth she might have been a very lovely blond person.

It was a Sunday afternoon in August 1909, and the Ohio River flowed so slowly it almost seemed to be a millpond. The houseboat was moored at the Portland wharf in the west end of Louisville, and Miss Singleton was fishing. I had been digging in the rubble of a once great hotel, long since destroyed by fire. It was known as the St. Charles Hotel, and the rubble thereof had produced interesting treasures. Once, some Mexican gold coins had been found. All I had found on this particular Sunday afternoon in 1909 were a few pieces of colored glass.

Miss Singleton was a person of education and good manners, and when I told her that I was interested in old-timey music and hoped to be a

# Granny and the Golden Ball

## (Niles No. 39 B)

hang - man's tree, To save ___ me from ___ this hang - man's tree?"

*(Dorian mode on E)*

### Granny and the Golden Ball (Niles No. 39 B)

1. From over the hills and far away,
   Came an old granny dressed in gray.
   "Oh pray, granny, pray, ere the trap do fall,
   Did you find my golden ball,
   Or did you bring me of your fee
   To save me from this hangman's tree,
   To save me from this hangman's tree?"

2. "Oh no, oh no, I have no fee
   To save you from this hangman's tree.
   I found no ball, no ball of gold,
   But I have come as you've told
   To see you hanged and hangèd high,
   And the hangman, he knows right well why."
   *(repeat last line of each verse)*

3. From over the hills and far away
   Come a young lover very gay.
   "Oh lover, oh lover, ere this trap do fall,
   Did you find my golden ball,
   Or did you bring me a little fee
   To save me from this hangman's tree?"

4. "Oh yes, I brought you gold and fee
   To save you from this hangman's tree.
   We lost that pretty golden ball,
   And we have never found it at all.
   But I can't see you hangèd high,
   And everybody knows right well why."

concert singer someday, she was greatly interested. The final result of it all was that she sang, and I sang, and then I sang along with her.

She said her name was Augusta Singleton, and furthermore that she was one of a party of four on board the little houseboat named *The Poppinjay,* and that they hoped to get as far as Paducah by the end of August.

From my field notebook I find that Miss Singleton sang about the Golden Ball. Not many versions of this earlier form of "The Maid Freed from the Gallows" have been recovered in the U.S., and these come from Maine and Virginia. Miss Singleton's singing was faint, but clear. Her intonation was quite accurate. Just before the hawsers were hauled in and the *Poppinjay* headed lazily for Paducah, Miss Singleton sang, and her melodic line was one I have never been able to forget.

In my notes I discover this information: ". . . an odd tune. I took it down as carefully as I could . . . she sang the first verse over many times, and I sang it with her."

# The Knight and Shepherd's Daughter

(Child No. 110)

## The Shepherd's Daughter and the King

(Niles No. 40)

Examples of this interesting ballad have been found in Massachusetts, Maine, Newfoundland, North Carolina, and Kentucky. The plot material is quite simple: boy meets girl, boy rapes girl, girl appeals to the highest authority in the land, boy is given two choices and decides on the lesser of two evils and marries the girl (the other evil being hanging).

The Kentucky text runs to 9 verses, and as such, is greatly concentrated. The characters in this version are indeed a hireling servant and the shepherd's daughter, who is just that and no king's daughter in disguise as she is in some of the English versions. This relieved the singer from what Child referred to as "humorous artifices which the lady practices to maintain the character of a beggar's brat." Child, who was easily bored, further declared that these artifices had been "exaggerated in later copies [of the ballad] to a point threatening weariness."

The forgetting that surrounds the process of oral transmission may account for some of the shortened versions found in North America, but in our family, verses were often struck out for fear that a restless or even a dwindling audience would be the reward of a verbose ballad.

## The Shepherd's Daughter and the King

(Niles No. 40)

This ballad came to me from my father, God rest him. He was a man who loved singing, dancing, the theatre, and was particularly fascinated by the black-face minstrels. I believe I can best describe him in the following quatrain:

*My father was a gay young blade,*
*Who raised his voice to sing,*
*And thought the terpsichorean toe*
*Was a very pretty thing.*

We never used the word ballad at home;

# The Shepherd's Daughter and the King

## (Niles No. 40)

*With gay abandon*

I— sing of a shep-herd's daugh - ter, Tend-ing sheep on a hill so high, When

one of them hire-ling ser - vants Came a-gai-ly rid-ing by, With a

ring, dong, down And a did-dle-a - la-di - do, Ring, dong, down And a did-dle-a - la-day.

*(Major mode on F)*

indeed, we did not know the word at all. What is now called balladry we called old-timey music; and if it were of a religious nature, it was called Old Baptist music. (This "Old Baptist" music belonged to no particular denomination, but consisted simply of shape-note hymns coming from *The Sacred Harp* or *The Southern Harmony*.)

In 1880, when my father was about 12 years of age, he lived not far from a broom factory in Louisville. The broommakers, male and female, sang at their benches. It was from them that he learned "The Shepherd's Daughter and the King."

My notes were copied into my records on August 12, 1917, as I was about to go off to World War I. My father said: "Write the verses carefully, boy. Someone else may have to read them. Neither of us may survive what's going on over yonder."

## The Shepherd's Daughter and the King (Niles No. 40)

1. I sing of a shepherd's daughter,
   Tending sheep on a hill so high,
   When one of them hireling servants
   Came a-gaily riding by.

   *Refrain:*
   > *With a ring, dong, down*
   > *And a diddle-a-la-di-do,*
   > *Ring, dong, down*
   > *And a diddle-a-la-day.*

2. I sing of a shepherd's daughter
   With shoes of rabbit's fur,
   And how that hireling servant
   Did come and robbèd her.
   > (*repeat refrain after each verse*)

3. Oh, she grabbed her pettiskirts in her hand,
   And she ran by the horse's side,
   And she ran twill she come to the river,
   And she swam that raging tide.

4. Oh, she swam twill she come to the drièd land,
   And she grabbed her skirts and she run,
   And she run twill she come to the King's
      highway,
   And she wasn't running for fun.

5. Oh, she walkèd up to the castle door,
   How boldly tingled the ring,
   And none was so spry as the King hisself
   At letting the shepherdess in.

6. "What matter, what matter, what matter, my
      maid?
   What matter, what matter?" cried he.
   "Oh, one of your hireling servants
   Has been and robbèd me."

7. "Oh, what, my maid, did he rob you of?
   Oh, what did he take away?
   Was it diamond rings or silver
   Or gold he took today?"

8. " 'Twern't no gold nor silver,
   'Twern't no treasure trove!"
   And she hung her head, and she wept for
      shame
   Like the note of a mourning dove.

9. Then cried the King: "If married,
   Hangèd he shall be.
   But if he's e'er a single man,
   He's bounden to marry ye."

# Johnie Cock

(Child No. 114)

### Fair John and the Seven Foresters
(Niles No. 41)

So far as I have been able to tell, this fine ballad has been found only a few times on the North American continent. I know of two examples from Virginia — one reported from Highland County, Va., on November 3, 1920, and the one in my collection, taken down in Marion, Smyth County, Va., in August 1933.

As in the Child texts, the American versions present Johnie Cock in the form of a gay, sport-loving young man who understands bows and arrows, hounds and hunting, and, besides all this, has a great appetite for venison. It seems that his hounds shared this latter interest.

The game laws mean nothing to Johnie Cock, and although his mother, according to the Child texts, weeps, wrings her hands, entreats, and finally takes to her bed in her grief, Johnie calls his hounds and goes forth to kill the dun or dark brown deer. The news of Johnie's expedition is carried to the foresters, or game wardens, by a palmer, or by a silly old man, and soon the battle is on. Johnie is wounded, but six of the foresters are killed outright, and the seventh is wounded too. A bird is called in to carry the tragic news to Johnie's mother.

Although neither of the American texts is complete, the bold outlines of the story are clearly indicated. Francis J. Child and Arthur Kyle Davis, Jr., thought well of this ballad, Child referring to it as a "precious specimen of the unspoiled traditional ballad."

## Fair John and the Seven Foresters
(Niles No. 41)

It was August 1933 and darkness had settled on White Top Mountain, in Washington County, Va. A folk festival was in progress up on the mountain, and as I have said before, all the way up and all the way down the newly cut road, one encountered automobiles beset by various difficulties.

I had given a delightful little white-haired octogenarian a lift. His name was Pete Johnson, and he was the singer of "Lady Margot and Love

228

Henry," indicated in this collection as No. 27. Pete Johnson left me at Konnaroch. Hardly had I gotten to the outskirts of the village before I ran over a small bundle of barbed wire and almost destroyed a rear tire.

As I was standing by surveying my bad luck, four men appeared out of the early night. They proved to be great people — strong, willing, and entertaining. They had been denied a chance to sing at the White Top festival, but they were still gay. Of course, a certain overconsumption of locally made corn distillate had helped to buoy their spirits.

They went at once to helping me change the damaged tire. After a bit, I discovered that two of them were brothers, Ed and Charlie Russell. Then there was the usual silent partner, who looked like a half-breed Indian. The fourth man was Roscoe Pulsifer: he proved to be the singer.

was then that Roscoe Pulsifer got around to the serious business of the evening. With the "help" of his three friends he sang what he called "Fair John and the Seven Foresters," which proved to be a thrilling variant of Child ballad No. 114, originally entitled "Johnie Cock."

After Pulsifer got well under way, Charlie Russell went to singing, too, but his contribution was not much more than tiresome interference. The audience we had collected presented a problem. They were ever ready with inane suggestions and odd remarks, calculated to amuse and distract. None of this made my task any easier; my notes make difficult reading today. I finally took down the following 12 verses and checked them against two additional performances, one by Pulsifer and one by me.

As I was putting up my dulcimers, Charlie Russell came to me and said: "Pardner, this old

As soon as the car was ready to go, they told me that they wanted to get to Marion, Va., and as I was stopping at a hotel in that town, it all worked out quite nicely. While we were driving along, they discovered my interest in balladry, and by the time we had arrived at the hotel (about 35 miles away) we had decided to hold our own folk festival in the peace and comfort of a Marion hotel.

I do not remember how many ballads I sang, but I do know that the management of the hotel was growing weary of our using the lobby for a concert stage. The suggestion was made that we "take the show back up to White Top." It

singer, this white-headed drunk-man, name of Roscoe Pulsifer, was once a teacher in a ladies' seminary over in the direction of Charlottesville. But drink and ladies ruined 'im. You see, in Charlottesville there was too much of both."

Then Pulsifer spoke up. "Charlie Russell, you oughta enter a liars' contest. You'd win, hands down!" He turned to me and said, "I quit school-teaching about thirty years ago, when I was thirty-five years of age, but my reasons are my own business, and they've got nothing to do with that snake-stomper Russell."

We shook hands all around, and they went out into the night.

# Fair John and the Seven Foresters

## (Niles No. 41)

*(Minor mode on F)*

1. He went to hunt the running buck,
   He went to hunt the doe,
   He dinged them to the very ground,
   His mother said him no.

2. Now Johnny he wore a coat of red
   With gold and blackish sheen,
   But when he hunted the running buck,
   Put on his Linkhorn green.

3. In yonders town of Broadalow,
   The foresters be seven,
   And for a drop of Johnny's blood,
   They'd go to hell or heaven.

4. Now Johnny saddled up his horse,
   He loosed his deerhounds three,
   And with his arrows at his side,
   He rode forth merrily.

5. When Johnny shot the running buck,
   He ate him heartily,
   And then he slept upon the ground
   Among his deerhounds three.

6. Now Johnny took his bugle-horn,
   And blew so loud, so clear.
   The foresters in Broadalow:
   "Young Johnny Cock is near!"

7. They rode o'er hills and mountains steep,
   They rode o'er valleys wide,
   When they did come where Johnny slept
   With deerhounds at his side.

8. The firstest arrow they did shoot,
   It hit fair John on the eye;
   But every time John pulled his bow,
   A forester did die.

9. "Woe be, woe be to seven men,
   Who struck me such a blow.
   They hain't a wolf in all this wood
   To come and treat me so."

10. His blood was like the roses red
    That dripped down from his crown.
    The foresters' blood was redder still
    As Johnny shot them down.

11. "Stand strong, stand strong, my hound-dogs
       three,
    The battle's almost done!
    There once was seven men to fight,
    And now there's only one.

12. "Oh pretty bird, oh singing bird,
    Come bode what I do say:
    My mother waits to hear the word,
    Come, take fair John away!"

# A Short Foreword
# Concerning Robin Hood

IN THE YEAR 1332 or thereabouts, a farmer's son was born at Cleobury Mortimer in Shropshire, England, and his name was William Langland. As a rule, the scholars and minor clerics of the 14th century left very little accurate information concerning their doings, and although William Langland left certain notes and papers concerning himself, the historians of the 20th century have not accepted this information as much more than conjecture. We believe that he was educated at Malvern, and that he lived what was then a long life in the Cornhill section of London with a wife by name of Kitte, or Kitty, and a daughter who was called Calote or Colotte, a name that might have been French in origin.

All this leads us to the fact that the world of letters has been considerably enriched by a poem which in modern English runs to more than 2400 lines, entitled *The Vision of Piers Plowman*. One school of thought has long attributed this truly remarkable poem to none other than the mysterious William Langland.

In *The Vision of Piers Plowman*, a character named Sloth comes to confession, "all beslobbered, with two slimy eyes," and after a few lines of mutterings, Sloth declares:

*"This day should I die, no duties for me!*
*Paternoster I know not, as priests intone it,*
*But rhymes of Robin Hood, or Randolph of*
*Chester . . ."*

Professor W. W. Skeat stakes his reputation on the statement that these lines must have been written before 1377.

So far as we can tell, this is the earliest notice of the fabulous Robin Hood, whom some serious scholars have confused with Randolph of Chester or "Randle, erle of Chester." The mystery deepens when we realize that there were several earls of Chester — one, the 2nd Earl of Chester, dating 1128 to 1153, and another, the 3rd earl, who took over in 1181 (not 1153, as one might suppose) and carried on for perhaps 50 years thereafter.

Following the reference above from *Piers Plowman* (1377), we find that in 1417 a charlatan who took the name of "Fryar Tuck" was committing many robberies in the English counties of Surrey and Sussex, and in 1420, a Scottish fragment of four lines concerns "Robyne Hude and Lytill Ihon." Again, in 1439, there is a petition to the English Parliament containing the following reference: ". . . and in manere of insurection, wente into the wodes in that contre, like as it hadde be Robyn-hode and his meyne."

No matter which school of thought one joins — whether the Skeat-Jusserand school, which attributes *Piers Plowman* to William Langland, or the one headed up by Professor J. M. Manly, which holds that as many as five different poets wrote it — the references therein concerning

Robin Hood still leave us incapable of identifying this delightful brigand, this magnificent archer, this foe of the mighty and friend of the poor as a true reality. Furthermore, when we add up all Robin Hood's fabulous accomplishments, we are convinced that no one person could have done it all, because no human being could have had all the cunning, the skill, the highmindedness, and the luck that it took. With all this in mind, I, who have drawn a bowstring myself, must join the ranks of those who say, with Francis J. Child, that "Robin Hood is absolutely a creation of the ballad-muse."

# Robin Hood and the Monk

(Child No. 119)

## Robin Hood and the Twenty Pounds of Gold

(Niles No. 42)

*Hit befel on Whitsontide,*
*Erly in a May mornyng,*

and, according to Child No. 119, Robin Hood, concluding that he had not "seen his Saviour" for some time, decides to go into Nottingham and hear mass. Twelve archers want to attend him on this perilous journey, but Robin takes only Little John.

On the way to church Robin and Little John shoot for a wager. An acrimonious argument follows: Robin insults Little John, and proceeds into Nottingham alone. Little John will have no more of him. Once in St. Mary's Church, Robin Hood is recognized by a monk, who calls the sheriff of Nottingham and all his deputies. They fight, and many are killed. But Robin's sword breaks over the hard head of the sheriff, and thereupon he is captured.

Not long after, Much and Little John capture the monk, who is carrying the glad tidings of Robin's arrest to the King. They do away with the monk, and dressed in the monk's clothes, carry the letters themselves. The King, in his delight, makes Much and John yeomen of the crown, gives them twenty pounds, and directs that Robin Hood be delivered into the King's presence unharmed.

All this is cause for great joy in Nottingham. The sheriff entertains Much and Little John, not knowing who they are, and while he is in a deep sleep brought on by an overconsumption of alcoholic beverages, Little John, Much, and Robin Hood escape. Later the King, who is greatly annoyed by all this, will hear no more talk about it, and declares that Little John "has begyled us all."

# Robin Hood and the Twenty Pounds of Gold

(Niles No. 42)

CHRISTIAN MATHERS was 78 years of age in August 1933, and he lived in a shambles of a cabin not a long way from Dalton, Ga. He had preached in the Primitive Baptist Church up until the turn of the century, but he quit preaching because what he thought in his heart and what the congregation expected him to say just didn't fit together. He then took up schoolteaching — all eight grades in one room. He had read history, and he knew the English language surprisingly well. He lived alone and avoided his relatives. In fact, he had been avoiding them for so long that he couldn't remember clearly who they were.

Mathers thought he remembered McGuffey as a man who came through the country every so often, selling little blue-backed reading and spelling books. Once upon a time a man whom he believed to be McGuffey was invited to eat dinner at a nearby family picnic. The tables groaned with food. In front of McGuffey was a great heaping platter of fried chicken. As the honored guest of the occasion, McGuffey was called upon to ask the blessing, and he was a man famous for his long-winded blessings. McGuffey rose to his feet, closed his eyes, and went on and on, literally preaching a short sermon. When at last the blessing had come to an end and McGuffey opened his eyes, there was nothing left on the chicken platter but some gizzards, some necks, and a few wings.

at the beginning of the ballad. Mathers said the moral belonged at the beginning because the singer might stop singing before the end or, more likely, the listener would quit listening, and then the moral would be lost. He said all preachers should preach their sermons backward, if the sermons were more than five minutes long, because the congregation usually went to sleep although their eyes might remain wide open. Christian Mathers was a great wit, and he was also thought to be "quare-turned."*

In an almost *sotto voce* aside, he told me he had once been married. At the time of my visit, however, his cabin was full of dogs and cats.

"Yes," said Mathers, possibly thinking that I was hoping for an explanation, "married life fit me like a sidesaddle on a ridge-runnin' boar-hog . . . and then, during my schoolteachin' days, I was a gay one. I was all for dancin' and singin' and a lot of gallivantin' like that, which don't pleasure some female-persons. My wife used to say I was a bold rooster and that I'd crow in any barnyard. And that's the way it was. Now I'm

Several years later McGuffey was back in the same country, and again he was called upon to ask the blessing at a summertime gathering where a magnificent platter of fried chicken lay before him. McGuffey rose, speared the juiciest breast of chicken he could find, held it down to the platter with his fork, closed his eyes, and blessed the food and the company for the next ten minutes.

In discussing his ballad, which Mathers called "Robin Hood and the Twenty Pounds of Gold," I said it was strange to find the moral of the story

* Slightly insane.

alone with my dogs and my cats. They never talk back . . ."

Mathers told me that when he was a young man teaching spelling, reading, and English composition he had quite a collection of "ballad sheets," and among them were several concerning Robin Hood.

In my notebook I find the following notation: "If Mathers only knew how drab his years are . . . think of being alone with 3 dogs and 5 cats at 78 years of age."

# Robin Hood and the Twenty Pounds of Gold

## (Niles No. 42)

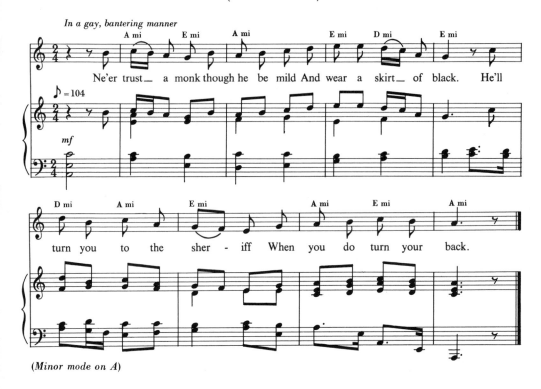

*In a gay, bantering manner*

Ne'er trust__ a monk though he be mild And wear a skirt__ of black. He'll

turn you to the sher - iff When you do turn your back.

*(Minor mode on A)*

1. Ne'er trust a monk though he be mild
   And wear a skirt of black.
   He'll turn you to the sheriff
   When you do turn your back.

2. When summer came, the skies were blue,
   The May leaves fine and long,
   And every forest was quite full
   Of birdies' chirp and song.

3. Then Robin Hood to Lovill John
   Said, "I must go and pray,
   For I have never prayed a prayer
   For many a livelong day."

4. Now Robin Hood should have taken men
   To holp him ere he fall
   Into the sheriff's jailhouse
   And be beyond recall.

5. But Lovill John was all he took,
   And they did part anon,
   When Robin went to pray alone
   In far-off Nottingtown.

6. He went into the sainties church,
   And it was very fair,
   And ne'er a one who prayed with him
   Knew Robin Hood was there.

7. A monk who knew good Robin Hood
   Made such a hue and cry,
   And called the sheriff and his men
   To quickly come there by.

8. Twelve men did bold Robin slay,
   By one, by two, by three,
   And many another wounded
   As he did fight for free.

9. Bold Robin broke his two-hand sword
   Upon the sheriff's haid,
   "Woe be, woe be, to any smith
   To make so poor a blade!"

10. "Light down, light down, fine holy man,
    And let me try my sword."
    And Lovill John led off his horse
    Into the deep green wood.

11. "How now, how now!" the King did cry.
    "My felon's in the keep.
    I'll give you twenty pounds of gold
    And make you wardens brave."

12. The sheriff said to Lovill John,
    "Come drink and sup with me."
    But late that night, when all did sleep,
    Bold Robin Hood was free.

13. Then said our King, "I gave them gold,
    I even gave them fee,
    But Lovill John loves Robin more
    Than ever he loves me.

14. "Bold Robin Hood is bound to him,
    No matter what befall.
    Speak no more of the fuel* thing,
    Young John has buggered us all."

* Perhaps "fool."

# Robin Hood's Death

(Child No. 120)

## Robber Hood's Dyin'
### (Niles No. 43)

**F**ROM TWO TEXTS given by Child under No. 120 we discover that (1) Robin Hood is ill, (2) he decides that he must be bled, (3) goes to Kirklees Priory to be treated with the bleeding irons, (4) is bled to death by the Prioress, (5) will not permit Little John to burn Kirklees, and (6) is buried with his sword at his head, his arrows at his feet, and his bow at his side.

The Child texts are 27 stanzas and 19 stanzas long. The American text offered herewith as Niles No. 43 tells the essentials of the story in 12 stanzas. This ballad has not been encountered very often in the United States. However, Arthur Kyle Davis, Jr., offers 17 wonderful verses (*Traditional Ballads of Virginia*), in which the original story is told quite accurately.

## Robber Hood's Dyin'
### (Niles No. 43)

TAKEN DOWN in Hazard, Ky., from the singing of Albert and Magilee Key, who lived in Martin, about 40 miles away . They said they were somewhere between 75 and 78 years of age. They were very alert, accurate, and quite gay. I tried to explain to them that the person who admitted Robin Hood into the "church and hall" was in reality a nun. They could not understand the word "nun." At first, they thought a nun might be a county health nurse or perhaps a relief worker. I finally hit on the idea of telling them that a nun was a kind of woman preacher. That seemed to be a satisfactory explanation.

The Keys' approach to almost everything was rather humorous. In their ballad, Robin Hood becomes Robber Hood, and when I asked them about this, they simply said, "He were a robber, were he not?"

I had to admit that Robin Hood was a robber, but I tried to explain that he robbed the rich to help the poor.

"Oh yes," said Mr. Key. "It was like it says in Holy Writ — robbin' Peter to pay Paul."

I asked whether his statement about Peter and Paul was really in the Bible.

"I ain't quite sure," retorted Mr. Key, "but if it ain't, it oughta be." And everyone had a small laugh. Yes, the Keys, man and wife, approached everything with a certain childish gaiety, and they sang with great willingness.

# Robber Hood's Dyin'

## (Niles No. 43)

(Dorian mode on C♯)

1. When Robber Hood came to church and hall,
   How tingled on the ring!
   And none was so gay at opening the door
   As the woman who lived therein,
   The woman who lived therein.

\* Wine?

2. "Come sit, come eat, for we be kin,
   Come drink the fine\* with me."
   "I can't not eat, nor will I drink,
   Until you've bleeded me."
   *(repeat last line of each verse)*

3. She quickly did bleed him from the leg,
   She bled him from the arm,
   And when he bled the livelong day,
   He knew he bled for harm.

4. Oh, Robber reached in, and Robber reached
      out,
   He tried to reach the door.
   He was too weak to raise himself
   From where he lay on the floor.

5. Oh, good Robber knew they meant him
      wrong,
   He knew they'd done him ill.
   He could not quit because of the length
   From ground to windowsill.

6. Oh, he gathered up his trumpet,
   He gathered up his breath,
   And he blew himself three long, low blasts
   To warn them of his death.

7. When Little John heard the trumpet-horn,
   He sat beneath a tree.
   Said, " 'Tis the note of a sick, sick man
   That I heard one, two, and three."

8. Then John ran quick to church and hall,
   And loud he struck thĕ door,
   And when they would not enter him,
   He smote it to the floor.

9. "Oh, pray, master, shall I kill this kin,
   Or shall I kill them all?
   Or shall I take thee from this bed
   And burn this cursèd hall?"

10. "Oh no, oh no," cried Robber Hood,
    "Spare kin, spare church, spare life.
    In this broad valley hit shall ne'er be said
    That I killed e'er a wife.

11. "Oh, go bring me yet my strong yow bow,
    That I may shoot an arrow.
    And where it falls, go dig my grave,
    So deep, so long and so narrow.

12. "Oh, leave me a length at my grave-feet,
    A full length more at my head,
    To room my arrows and my bow
    Beside me when I'm dead."

# Robin Hood and the Potter

(Child No. 121)

## The Potter and Robin Hood

(Niles No. 44)

On May 20, 1934, I came upon Preston and Mattie Cobb quite by accident. It was near a community called Big Hill in Madison County, Ky. I had been trying to photograph some wildflowers, and the Cobbs, man and wife, went to helping me. They said they were visiting in Berea, just a few miles away, and planned to return to Manchester, a town on Goose Creek in Clay County. Mrs. Cobb called her husband Potsie. She said, "Hit's a sweet name for Preston." Mr. Cobb, a onetime blacksmith, smiled. He was the silent type.

Mattie Cobb said that in her youth she knew many "ballards" and many songs about church subjects. Potsie Cobb smiled again and suggested that it was time they began going to church, "and regular." He added, "The frost is on the pumpkin." She said that she went to church every Sunday of her life except when she was in childbed. He had no answer to this. I thought he looked rather sad.

It was very easy to get Mattie Cobb to sing. In fact, I had certain difficulty in getting her to stop, for after singing her song about Robin Hood and the Potter, she went on to the good old hymns right out of the hymnbook. In an attempt to get her back onto traditional music, I tried to squeeze a song in edgewise, and did succeed in singing several carols. "The Seven Joys of Mary" was received with hand-clapping and shouted amen's, as if it were a revivalist device.

Mrs. Cobb said that I should come to Manchester, down on Goose Creek, because they were planning a revival soon, and I would be such a comfort to the preacher. I gave them a half-hearted promise, and went to discussing hand-forged hinges with Potsie Cobb, the onetime blacksmith. Later I toted them back to Berea.

Mrs. Cobb sang the ballad of "The Potter and Robin Hood" without a pause. In fact she sang the verses so fast that I could hardly get them written down accurately. On the other hand, she was willing to repeat as often as necessary. Mrs. Cobb was the small, wiry, nervous type. She said she had birthed seven children in her time.

When we came to the end of the singing, I tried to make talk with Preston Cobb by asking him if he too were a singer. He shook his head sadly and said: "No, mister," and then, as an afterthought, he continued, "I'm what you might call the fifth wheel." (He was referring to the fifth wheel on a jolt-wagon.)

At this point, I thought that Mrs. Cobb looked sad. She hung her head a bit. Then, to my great surprise, Potsie Cobb took up the conversation on his own. He said: "Mister, do you get any fun out of this business — this singin' of old-timey songs and writin' 'em down in little books?" I assured him I did have fun in my strange business, and that my greatest enjoyment came from associating with the wonderful people who sang the old-timey songs.

# The Potter and Robin Hood

## (Niles No. 44)

*In a gay, confident manner*

There— was a pot-ter bold, Who came one spring-time day, And said to our strong Rob-in— Hood: "No tri-bute will I pay."—

(Major mode on C)

"I'm glad for you, mister," said Potsie. " 'Cause outside of blacksmithin' I ain't had much fun."

Mrs. Cobb shook her head and said, "Potsie, Potsie . . ."

It might be a good idea to explain some of the omissions in Mrs. Cobb's text. According to the original legend, Robin Hood and the potter fight, and the potter is indeed victorious. Thereupon Robin, seeing a chance to get at the sheriff of Nottingham in what he hopes is a safe disguise, puts on the potter's clothes, trades horses with him, and drives off with the potter's horse and wagonload of pots. He goes into Nottingham, where he sets up a street stall just beside the sheriff's jailhouse.

He sells the pots so cheaply that presently there are only a few pots left, and these he sends into the jail as a gift to the sheriff's wife. (I have always imagined the sheriff's wife as a young, attractive woman and the sheriff as a tiresome, mean-natured, cruel old man.) Young or old, the sheriff's wife invites Robin Hood, still in the disguise of the potter, into the jailhouse for a rather sumptuous dinner. At this dinner, attended by a considerable company, some of the sheriff's men propose a shooting match with a purse of 40 shillings. Robin Hood joins the shooting party at the butts and distinguishes himself as an archer.

Later, Robin Hood, still acting the part of the potter, offers to take the sheriff into the greenwood, where the outlaw Hood resides. Next morning the two of them go forth in the direction of Sherwood Forest, the sheriff riding his horse and Robin Hood driving the potter's horse to the wagon. When at last they come to the greenwood, Robin blows a long blast on his horn, and the merry men come forth, seize the sheriff, relieve him of his horse and other valuables, beat him soundly — but spare his life because of the charm of his wife.

Ultimately, the sheriff arrives home, walking and leading a white palfrey, which is a gift to his wife. (No explanation is given for his walking, when he might have ridden the gift palfrey.) From his conversation with his wife, it appears that she had been aware of the potter's true identity from the very beginning. She chides the sheriff on his failure to bring Robin Hood back to jail, and the sheriff says, "The devil speed Robin Hood."

This lively dramatic ballad has been turned into a farce comedy by my son, John Edward Niles.

## The Potter and Robin Hood (Niles No. 44)

1. There was a potter bold,
   Who came one springtime day,
   And said to our strong Robin Hood:
   "No tribute will I pay."

2. And they did fight with stem and stick,
   And Rob was thrown to the ground,
   And there the potter, tongue in hand,
   Did beat our Robin sound.*

3. So Robin took the potter's pots
   And set a little stall
   Beside the sheriff's jailhouse,
   And sold the pots full all.

4. Next morn they left the sheriff's wife
   And thanked her full merry.
   The sheriff's heart was very light
   The greenwood for to see.

5. "Here's for your wife a horse of white
   And for her, too, a ring."
   And they would kill him very sure
   But she did many kind thing.

6. "How fared you in the forest green,
   And brought you Robbie home?"
   "He is the very devil's skin,"
   Said the sheriff with a moan.

7. "And we shall pay you for your pots
   And with our gold make free.
   And when you to the greenwood come,
   Welcome, my potter, to me."

---

* At this point, Potsie Cobb explained that the "tongue" was the tongue of a two-horse wagon. If this were so, it was indeed a formidable weapon, about 7 feet long and perhaps 2 inches by 4 inches — and made of hickory.

# Robin Hood and Little John

(Child No. 125)

## Robin and John

### (Niles No. 45)

A SEVEN-FOOT GIANT named John Little encounters Robin Hood on a narrow bridge. Robin is at this time a 20-year-old forester with a company of three-score-and-nine bowmen. However, Robin directs them to stay out of sight, but to come quickly if they hear his horn.

Robin refuses to give way to the tall stranger. At first, he considers shooting an arrow into him, but then decides that this would be poor sportsmanship since his antagonist is unarmed, save for a staff. Robin then provides himself with an oaken staff, and the fight is on. The rules of the game are simple: whoever is thrown off the bridge into the river has lost the play.

Robin Hood is tumbled into the water, and blows his horn for his merry men. They come quickly, and at first plan to duck John Little. Robin Hood will hear none of this, but offers John Little a place in his company. Little accepts, and with his name changed from John Little to Little John, he becomes one of Robin's most dependable associates.

## Robin and John

### (Niles No. 45)

IN MY FIELD NOTEBOOK I find the following information:

"July 8, 1932, night. Gilly [Gilbert] Sizemore, W. Va. miner out of a job. About 60. He was in jail in Hazard, Ky., for being involved in a drunken brawl. I visited him in his jail; I sang for the boys, and they sang for me. They thought it was quite swell, and so did I. Gilly Sizemore was the best singer of them all. He sang 'Robin and John,' and I took it down. I wrote the music across the page in pencil, and later rewrote it here in ink. It [the jail] was so hot we could hardly stand it. The jail smelled terribly. Drunkenness being no novelty on Saturday nights, there was no formal charge against Gilly, so after the usual cooling-off period, he will probably be free to go back to Coeburn, Va., and do whatever mining there's to be done.

" 'Drinkin' is a bad thing,' said Gilly, and I feared he was going into a temperance lecture. But instead he rationalized the entire process by saying: 'Of course, it eases a man a bit, takes the

247

# Robin and John
## (Niles No. 45)

*Gay and rollicking*

When Rob - in Hood was twen - ty - one, With a low down down by the riv - er down, When Rob - in Hood was twen - ty - one, He then did meet with Lit - tle John, Who lived a - far in North - ern - town, With a down by the riv - er down.

*(Dorian mode on E)*

weight off of his shoulders for a spell. Now, in my case, it takes more to ease me, 'cause I'm old and I been at it a long while. You know, like a feller says, an old sack needs a power of patchin'.'

" 'You write down everythin' everybody says to you?' demanded Gilly after a pause. I was writing furiously, and sweating, too. I tried to explain myself, but I had long ago discovered that no form of explanation really explains a man who spends his time making notes in a little black book. I just went on listening and writing.

" 'Powerful hot in here,' said Gilly. 'I'm as uncomfortable as a stewed witch. And don't this place stink? My, oh me . . . Still an' all, the jail-house is the safest place for a man of a Saturday night. What with womenfolk pawin' at you fer yer pay, and landlords pawin' at you fer their rent, hit ain't safe to be out in the open.' "

Here is how Gilly Sizemore condensed the 39 stanzas of the original ballad into 6 of his own.

## Robin and John (Niles No. 45)

1. When Robin Hood was twenty-one,
   *With a low down down by the river down,*
   When Robin Hood was twenty-one,
   He then did meet with Little John,
   Who lived afar in Northerntown,
   *With a down by the river down.*

2. They met upon a narrow bridge,
   *With a low down down by the river down,*
   They met upon a narrow bridge
   And neither then would give away
   Until they had some Northern play,
   *With a down by the river down.*

3. So thick, so fast they laid it on,
   So thick, so fast they laid it on,
   They flourished staffs and sticks of oak,
   And heads they bashed and bones they broke.

4. Now John struck Robin such a blow,
   Now John struck Robin such a blow,
   He topped poor Robin into the tide below,
   *With a low down down by the river down.*

5. "How now, how now?" John Little cried,
   "How now, how now?" John Little cried.
   "The water in his tide is cold,
   You've won, you've won, my warrior bold."

6. Brave John put on the all-of-green,
   Brave John put on the all-of-green.
   He then did join the merry men
   And lived with them in the greenwood glen.

# 46

# The Bold Pedlar and Robin Hood

(Child No. 132)

## The Bold Peddler

(Niles No. 46)

ROBIN HOOD and Little John encounter a peddler and bother him with their usual sort of teasing. They ask the peddler what he is carrying in his pack, and he truthfully tells them that he has several green silken suits and some silken bowstring. Thereupon Little John declares that he will have one half of the peddler's pack. The peddler offers to give up the entire pack if he can be pushed one perch* from where he stands. Little John and the peddler fight, and the peddler forces John to cry hold. Robin Hood engages the peddler with the same result.

Robin Hood and Little John disclose their identity, and the peddler reluctantly admits that he is fugitive from his own country and that his name is Gamble Gold. Robin recognizes the peddler as his own cousin, and after everyone has sheathed his sword they retire to a convenient tavern for food and drink. Of course the bold peddler joins Robin Hood's company of merry men.

Broadsides of the above legend were found in England during the middle years of the 19th century.

## The Bold Peddler

(Niles No. 46)

THE YEAR WAS 1912, and I was traveling northward from Corbin to London, Ky., in an automobile of 1910 vintage. The going was slow. The road was very poor. North of Corbin there is a fork in the road, one branch going off in the direction of Middlesboro. It was at this road junction that I stopped to repair a tire and, while

doing so, made friends with a large, jovial, middle-aged woman named Aunt Etta Smithy. She wanted to be remembered as a good Bible-reading Methodist and one who would not listen to the scandals and back-bitings of the local Baptists and the Rollers. She was particularly bothered by the youth of 1912 — how they had

---

* A perch may be a measure of length, especially for land, and is generally accepted as 5½ yards, but it varies locally. It may also be used as a measure for solid stone construction. In this case a perch is: 1 foot wide, 1 foot deep, and 25 feet long.

# The Bold Peddler

## (Niles No. 46)

*(Major mode on F)*

no respect for their elders and were always on the go. "Lollygogglin', kilfliggin', rampin' up and down these roads," said she. "Why, it's bad enough now, when they drive horses to top-buggies. But just you wait and see — in time they'll be drivin' automobiles!"

Her nephew had died, and she was still in mourning. "Yes," she said, "that boy upped and married a widow-woman with a grown daughter. 'Treckly, he had two back doors to his house,* and meanwhile, he was workin' himself to death, supportin' that triflin' lot. I told him there was

\* Meaning that the widow-woman and her daughter entertained other men when the husband was away at work.

no pockets in a shroud. But now he's gone, and his women took his house-plunder and left the day after the funeral."

Aunt Etta said that when she was a young woman, she had a great collection of ballad sheets, and among them was the song about the peddler. Her pitch was variable, but her natural method of projection might have been a model for public performers. I sat with her long into the afternoon, ate some victuals, and drank some coffee. In 1940 I discovered that a gas station occupied the spot where her cabin had stood in 1912.

Below one will find Aunt Etta Smithy's version of "The Bold Pedlar and Robin Hood," which, by the way, has a happy ending.

## The Bold Peddler (Niles No. 46)

1. There was a peddler bold,
   A peddler bold was he.
   He tied his pack upon his back
   And traveled the wide country,
   And he traveled the wide country.

2. He met two gay young blades
   Who bothered him anon,
   And one of them was Robin Hood
   And the other Little John.
       (*repeat last line of each verse*)

3. "What's in thy pretty bag?
   Come tell us speedily."
   "It's I have silken suits of green,
   By one, by two, by three."

4. "If you have suits of green
   And silken suits of gray,
   What ho! what ho!" cried Little John,
   "It's I'll take one away."

5. "You shall not thieve my gray,
   Nor thieve me of my green,
   Nor thieve me of a single strand
   Of bowstring in between!"

6. Now John took out his sword,
   The peddler swung his wand,*
   And oak against the metal banged.
   Said, "Peddler, hold your hand."

7. Then Robin drew his sword,
   The peddler swung his wand,
   And there was blood and bruises
   When the peddler held his hand.

8. "What name, my peddler bold,
   Come tell us quickily."
   "My name I'll never, never tell
   Till you two do tell to me."

9. "Yes, I am Peddler Goldy,
   From a far country,
   And for a drop of my heart's blood
   The sheriff would give three."

10. "If you are Cousin Goldy,
    Then welcome unto me.
    No sheriff will e'er hold you long
    Beneath the greenwood tree."

* As I remember, "wand" rhymed with "hand."

# 47

# Robin Hood Rescuing Three Squires

(Child No. 140)

## Robin Hood and the Old Maid
### (Niles No. 47 A)
## Robin Hood and the Old Woman
### (Niles No. 47 B)

IN THIS CASE, the original story is as follows: Robin Hood is on his way to Nottingham. He encounters an old woman who is weeping because her sons will be executed that day by the sheriff of Nottingham. Robin Hood borrows the clothing of an old man (a palmer or a beggar) and continues on his way to Nottingham. Once there he offers to be the sheriff's hangman. Having been given the job, he blows his trusty horn. His merry men appear, release the three young men, and hang the sheriff.

## Robin Hood and the Old Maid
### (Niles No. 47 A)

THE READER has already discovered by way of "Oh Judy, My Judy" (Niles No. 16 C) that Pete Mulleneoux burned charcoal and raised watermelons. He also made an intoxicant (distilled from fermented cornmeal) sometimes called moonshine.

I visited Pete and other members of the Mulleneoux clan quite often during the summer of 1909. They lived in what was then called the Wet Woods, in the south end of Jefferson County, Ky. About 12 miles away the great populous city of Louisville occupied a large portion of the northern end of the same county. On a clear night, one could see a glow on the northern skyline from Pete's farm.

Pete sang lustily. He enjoyed the idea of hanging a sheriff. He called the song "Robin Hood and the Old Maid."

# Robin Hood and the Old Maid

## (Niles No. 47 A)

(Dorian mode on G)

1. "What news, what news, my silly old maid,
   What news have you for me?"
   "I know three gay and merry men
   In Northbeetown will die,
       I know three gay and merry men
       In Northbeetown will die."

2. "Oh, did they burn or did they steal,
   Or were twelve preachers slain?
   Or have they rapèd virgin girls
   Or with some pretty wives lain?"
       (*repeat last 2 lines of each verse*)

3. Now Robin Hood's gone to Northbeetown,
   With a down-down-down and a derry-down-
   dey,
   And there he met a preacher-man
   As he walked the King's highway.

4. "Come change, come change, come change
   with me,
   Come change your clothes for mine,
   And I will give you market gold*
   To eat on meat and wine."

5. Now Robin went up to the sheriff,
   Said, "Pray do hear of me.
   What will you pay a poor old man
   Who will your hangman be?"

6. "I always pay my hangman well,
   And you shall be paid more —
   A suit with no cloth patches
   Because you are so poor."

7. Now Robin blew a mighty blast,
   He blew one, two, and three,
   And see his men spring quickly out
   And shout most merrily.

8. The door is down, the prisoners out,
   The gallows is on the hill.
   And there they hanged the sheriff,
   And he must be hanging still.

# Robin Hood and the Old Woman
## (Niles No. 47 B)

THIS WAS taken down on the roof of the Civic Building in Asheville, N. C., on August 3, 1934, from the singing of an old man named Vital Bean. I asked him where he lived, and he simply said, "Nearby." I have encountered many so-called silent types; Mr. Bean was one of these. His singing was low and timid but quite accurate. Contact with him was made through a member of the Farmers' Co-operative. His clothing was threadbare, but washed clean and bright. I thanked him for coming into town and singing for me. He said he had to come anyway, for, being childless, he enjoyed visiting his sister's children once each week. When he finished singing "Robin Hood and the Old Woman," without any prompting he sang a quite wonderful version of "The Holy Family."

* Minted gold.

The ballad of Robin Hood as sung by Vital Bean was, in fact, a combination of two ideas: one, "Robin Hood Rescuing Three Squires" (Child No. 140) and the other, "Robin Hood and the Bishop" (Child No. 143). In the first of these, three young men are rescued by Robin Hood disguised as a palmer; while in the second, Robin Hood gets the best of the Bishop (one of Robin's greatest enemies) in the guise of an old woman. To make the deception complete, the old woman puts on Robin's coat of green and even carries his bow and arrows. She is captured by the Bishop, who is convinced he has caught Robin Hood. Later when she reveals her true identity and the Bishop refuses to believe her, she cunningly proposes the acid test, as follows:

# Robin Hood and the Old Woman

## (Niles No. 47 B)

(Major mode on G)

*"Why who art thou," the Bishop he said,*
  *"Which I have here with me?"*
*"Why, I'm an old woman, thou cuckoldly bishop;*
  *Lift up my leg and see."*

Ultimately, the Bishop is captured by Robin Hood and his merry men, and the profit on this capture is not only the person of the Bishop but also 500 pounds sterling, and the Bishop is further belittled by having to sing mass while tied to a tree.

But Vital Bean knew none of this. Rescuing three young men was something he could understand. I doubt if he would have recognized the word "bishop." His ballad, however, has Robin

Hood changing clothes with an old woman, as in Child No. 143.

At the end of the singing, I worked up the courage to ask Mr. Bean about his name. He said Vital was a family name, and the discussion was closed. I thought how unfair it was of parents to choose names for their children which in combination with the family name could become descriptive terms.

While Vital Bean had been singing and I had been taking notes, a group of young dancers had collected, and almost at once they began rehearsing the complicated figures of a dance they planned to display at the folk-dance festival later in the evening.

It seemed to me that Mr. Bean was watching the dancers with a touching kind of wistfulness.

It must have been years since he had had so much fun. He turned to me and said, "Young folks is ahead of themselves these days, particularly the girls . . ." The dancers went on and on, the boys smiling as they wove in and out, bowing, swinging their partners, the girls curtsying in a swirl of skirts. "Yes," said Mr. Bean, "they don't give themselves time to grow up. It's like old folks used to say — quick ripe, soon rotten."

I thanked him again, we shook hands rather ceremoniously, and he turned away quickly and lost himself among the dancers who were so far ahead of themselves . . . The sun was down, the city lights were coming on. I was hungry. The Battery Park Hotel was nearby. I could almost see the window of my room from the roof of the building where the dance was in progress.

## Robin Hood and the Old Woman (Niles No. 47 B)

1. "Oh why, oh why do you weep, old woman?
   Or is it that you're an old maid?
   Or do you want the gold I've got,
   Or are you sore afraid,
   Or are you sore afraid?"

2. "I am no maid, but I am a widow.
   My man was a soldier brave.
   And now I weep for my three fine sons,
   Who soon will be in the grave."
   (*repeat last line of each verse*)

3. "Come give me your dress and give me your
        jump,*
   And give me your worn-out shoes
   And pray give me a piece of leathern
   To make me a pair of thews."†

4. He's off to town, he's off to jail,
   He's begging all the way.
   He's begging the sheriff for three young men
   Who were to die today.

5. He's blowing his horn by one, two, and three,
   He's calling his men to bide,
   And there they took the cruel sheriff
   And tied him well inside.

6. They've left the jailhouse far behind,
   And this is what they tell:
   The widow's weepy eyes were dry,
   She thanked bold Robin well.

7. The people in the city
   Did cry with joy and glee.
   The sheriff was the only one
   To shine on the gallows tree.

* Jumper or jacket.        † Laces.

# Queen Eleanor's Confession

(Child No. 156)

## The Dying Queen
(Niles No. 48)

IN THE ENGLISH VERSIONS of "Queen Eleanor's Confession" we find the Queen of England dying. She asks for two priests to receive her last confession. The priests arrive in cowl and hood. They are, however, not actual priests but the King, husband of Queen Eleanor, and a man called the Earl Marshal, whom the King suspects as the Queen's lover. Moreover, the King has made a solemn promise that no matter what the Queen says, he will not hold it against the Earl Marshal.

The Queen proceeds to reveal a past life involving the Earl Marshal. She then confesses that she has poisoned Rosamond Clifford, the King's mistress. Finally, the King has heard enough. He steps out of his priestly robes, and the Queen screams that she has been betrayed.

But let us go back to the early days of Queen Eleanor's life, when indeed she was Eleanor of Aquitaine. Born she was in 1122 in the south of France (Bordeaux and Belin both claim to be her birthplace). Neither her father, William X, Count of Poitou and Duke of Aquitaine, nor her mother could have had any premonition of what history-making fate lay "so low in swaddling clothes."

Eleanor's early youth was spent in a peace-loving court, where the songs of the troubadour had largely displaced the clang of armor, where courtly love and the production of poetic literature concerning love were thought to be of first importance. Her grandfather, William IX, had been a well-known loser of battles but an equally well-known winner of women. In 1101 William IX went forth, an unwilling crusader, lost nearly all his forces in the Holy Land, and returned to compose a sad song about the entire wretched enterprise. This doughty nobleman was continually at odds with the Church, and once contemplated a small abbey, or nunnery, wherein the good ladies would all be prostitutes. Indeed, he tried the patience of Rome no little bit.

Eleanor's father, William X, followed in his father's footsteps by battling churchmen, encouraging troubadours, chroniclers, poets, and minnesingers, being defeated in local wars, engaging in all the delightful vices the nobility could invent, and finally dying within sight of the shrine of St. James of Compostella. He had made the pilgrimage to the shrine as a contrite penitent, and he was finally buried before the main altar at Compostella. His last official act was to offer his daughter Eleanor in marriage to Louis Capet, heir apparent to the French throne.

On Sunday, July 25, 1137, at the Church of St. Andrew in Bordeaux, Geoffrey, Archbishop of Bordeaux, married Louis Capet and Eleanor of Aquitaine. Eleanor of Aquitaine had become Queen Eleanor of France, and the French kingdom was enormously enlarged and enriched by the addition of the vast lush lands of Aquitaine and Poitou.

As the years passed, Queen Eleanor discovered that Louis Capet, now Louis VII, was a weak man, possessed of a strange, psychopathic religiosity, which must have been tiresome, to say the least. She did accompany the King on that most tragic Second Crusade of 1147. While Louis lost battles to the infidels, Queen Eleanor was accused of making merry with an enemy general. Indeed, in Section 7, Vol. II, of the *Reliques of Ancient English Poetry,* we find Bishop Percy's report that Eleanor had "fallen under some suspicions of galantry with a handsome Saracen."

Shortly after Louis VII returned from his costly, fatuous failures in the Holy Land, a young man of 18 years named Henry Plantagenet came up to Paris to pay homage. This young man, already Duke of Normandy, Count of Anjou, Touraine, and Maine, captured the attention of Queen Eleanor almost at once.

Those who were privy to Eleanor's thoughts knew that she considered Louis more a monk than a man, and none of these was surprised when it became known that Eleanor and Louis were divorced — or, at least, that the marriage had been annulled on the trumped-up grounds of nearness of kin.

No one ever made bold to accuse Henry Plantagenet of being handsome or polite or gentle, or failing in ambition. He was indeed a boisterous, redheaded, heavily built nobleman, with the distant blood of William the Conqueror in his veins. His bandy legs were said to be the natural result of his interest in horses, hounds, and the chase.

The decree of separation of Queen Eleanor and Louis VII of France was announced on March 21, 1152. Just under two months later, Eleanor (aged about 30) and Henry Plantagenet (19) were married. At first, the disparity in their ages did not seem to matter much, because Eleanor had come into the full loveliness of her maturity. She had indeed discovered how to comfort a man, to mother and rear children, to sing the songs of the countryside, to break bread with nobles, kings, and clergy, to talk diplomacy behind her hand, to ride a horse, listen to the bay of a hound, and feed a falcon. She was the kind of queen to stir a king to conquest.

In 1154, Henry, Count of Anjou, became Henry II, King of England, and Eleanor became Queen, and in the fullness of time produced five sons and three daughters. Two of her sons became kings of England, and her husband, Henry II, earned doubtful honor as the most unfaithful husband in the Plantagenet family. The history of Eleanor as Queen of England is splashed with the names of Thomas à Becket, Archbishop Thibault, Frederick Barbarossa, Malcolm of Scotland, Rosamond, the fair daughter of Walter, Lord Clifford, and Richard, Heart of a Lion, and John Lackland (these last two being her sons), and a host of others. She died at peace with the world in the 83rd year of her life and was buried at the convent of Fontevrault in France. Her tomb is between those of her husband Henry II and her son Richard, the Lion-Heart.

Although Henry II did have two illegitimate sons by fair Rosamond, and although he did build her a house in the middle of a fabulous labyrinth, or maze, there are those who doubt whether Queen Eleanor actually poisoned Rosamond Clifford. Nor is it likely that Queen Eleanor went to the trouble to extend her "gallantries" as far as the Earl Marshal. Furthermore, it seems almost preposterous to think that Queen Eleanor, as clever as she must have been, could have cuckolded Henry Plantagenet to the extent of passing off the Earl Marshal's son as royal get. This is indeed more than logic can accept; but gossip was always more art than science, and can swallow most anything.

The marriage of Henry II, Plantagenet, and Eleanor of Aquitaine, at first a glittering political success, ultimately proved to be one of the most dismal marital failures in history. In conclusion — lest the reader wonder why I have dealt at such length with them — I must confess that Henry II and Eleanor of Aquitaine are two of my choice people: Henry because he rode to hounds and hunted the fox with such glee and Eleanor because she loved the sound of the lute and the singing of the epic ballad.

# The Dying Queen
## (Niles No. 48)

*(Minor mode on E)*

# The Dying Queen
## (Niles No. 48)

MY INFORMANT, who asked that her name not be mentioned, was of undetermined but far advanced age. Her cabin, about six miles from Murphy, N. C., was falling down. When I came upon it I thought it was deserted, until I heard her voice calling to me from a nearby cornfield. She emerged, bare of head and foot, hoe in hand, and wearing a gunny sack for a dress.

Her husband had died, and her daughters had taken to the road, but her corn crop was one of the best, and her garden was a thing of beauty. Every vegetable the land could produce was there in great abundance.

My eyes must have betrayed me, for she seemed to know that I was taken aback at her appearance. It was then she said, "John, you should have seen me in my flash!"*

"Yes," I said, not knowing what else to offer.

"My hair was red, and the boys used to say my skin was the color of fresh milk."

Sixty years earlier I might have beheld the gay little redhead with the milk-white skin — the gay little redhead who at the end of her life was a withered old woman with a mop of rusty-white hair, living in the corner of a "down house." But, undaunted, she sang with gay abandon, and laughed as she told me how she had thrown a rock at a rattlesnake earlier that afternoon. According to her story, the rattler had slithered away reluctantly.

Her singing was fairly accurate, and her eyes glowed when I handed her a chip-basket filled with the most simple necessities. One thing she wanted above all else was some Railroad Mills snuff.

"Them six little cans of snuff is worth a king's ransom to me, John," she said.

Of course, my informant knew nothing of Eleanor of Aquitaine, and the mention of Henry II, Plantagenet, would have been a mystery to her ears. As we talked on, I found that my onetime little redhead had never gone to school at all. But she did sing one of the rarest ballads in all my collection. She said she had learned it as a child, from her granny.

As we said before, the dramatic death detailed in this ballad is entirely at variance with the facts. The Queen died in France, at peace with the world, on March 30, 1204, and by that time Henry II had been dead 15 years.

In France, Italy, Germany, and Denmark, we find folk tales in which a husband disguises himself as a priest and receives his wife's confession. Boccaccio manages the situation very nicely: he has the wife recognize the disguised husband and, by her confession, worm herself out of an embarrassing situation and convince everyone of her innocence.

## The Dying Queen

1. The Queen is sick, and she will die,
   *Fa-la-le-la, fa-la-le-lu,*
   The Queen is sick, and she will die,
   Send her two preachers speed-ee-lie,
   *Fa-la-le-la, fa-la-le-lu.*

2. The King was one, the Captain 'tother,
   *Fa-la-le-la, fa-la-le-lu,*
   The King was one, the Captain 'tother,
   My firstest child was got by another,
   *Fa-la-le-la, fa-la-le-lu.*

3. My daughters were not Henry's get,
   Their beauty you could not forget.

4. My second son, I liked him least,
   He looks like one who is this priest.

5. I carried pizen in a bag
   To pizen them as did me bad.

6. I pizened that fair Price-ee-mond.
   She bare the King two little sons.

7. The King took off his preacher's gown
   And gave the Captain many a frown.

8. The Queen made moan and died in baid,
   She shrieked and cried she was betrayed.

* Her early teens.

# 49

# King Henry Fifth's Conquest of France

(Child No. 164)

### The Fency King and the English King
(Niles No. 49 A)

### Henry's Tribute
(Niles No. 49 B)

### The Tennis Balls
(Niles No. 49 C)

FROM THE TEXT of this ballad as given by Child we gain the idea that Henry V was in the habit of collecting a tribute of gold coinage from Charles VI, King of France. At one point, with the tribute long overdue, Henry V sends a messenger to France to remind the French ruler of his delinquent payments. Although Henry V was almost 28 years of age, the French, instead of paying the tribute, go out of their way to belittle the English king by sending him some tennis balls. (All this according to Child ballad No. 164.)

We are quite certain that the idea of tribute is entirely manufactured, and we are even doubtful of the tennis balls, although one chronicler goes so far as to speak of "a tonne of tenys-ballys." The idea, of course, behind the gift was that Henry V and his lords would then be able to indulge in the game of tennis, which was extremely popular among the nobility of the period.

The ballad reporting of the Battle of Agincourt, in which Henry V defeated the French in 1415, is endlessly inaccurate. In stanzas 10–13, we find that between drums and trumpets shots were fired, 10,000 Frenchmen were killed, and the English armies marched into Paris. We are positive that none of this took place quite as reported. History tells us, however, that there was a girl, Catherine of France (mentioned in the 14th stanza of Child No. 164), and there was a battle, at first unnamed. And when it was over the flower of French and English manhood lay scattered about in careless little piles. The thickets and swamps of Maisoncelles were choked with knights dead in their armor, with bowmen face down as if sleeping, with wounded horses whinnying in agony, and with French peasants looting for treasure.

Henry, fifth of the name to be King of England, turned his eyes to a turreted castle on an eminence in the distance, a castle as gray as a rain cloud. A chronicler stood by, gathering the facts of the battle.

"My lord," said King Henry to the captured Duke of Orleans, "by what name do they call yon turret?"

"Sire, it is called Agincourt —" And his voice faltered, for his spirit had died.

"Be it so," said Henry, and, turning to the assembled company, he continued, "My lords,

God looked upon us with mercy. We have just fought the Battle of Agincourt, and if God continues to favor our arms, we may have won it."

It was not until after they had sung a Te Deum, counted their dead, bound up their wounds, scouted the enemy, and started on the long road to Calais — in fact, it was not until the next day — that they were sure of victory. No one knew quite what had happened, not even Henry, and much less the bewildered, defeated French. History would later tell that they had fought one of the most often, and least accurately, reported battles in all the long, bitter history of arms. Military men are quick to admit that Agincourt was one of Britain's most fabulous victories.

The English army under Henry V had left London quite gaily on a June morning in 1415. They left Porchester on August 7 and Henry was taken to his ship, *The Trinity,* at Southampton. Later in August they landed in France and laid siege to Harfleur, staying there until early October. After skirting the Somme River, they made a crossing at the village of Voyennes. The Battle of Agincourt was fought during that 24-hour period between October 24 and 25, 1415. So few hours of battle never produced such world-wide results in the world as it existed in 1415.

What was left of the English forces after Agincourt continued to Calais, unmolested, and embarked once more for England on November 16. Already winter was setting in. The landing in England was made in very inclement weather. Henry V and his victorious though bedraggled army arrived in London once more, on November 23, and their entry was no doubt more tumultuous than all the tumults of Agincourt.

If the simplification of history found in the ballad of "King Henry Fifth's Conquest of France" could be substituted for historical fact, how delightful it would be! But the ballad and the facts are far apart. They have in common the central character Henry V, and a more romantic character would be hard to find, either in history or in ballad literature.

Henry V, son of Henry IV and Mary de Bohun, was born at Monmouth Castle in 1387; became King of England in 1413; fought and won the Battle of Agincourt in 1415; married Catherine of Valois in Troyes in 1420; died in France in 1422. He was a medieval hero, the likes of which have seldom walked the earth. His achievements were as dazzling as his failures were consuming. At one time he was not only King of England but ruled over much of what is now France.

It is interesting to note that the ballad mentions Catherine of Valois, although her marriage to Henry V did not take place until five years after the Battle of Agincourt. In Child No. 164, she is mentioned as "the finest flower that is in all France" or "the fairest flower in all French land." The idea, however, that she is to be given to Henry "for free" is nonsense. Since the beginning of time, daughters have seldom been free. They are usually very costly items, and this one, Catherine, beautiful beyond the telling save for the Valois nose, was perhaps the most expensive daughter priest ever joined to man in holy wedlock.

All the blood of Agincourt and the treasure collected through the taxes of years on end went into the mating of this slender girl to Henry V. The son born of this union made a sorry spectacle as Henry VI of England and France. But after Henry V's death in 1422 Catherine married a Welsh knight named Owen Tudor, and thereby became the grandmother of Henry VII and, of course, great-grandmother to Henry Tudor, eighth of the name. Thus, every Tudor from 1428 on had some Valois blood in his veins. The ghost of Catherine of Valois — ultimately Queen Catherine of England, whose early life had been so tragic and who was so shabbily treated after Henry V's death — must have had many a satisfying laugh as it watched the 16th and 17th centuries unfold.

The ballad of "King Henry Fifth's Conquest of France" has not been encountered very often in the United States. Special mention should be made of the work done by Mr. and Mrs. Mellinger E. Henry in recovering two excellent texts and one tune of this rare ballad. I have been fortunate in recording one text with music and two fragments without music.

# The Fency King and the English King

## (Niles No. 49 A)

Oh, King Hen-ry lay a — mus-er-ing Up-on his bed — so fine: — "The King of Fence-'s trib-ute Has been ow-ing quite some time. Far-la-la-la-la, fa-la-la-la-la, 's been ow-ing quite — some time."

*(Dorian mode on G)*

# The Fency King and the English King

## (Niles No. 49 A)

HER NAME was Aunt Flory French, and she was born in Mount Sterling, Ky., in about 1858. She did not know her age, but these vital statistics were passed on to me by a friend. She was toothless and gay and a very unwilling singer when I encountered her in 1932 at the Daniel Boone Hotel in Whitesburg, Ky.

At a very early age, Aunt Flory had married Richard ("Paddy") French. I never discovered her maiden name. I said, "Captain French? Captain of what army?" knowing that the cavalier Confederate general John Bell Hood had been born in Mount Sterling and expecting to discover that her husband had fought with General Hood. But she threw back her head and cackled out a long laugh and said, "Young man, my husband was a captain of soldiers." Aunt Flory had an answer for everything.

I believe she was as thin a person as I've ever seen. She said, "Don't buy me no food, food don't do me no good. I eat continual, but I gum my vittles, and so I'm as thin as a snake." (She had no teeth.)

She was holding an audience in direct competition with the radio broadcast of the Democratic National Convention of 1932. (Perhaps I should explain that in those days, very few homes in the Kentucky mountains had radios, and thus people from all around gathered in the lobby of the Daniel Boone Hotel in Whitesburg to listen to the events being broadcast from Chicago over the hotel radio.) A great many people were listening to the radio, but Aunt Flory had her listeners, too.

Her voice was wispy and, as I said before, she was an unwilling singer. Furthermore, she was not really interested in singing, or in my process

## The Fency King and the English King

1. Oh, King Henry lay a-musering
   Upon his bed so fine:
   "The King of Fence's tribute
   Has been owing quite some time.
   *Far-la-la-la-la, fa-la-la-la-la,*
   'S been owing quite some time."

2. He called upon his youngest page,
   His youngest page called he:
   "Go over to the Fency King,
   And that right speedily."
   (*repeat refrain & last line of each verse*)

3. "Oh, worthy, mighty King of Fence,
   Some gold is due in England.
   And you will send this tribute home,
   Or Fence will feel great England's hand."

4. "Your master's in his tender age,
   And does not know my high degree.
   Here, take him three fine tenny-balls
   That he may learn to romp and play."

5. "What news, what news, my little page,
   What news bring you to me?"
   "It's I can tell you anyhow
   That you will not agree.

6. "He says you're young, of tender age,
   And can't not know his high degree,
   And he has sent you tenny-balls
   That you may learn some skip-er-ee."

7. When proud Henry marchèd through the Fence,
   A-drumming merrily,
   They killed ten thousand Fencermen,
   And their king left speedily.

8. "It's I will send his tribute home,
   I'll send him gold and fee,
   And I will send my daughter,
   And she will be for free."

of writing down what she sang. Then, too, she was determined to make an act out of everything. But she was as cunning and as humorous a person as I've ever encountered. At one point I asked her whether she knew any other ballads, and she said: "I know more ballards than a dog has fleas, but I hain't a-goin' to sing any more because I'm plumb sung out, and this here radio-machine is a lot more interesting than you or your singin'."

I then asked her — much to the delight of her increasing audience — what a tenny-ball was. She came up with a surprising answer: "A tenny-ball is a ball what grows on a tenny-tree, just like a sycamo' ball grows on a sycamo' tree."

Next I tried to straighten out the pronunciation of the word "France," but to her it was Fence and Fencermen. I asked her where Fence was. She declared it was a place far, far south — south even of Texas. I assumed she was thinking of Mexico.

Finally, I asked her where she lived.

"In Kentucky, of course," she said with pursed lips.

"I know, but where in Kentucky?"

"With some no-count, tore-down in-laws and grandchildren."

"But where, exactly?" I demanded.

"Hain't no exactly about it, young feller. Hit's up the second holler on the left."

Meanwhile, I had bought her a ten-cent bottle of perfume. It was a kind of perfume called Jockey Club. Aunt Flory opened the tiny bottle and daubed it all over her face and arms. Turning to her admiring public, she said, "Hot dog! I stepped in a mudhole and come up with a shoeshine!"

I concluded she was positively irrepressible.

# Henry's Tribute

## (Niles No. 49 B)

TAKEN DOWN from the recitation of Porter Roberts in the Hibbler Hotel, Hazard, Ky., July of 1932:

Oh, Henry lay a-restin'
Upon his bed of silk.
The King of France's tribute
'S been owin' so long,
　　We have no bread and milk.
The King of France's tribute
'S been owin' so long,

We have no bread and milk.
Oh, fa-la-la-la-la, bugger-i-loo,
Oh, fa-la-la-la-la, owl says "Hoo."

There had been a hotel fire in Hazard, and the remaining lower floors of the hotel were being restored and redecorated. Porter Roberts told me how lucky he was to have a good paying job, working in the hotel. The depression of the '30's had caused great hardship in the southeastern mountains.

# The Tennis Balls

## (Niles No. 49 C)

As SUNG by a blacksmith's helper named Gil Napier (pronounced "Napper") in Hazard, Ky., in July of 1913. The music was either lost or was not taken down.

1. 'Twas night when our King Henry
   Did lay him down to rest.
   'Twas morning when he spoke his mind:
   "That French King must be pressed, pressed, pressed,
   That French King must be pressed.
   *Refrain:*
     *Oh fol-de-lol, oh fol-de-lay,*
     *A dolly-down-diddle and a nay-nay-nay."*

2. He called for his lovely page,
   His lovely page called he.
   "A tribute from the Frenchman
   Has long been due me, me, me,
   Has long been due me."
     (*repeat refrain after each verse*)

3. Then went away his lovely page,
   He rose so speedily,
   And when he came to the King of France
   Low fell he on his knee, knee, knee,
   Low fell he on his knee.

4. "My master greets you, greets you, sir.
   One ton of gold is due he:
   That you will send his tribute soon,
   Or sooner him you'll see, see, see,
   Or sooner him you'll see."

5. "Your master is of tender years,
   Your master's shift is short.
   I'll send him three round tennis balls
   That he may learn to sport, sport, sport,
   That he may learn to sport."

Incomplete as it is, this text of 5 five-line stanzas was always interesting classroom material. There was a certain charm about the poem, and the students found it humorous. It should be noted, too, that all three examples of No. 49 in this collection come from the same area — two are from Hazard and 49 A is from Whitesburg, which is nearby — and doubtless two of them originate from the same source. Aunt Flory's version, however, differs from the two recorded in Hazard, and it should be remembered that though I met her at Whitesburg, she was born in Mount Sterling, which is on the edge of the Blue-grass country, some distance away.

# The Death of Queen Jane

(Child No. 170)

The Death of Queen Jane
(Niles No. 50)

I<small>N</small> F<small>EBRUARY</small> 1776 the following text was written down from memory by one Mrs. Bernard, the mother of the Dean of Derry. The Dean of Derry later delivered the writing to Lord Percy, and thereupon the ballad, "The Death of Queen Jane," became a part of the Percy Papers.*

*Queen Jane was in labour full six weeks and more,*
  *And the women were weary, and fain would give oer:*
*'O women, O women, as women ye be,*
  *Rip open my two sides, and save my baby!'*

*'O royal Queen Jane, that thing may not be;*
  *We'll send for King Henry to come unto thee.'*
*King Henry came to her, and sate on her bed:*
  *'What ails my dear lady, her eyes look so red?'*

*'O royal King Henry, do one thing for me:*
  *Rip open my two sides, and save my baby!'*
*'O royal Queen Jane, that thing will not do;*
  *If I lose your fair body, I'll lose your baby too.'*

*She wept and she waild, and she wrung her hands sore;*
  *O the flour of England must flurish no more!*
*She wept and she waild till she fell in a swoond,*
  *They opend her two sides, and the baby was found.*

---

* The Percy Papers, or, in edited and published form, the *Reliques of Ancient English Poetry*, was the work of Thomas Percy (1729–1811), Bishop of Dromore (Ireland). Percy died September 30, 1811, and is buried in Dromore cathedral. His *Reliques* was based on a manuscript written probably in the mid-17th century which contained 191 sonnets, ballads, historical songs, and metrical romances, either in whole or in part. Percy came into the possession of this collection from the hands of a housemaid who was about to light a fire with it. All this happened in the household of Humphrey Pitt, who lived in Shropshire. There were many imperfections in the original MS, and the restoration and the editing of these imperfections by Thomas Percy and his nephew were the central reasons for a long-drawn-out controversy, which is still going on. The *Reliques* was first published in 1765.

*The baby was christened with joy and much mirth,*
  *Whilst poor Queen Jane's body lay cold under earth:*
*There was ringing and singing and mourning all day,*
  *The princess Eliz[abeth] went weeping away.*

*The trumpets in mourning so sadly did sound,*
  *And the pikes and the muskets did trail on the ground.*
    *(Unfinished verse)*

An imported French headsman executed Anne Boleyn in the Tower courtyard during the early hours of Friday, May 19, 1536. Already the courtship of Jane Seymour had begun. Throughout the days of Anne Boleyn's trial, Henry VIII had been riding up and down the Thames in a lighted and festooned barge, "taking the water, to visit and have conversation with his love [Jane Seymour]." Anne Boleyn was allegedly guilty of certain plots and adulteries, but her most deadly sin was the birth of a girl child, Elizabeth, and finally a dead male child.

Henry believed — no one knew why — that Jane Seymour could, and would, produce him a male heir. Eleven days after the execution of Anne, Henry and Jane were married in the Queen's closet at York Palace. Two days after their marriage, however, trouble started and went on almost continually.

It is reasonable to suppose that Queen Jane gave birth to her child in a normal manner, rather than by Caesarean section, as stated in the ballad. The baby was born about two o'clock in the morning, October 12, 1537. It was a boy, named Edward. He was destined to become Edward the Sixth of that name, to be King of England, and to die in his seventeenth year. As for his mother, Queen Jane, she died twelve days after his birth.

Edward was a precocious child, and far better educated than his father, Henry VIII. At the age of 9, Edward became King of England and Ireland, and supreme head of the Church of England. Although he died very young, he lived long enough to associate his name with the first Anglican prayer book, the *Book of Common Prayer* (1549), or the First Prayer Book. Edward VI died on July 6, 1553. The Catholics said the Protestants had poisoned him, and the Protestants said the Catholics had poisoned him, and everyone seemed to be quite well agreed.

As a matter of comparison, it will be interesting to observe the following text quoted by Child from Kinloch's *Ancient Scottish Ballads*. There is a definite similarity between Kinloch's verses and the American survival taken down in Letcher County, Ky.

*Queen Jeanie, Queen Jeanie, traveld six weeks and more,*
  *Till women and midwives had quite gien her oer:*
*'O if ye were women as women should be,*
  *Ye would send for a doctor, a doctor to me.'*

*The doctor was called for and set by her bedside:*
  *'What aileth thee, my ladie, thine eyes seem so red?'*
*'O doctor, O doctor, will ye do this for me,*
  *To rip up my two sides, and save my babie?'*

*'Queen Jeanie, Queen Jeanie, that's the thing I'll neer do,*
  *To rip up your two sides to save your babie:'*
*Queen Jeanie, Queen Jeanie, traveld six weeks and more,*
  *Till midwives and doctors had quite gien her oer.*

*'O if ye were doctors as doctors should be,*
    *Ye would send for King Henry, King Henry to me.'*
*King Henry was called for, and sat by her bedside,*
    *'What aileth thee, Jeanie? what aileth my bride?'*

*'King Henry, King Henry, will ye do this for me,*
    *To rip up my two sides, and save my babie?'*
*'Queen Jeanie, Queen Jeanie, that's what I'll never do,*
    *To rip up your two sides to save your babie.'*

*But with sighing and sobbing she's fallen in a swoon,*
    *Her side was ript up, and her babie was found;*
*At this bonie babie's christning there was meikle joy and mirth,*
    *But bonnie Queen Jeanie lies cold in the earth.*

*Six and six coaches, and six and six more,*
    *And royal King Henry went mourning before;*
*O two and two gentlemen carried her away,*
    *But royal King Henry went weeping away.*

*O black were their stockings, and black were their bands,*
    *And black were the weapons they held in their hands;*
*O black were their mufflers, and black were their shoes,*
    *And black were the cheverons they drew on their luves.*

*They mourned in the kitchen, and they mourned in the ha,*
    *But royal King Henry mourned langest of a':*
*Farewell to fair England, farewell for evermore!*
    *For the fair flower of England will never shine more.*

# The Death of Queen Jane

## (Niles No. 50)

ON JULY 8, 1932, in the city of Whitesburg, Ky., Aunt Beth Holcolm sang this text and tune concerning the death of Jane Seymour, wife of Henry VIII and mother of Prince Edward.

Earlier in these pages I have written considerably about the Holcolms, Solomon and Beth. All things considered, these two wonderful old people, then far past 70, were perhaps the most gifted and informed singers of serious balladry I have ever encountered. (I say this after more than 50 years of folklore collecting.) Perhaps I should have asked them where they acquired their vast storehouse of folk music. But my early training as a soldier made me more concerned with results than with reasons, and here before my eyes were results beyond anything I had ever hoped to find.

The text of this ballad might lead one to believe that Queen Jane was buried in a rather simple manner. From historical accounts we

# The Death of Queen Jane

## (Niles No. 50)

**Slowly and very sadly**

Queen Jane lay in la - bor for six days or more, Twill the wom - en - folk grew wear - y and the mid - wives gave o'er. King Hen - ry was sent for with horse - back and speed For to be with Queen Jane in her hour of need.

*(Minor mode on F)*

learn that Queen Jane was buried with great pomp and circumstance. After three long weeks of obsequies, during which more tapers were burned than at the death of Henry's mother (Elizabeth, daughter of Edward IV), the funeral procession started for Windsor Castle. The head of the procession was at Windsor before the end of the procession had left Hampton Court.

## The Death of Queen Jane (Niles No. 50)

1. Queen Jane lay in labor for six days or more,
   Twill the womenfolk grew weary and the midwives gave o'er.
   King Henry was sent for with horseback and speed
   For to be with Queen Jane in her hour of need.

2. He went to her bedside: "How comes this, my flower,
   I come to ye direct in less time than an hour."
   "King Henry, King Henry, I take you to be,
   Pray cut my side open and save your baby."

3. "Ah, no," said King Henry, "that never could be,
   If I can lose my pretty flower, I can lose my baby."
   Queen Jane turned over, went into a sound —
   Her side was cut open and her baby was found.

4. Her baby was christened the very same day,
   While hits dear dead mother a-moulderin' lay.
   Six men went before her, four men followed on,
   King Henry stumbled after with his black mournin' on.

5. Oh, he weepèd and he mournèd untwil he was sore,
   Said, "The flower of England will flourish no more."
   And he sat by the river with his head on his hand,
   Said, "My merry England is a sorrowful land."

# 51

# Mary Hamilton

(Child No. 173)

## Mary Hamilton
(Niles No. 51 A)
## The Purple Dress
(Niles No. 51 B)

ACCORDING TO Leslie's *History of Scotland* (1830), Mary Stuart embarked at Dunbarton for France in 1548, and with her, among a great company of retainers, went "four young virgins," all by the same name of Mary. The Maries, as they were called, were the daughters of noblemen, about the same age as Mary Stuart, "being of four sundry honorable houses, to wit, Fleming, Livingston, Seaton, and Beaton of Creich." In the ballad, the names of Fleming and Livingston were dropped, and the names Carmichael and Hamilton were substituted.

Writing a great many years later, T. F. Henderson said: "If this corps continued to consist of young virgins, as when originally raised, it could hardly have subsisted without occasional recruits; especially if we trust our old bard and John Knox." These recruits may have included Mary Carmichael and Mary Hamilton.

The four Maries, whether or not their number and their morals were supported by recruits, remained with Mary Stuart all the while she was in residence in France, and returned only in 1561, some 13 years after their departure. According to Knox's *History of the Reformation* many things happened at the court in Edinburgh that were open to question. "But yet," says Knox, "was not the court purged of whores and whoredoms; which was the fountain-head of such enor-

mities; for it was well known that shame . . . hasted marriage betwixt John Sempill, called the Dancer, and Mary Livingston, surnamed the Lusty. What bruit the Maries, and the rest of the dancers of the court had, the ballads of the age do witnesse, which we for modestie's sake omit."

If the ballad of Mary Hamilton represents historical fact, then it might stem from one of the following situations:

1. An affair between Mary Hamilton and Henry Darnley, husband of Mary Stuart, which produced an illegitimate son who was thrown into the sea. To support this we have a ballad as follows:

*O Mary Hamilton to the kirk is gane,*
  *Wi ribbons in her hair;*
*An the king thocht mair o Marie*
  *Then onie that were there.*

*Mary Hamilton's to the preaching gane,*
  *Wi ribbons on her breast;*
*An the king thocht mair o Marie*
  *Than he thocht o the priest.*

*Syne word is thro the palace gane,*
  *I heard it tauld yestreen,*
*The king loes Mary Hamilton*
  *Mair than he loes his queen.*

2. The troublesome business at the court of

Empress Catherine of Russia. In a publication titled *Slovo y Dyelo* (St. Petersburg, 1885), one M. I. Semefsky offered as history the tragic tale of a maid-of-honor to Empress Catherine. This Englishwoman was of extraordinary beauty, and her name was Mary Hamilton. According to the above document, Mary Hamilton carried on an affair either with Ivan Orlof, aide-de-camp to Tsar Peter III, or with Peter himself, and produced a child, who was destroyed at birth. The law of the land being what it was, the maid-of-honor was executed in a white silk dress, and Tsar Peter was so disturbed as to be reduced to tears.

3. The least likely solution is one proposed by Sir Walter Scott, who was inclined to ascribe the ballad to "an incident involving a French woman that served in the Queen's chamber, who had played the whore with the Queen's [Mary Stuart] own apothecary. The woman conceived and bare a child, whom, with common consent, the father and the mother murthered."

I offer these three solutions for what they are worth, with the conviction that no source, historical or fictional, could ever dim the effect of the ballad of Mary Hamilton.

# Mary Hamilton

## (Niles No. 51 A)

I HAVE ALREADY indicated that my father, John Thomas Niles, was "a gay blade who raised his voice to sing," that he loved to dance till the night grew gray, and that on one occasion he danced with my mother till she had a hole in the middle of her dancing slipper. But there are other things about him, too.

As a young fellow he was an enthusiastic baseball player and swimmer, who spent much of his free time in the treacherous currents of the Ohio River. While still in school, he worked part time at matching straws in a broom factory, helping to support his widowed mother and yearning all the while for the theatre.

What he wanted most was to be a singer in a black-face minstrel company. When I was a child there was much talk of Al G. Fields and "Honey Boy" Evans and Primrose and Lew Dockstader. Father never made the theatre, nor did he ever sing or act in minstrel shows. But he was still the gay blade who raised his voice to sing and thought the terpsichorean toe was a very pretty thing. And, if I may quote, "he was a man, take him for all in all, I shall not look

upon his like again." He died when he was 54.

I see that at Christmastime 1916, I wrote down in my notebook 11 verses and a magnificent tune for a ballad titled "Mary Hamilton." My father was the informant. After a careful study of the existing American folklore collections, I am almost certain that the Niles-family version of "Mary Hamilton" is the only complete one, and that the other reported texts are fragments. I know that I could be mistaken about this, because in the collecting of folklore the last word is hardly ever spoken.

As a rule, the best ballad tunes are modal tunes (Dorian, Mixolydian, and Aeolian being the modes most frequently employed); but in the case of my father's singing of "Mary Hamilton" we have the simplest kind of major-scale melody — and, at the same time, a melody of rare grace and beauty.

I have sung this version of "Mary Hamilton" all the way from Estonia to Victoria on Vancouver Island, and in 42 years of performance, I've never known it to fail.

# Mary Hamilton

## (Niles No. 51 A)

*(Major mode on F)*

1. "Rised up, rised up, Mary Hamilton,
   Rised up and tell unto me:
   What did you with that sweet little boy
   You dandled on your knee,
   You dandled on your knee?"

2. "Speak not, speak not agin my name,
   And let your folly be.
   It was no baby ye heard cryin'
   But misery that pained me."
   *(repeat last line of each verse)*

3. She had not been to the King's high court
   A twelvemonth and a day.
   Oh, it's never went she to comfort the Queen
   But often went she to play.

4. Queen Mary came a-trippeling,
   Her hair so fair to see:
   "What did you with that sweet little boy
   You dandled on your knee?"

5. "I rowed him in my handkerchief,
   I thowed him in the sea.
   I could not have him come between
   The prince's bed and me.

6. "Oh, it's little did my mother know
   The day she held up my head,
   What lands my foot would fall upon
   Or how I'd earn my bread.

7. "Oh, it's little did my father think
   The day he gathered me in,
   That I would go in furrin land
   And die on gallows' pin."

8. She would not wear the velvet gown,
   She would not wear the brown.
   "Oh, it's dress me up in red and scarlet
   When I pass through the town.

9. "Cast off, cast off my scarlet gown,
   And then a napkin tie
   Around my eyes lest I shall see
   The death I am to die.

10. "Last night Queen Mary had four Maries,
    This night she'll have only three.
    'Twas Mary Seaton and Mary Beaton
    And Mary Carmichael and me.

11. "Last night I washed Queen Mary's feet
    And combed her golden hair.
    The gallows' pin is my reward
    And shame beyond my share."

# The Purple Dress

## (Niles No. 51 B)

AS RECITED by a maid in the Battery Park Hotel, Asheville, N. C., in August 1934. Her name, according to my notes, was Annie Matesby. There was no music.

1. "Take off, take off my purple dress,
   But let my petticoat be.
   Tie a rag around my eyes
   So death I cannot see.

2. "Last night I washed Miss Mary's feet,
   Tonight I wet her hair,
   Tomorrow my reward will come —
   I'll walk that gallows stair."

# 52

# The Gypsy Laddie

(Child No. 200)

## The Lady and the Gypsy
(Niles No. 52)

W HEREVER this ballad appears, be it in England, Scotland, or America, the general outlines of the story are in agreement. It was published in England, we think, as early as 1720, and the Scottish form is supposed to have appeared in the 4th volume of Ramsay's *Tea-Table Miscellany* in 1740. Since then, the ballad has been reprinted many times, either with traditional or arbitrary variations.

From Volumes III of Robert Pitcairn's *Criminal Trials in Scotland* and IV of the *Acts of the Parliaments of Scotland* and from other source materials we discover that Johnny Faa was a prominent and frequent name among known gypsies, that one of this name had been recognized by James V of Scotland in a document under the privy seal of February 15, 1540, as having right and title as lord of and earl of Little Egypt. The next year, however, on June 6, by an act of the Lords of Council, all Egyptians were ordered to leave the realm within 30 days or suffer death. (The term "gypsy" comes, of course, from "Egyptians," and the gypsies of these times were indeed thought to be of Egyptian ancestry.)

In 1609 all Egyptians were once more expelled from Scotland by Act of Parliament. But Johnny Faa and three other gypsies remained and were sentenced to be hanged in 1611. On January 24, 1624, Johnny Faa and seven others were finally hanged. Obviously, then, there were several people named Faa, for if the original Johnny Faa was old enough in 1540 to be recognized by the Scottish king, he would have been too old for hanging in 1624. I was told by an eminent Scottish lawyer that James V did not mind Johnny Faa's running off with the wives of the nobles, but when Faa went to stealing horses as well, the King decided to call in the hangman.

The other source of background material is a legend, backed up by certain written evidence, concerning John, the 6th Earl of Cassilis, who married one Lady Jean Hamilton when the lady loved not him but a man named Sir John Faa of Dunbar. (Here again the name of Faa crops up, but this time John Faa is assumed to be a born Scotsman and no gypsy.) Next we find Lord Cassilis attending the Westminster Assembly. While he is gone, Lady Jean, although by then the mother of two of Cassilis's children, runs away with a band of gypsies headed up by Sir John Faa himself, disguised as a gypsy. The Earl returns in time to give chase, capture the entire party, and hang eight gypsies. Lady Jean is then banished to what seem to have been rather comfortable quarters in a tower at Maybole.

In the North American versions — and there are many of them — the story resolves itself into a somewhat happy ending. A North Carolina text, however, indicates that her ladyship will be kept locked in an upper room, where the Egyptians can't get at her.

I have always been a little amused at the performances of the young American girls who sing a song about the "Black-Jack Davy-O," never, we hope, knowing or understanding the triangular connotations. In fact, many of the texts sung by Girl Scouts and Camp Fire Girls and the summer-camp lassies of this and that lake, from Maine to North Carolina, have been adroitly rewritten to avoid what may be called "the blush of shame."

# The Lady and the Gypsy
## (Niles No. 52)

ACCORDING TO my notes, I was resting over in Louisa, Lawrence County, Ky., with the idea of going on to Whitesburg later in the afternoon. It was lunchtime, and as usual I was very hungry. In 1932 there was an excellent restaurant in Louisa, which was my destination, but as I drove into the town I observed a pair of street musicians plying their trade. They were shabbily dressed, and presently I discovered that the man, a guitar player, was blind. At least, he was being led by a woman. The woman had a battered banjo tied on her back. Together they made a pathetic and romantic picture.

At lunch I inquired about the blind guitar player, and was told that he was from upriver (Sandy River), on the West Virginia side. The man's name was Pete Carter. He had been a coal miner until he lost his eyesight in a mine explosion. After that he played on the streets of several Big Sandy towns, and drank up most of each day's collection almost as fast as the collection was taken up.

I stood on the fringes of his audience for a while, and listened to a rather poor performance of hymns. When the audience thinned out, I engaged the Carters, man and wife, in conversation. At first, Mrs. Carter thought I was some local preacher bent on reforming her husband and curing him of the drink habit. This was a brand-new role for me, and I declined the honor quickly.

Ultimately, I bought them their lunch, although I was inclined to believe that Carter would have preferred a pint of white whiskey. In the restaurant there was much good-natured teasing and banter, and finally I got the Carters back to my car, where I unpacked a dulcimer and sang a bit for them. Again an audience collected, and Mrs. Carter had the tin cup handy for any pennies or nickels which might fall. The local police were not overly delighted with our operation, and recommended that I take the Carters and the show into a side street. Even in the side street the collection was excellent.

It must have been about three o'clock before Carter seemed to understand the object of all my efforts. Perhaps he never really understood at all. His wife, however, was a great help, and Pete Carter was used to her way of thinking and to her way of guiding him.

Many highly informed people have confused folk songs like "Sweet Betsy from Pike" with the classic ballads, which can be traced to the Child collection. The confusion is even greater in the minds of people like Mr. and Mrs. Carter. But, again, time and patience and a twist of Brown Mule chewing tobacco paid me a true reward. The reward was what the Carters called "The Lady and the Gypsy," which was in fact "The Gypsy Laddie," Child No. 200.

I had been singing "The Gypsy Laddie" a long while — years and years on end — but never had I sung as truly magnificent a melodic line in support of a convincing set of verses as Pete Carter did that day in July of 1932.

"If I was to sing 'The Lady and the Gypsy'

# The Lady and the Gypsy
## (Niles No. 52)

Last night she slept in a goose - feath - er bed, Last
night she slept with her ba - by - o, But to - night she sleeps on the
cold, cold ground, But she sleeps with the black - jack
gyp - sy - o, She sleeps with the black - jack gyp - sy - o.

*(Major mode on B♭ )*

on the streets, people would throw rotten apples at me," Pete said sadly.

"Folks likes hymns best," agreed Mrs. Carter.

"Too bad," said I, as I corrected a verse and made sure of the octave skips in the tune.

I did what little I could for the Carters. The

## The Lady and the Gypsy (Niles No. 52)

1. Last night she slept in a goose-feather bed,
   Last night she slept with her baby-o,
   But tonight she sleeps on the cold, cold ground,
   But she sleeps with the black-jack gypsy-o,
   She sleeps with the black-jack gypsy-o.

2. "Go saddle up my milk-white steed,
   Go blanket up my roan-o,
   And I will ride o'er the countryside,
   And search for the black-jack gypsy-o."
        (*repeat last line of each verse*)

3. He rode twill he come to a village-town
   On the side of the River Dee-o,
   And oh, how the tears come a-rollin' down
   When he spied his own fair lady-o.

4. "Come back, come back, come back, my miss,
   Come back, come back, my honey-o,
   And I'll swear by the sun and the moon and the stars
   You never will want for money-o."

5. "Ah no, ah no, I'll not come back,
   And I'll not be your honey-o,
   For I'd rather have a kiss from the gypsy's lips
   Than all of your lands and money-o."

6. "Pull off, pull off those high-heeled shoes,
   Those gloves of snow-white leather-o,
   And give me the touch of your lily-white hand
   And bid me farewell forever-o."

7. She pulled off her high-heeled shoes,
   Her gloves of Spanish leather-o,
   And she handed him down her lily-white hand
   And bade him farewell forever-o.

8. Last night she slept in a goose-feather bed,
   His lordship slept beside her-o,
   But tonight she sleeps on the cold, cold ground
   With the gypsies all around her-o.

local police assured me that if I gave them cash it would all go for white whiskey as soon as the sun set. But both the Carters needed shoes, and Mrs. Carter wanted a pair of shiny stockings. I thought she was referring to a kind of rayon stocking then in vogue.

Before store-closing time, they had their shoes and Mrs. Carter had her stockings, and I had a text and tune of "The Gypsy Laddie." I drove through the gathering dark to Whitesburg.

A year later I discovered to my sorrow that Pete Carter had fallen asleep in a gutter, and had apparently been crushed by a passing truck. It all happened at night.

# 53

# Geordie

(Child No. 209)

## The Death of Geordie
(Niles No. 53)

IN THE consideration of this ballad, one is inclined to ask whether the Scottish versions were colored by the English versions, or whether the English versions were colored by the Scottish versions. The many variations were noted by Motherwell, particularly among "reciters" of the ballad.

Most of the Scottish examples of this ballad are powerful, and conform closely to what a true ballad should be — that is, they tell a proper story. In these examples, we find that a battle has been fought somewhere in the north, an important person named Sir Charles Hay has been killed, and Geordie has been accused of the murder. The central figure of the ballad is either Geordie Gordon of Gight, or Geordie Gordon of the Bog of Gight, or George Gordon, 4th Earl of Huntly. In nearly all the Scottish texts, the ballad opens with the sad news that Geordie is in prison and is accused of being either a rebel or a murderer, or both, and is about to be executed. His life is saved by the arrival of his lady (whom we suppose to be his wife) and her payment of a huge ransom in gold crowns.

In the Appendix for this ballad, Vol. IV, pp. 140–42, Child offers two examples of this ballad from English sources. One is concerned with the death of George Stoole and the other with the "life and death of George of Oxford." In these examples, we find Geordie, now known as Georgy, to be an out-and-out horsethief. In each of these two examples, a fair lady pleads the cause of the accused, but neither tears nor gold can save him. It is safe to say that the American survivals of this ballad, and particularly "The Death of Geordie" (Niles No. 53), stem directly from the second of these English examples, "The Life and Death of George of Oxford."

## The Death of Geordie
(Niles No. 53)

IT WAS OCTOBER, and it was raining, and the year was 1932, and I was hoping to get as far as Marion, Va., before nightfall. I had made a fruitless voyage, involving nearly 100 miles of driving, from Johnson City to Kingsport, Tenn., and then on to Bristol and to Abingdon, Va., and

# The Death of Geordie

## (Niles No. 53)

*With increasing sadness*

As I walked o-ver Lon-don Bridge, One morn-ing that was fog-gy, — I o-ver-heard a fair one — say, "Pray save the life of Geor-die!" — I o-ver-heard a fair one — say, "Pray save the life of Geor-die!" —

*(Minor mode on A)*

to the left I drove over to Damascus and then back to Meadowview, Va., and then over a rocky road to Glade Spring and on to Saltville, and back over a much more difficult road to Route No. 11, and then eastward to the warmth and comfort of my hotel in Marion. I had the names of men and women in all these towns and villages who were said to be singers of old-timey music. The list contained 10 names. Not one of them would, or even could, sing. This was not unusual. I had spent many such days, but on this day, I was wet, I was weary, and I was terribly hungry.

Hardly had I finished supper when an employee of the hotel came to me with news of a fiddle-playing contest, and off I went again, hoping that there might be a singer somewhere on the fringes of the crowd. But there was no folk singer, and the fiddle-playing contest was not overly interesting. In fact, when it degenerated into a political speaking, I left.

Next morning, however, as I was having my car serviced at a local garage, I spied a bearded old man sitting in a farm truck, and beside him sat a young girl picking a battered guitar.

The old man's name was Clyde Russell, and he was as glum a person as I have ever encountered. No amount of singing on my part brought more than a sad nod of approval. The guitar-picking granddaughter admitted that "fun fits granddad like a shirt fits on a gate post."

Granddad Russell never did warm up, but he sang the tragic ballad of "Geordie," and as soon as I learned it, I took to singing it, and I have continued singing it for nearly 27 years.

## The Death of Geordie (Niles No. 53)

1. As I walked over London Bridge, one morning that was foggy,
   I overheard a fair one say, "Pray save the life of Geordie!"
   I overheard a fair one say, "Pray save the life of Geordie!

2. "Go saddle up my milk-white steed for I must ride miles forty,
   Far over and away to the Lonecastle fair, to plead for the life of Geordie."
   (*repeat last line of each verse*)

3. She rode all day, she rode all night, till she come, wet and weary,
   A-combin' out her golden locks, and a-pleadin' for her deary.

4. Then out of her pocket come a purse, the likes I ne'er saw any,
   Sayin', "Lawyers come and fee yourselves, for I'll spend every penny!"

5. Then George in dock was standin' by, said, "I ne'er did kill nobody,
   But I stole sixteen of the King's white steeds, and sold 'em at Gohoody."

6. The oldest lawyer at the bar said, "George hit is a pity,
   By your own words you're condemned to die — you ought to 'ave been more witty!"

7. Now George walked through the lined streets, and bid farewell to many,
   He bid farewell to his own true love, and hit grieved him more than any.

8. George was hanged with a mighty chain of gold that was so weighty,
   'Cause he was from a noble line, and he courted a virtuous lady.

9. I wish I was on yonder hill where kisses I had often —
   I'd stab myself with a pointed blade beside my lover's coffin.

# 54

# The Braes o Yarrow

(Child No. 214)

### The Lady and the Shepherd
(Niles No. 54 A)
### The Dreary Dream
(Niles No. 54 B)
### In the Lonely Glens of Yarrow
(Niles No. 54 C)

THE STORY told in the original examples offered by Child runs along the following lines:

A brawl, growing out of a drinking bout, leads to combat. Nine men in some cases (in others, the number is six or three, or even more) challenge one man, sometimes identified as a shepherd, who has married a very desirable young woman of wealth and position in a somewhat surreptitious manner. There is usually another man involved in the combat, a brother to the young woman — a brother "who takes no heart for fight." This brother feels that the marriage will be personally detrimental to him. In one example he is referred to as "a cowardly 'loon'" and in another he has a "rusted rapier."

After the challenged man has dispatched all his enemies — be they nine, six or three — the "cowardly loon" slips up from behind and slays the champion by driving the rusted rapier through his heart.

The young woman is naturally bowed down with grief, which her father urges her to restrain, telling her that he will wed her to as good a lord as she has lost or even a better one. She rejects all forms of comfort, being already great with child by her slain loved one, and dies in her father's arms.

Elements of this legend are found in the Scandinavian ballad "Herr Helmer" (Afzelius, ed. Bergström, I, 264, and elsewhere).

The three examples of "The Braes of Yarrow" offered herewith contain fragments of all 19 examples offered by Child. But they are even closer to a ballad submitted by Child in the volume that includes "Additions and Corrections." There, in Vol. 5, pp. 255–56, we find "The Dowie Dens o Yarrow" (Findlay MSS, I, 181) in 14 stanzas. My No. 56 A runs to 8 stanzas, and omits some of the concluding ideas in the Dowie Dens, but still tells a great deal of the story in a touchingly poetic manner.

The other two examples — Nos. 54 B and C — do not tell all the story by any means, but what they lack in legend they surely make up in poetry:

*Oh, gentle wind, oh tender wind,*
*How blow you, north or south?*
*Go take this kiss to her true love*
*And place it on his mouth.*

# The Lady and the Shepherd

## (Niles No. 54 A)

NOT FAR FROM Virgie, Ky., a man and two small children sat down beside me and offered to help me eat my lunch. Fortunately, I had what seemed to be an endless supply of food. Milk was sold in glass bottles in those days, and I had two such quart bottles with me. It was worth a lot to see those youngsters drink up the milk. They were very grateful, and the man asked me what had brought me to these hills. When I told him, he practically took me by the hand and led me to a pair of singers who, he said, would delight me "endless."

I never knew the names of the man and the two small children, but my singers were Ed Mullins and Creswell Tolliver. They were living in a lean-to and sleeping on a bed made of old newspapers. There were unopened copies of the Knoxville, Chattanooga, Lexington, and Louisville papers. I noticed a copy of the Louisville *Courier-Journal,* announcing the forthcoming (1932) Democratic convention in Chicago. I noticed, too, that there were no very recent papers, but I asked no questions about the papers or their way of life. Both of them were gay and tattered, and old and bearded. They had been working about three days a week in a local sawmill.

On discovering the reason for my visit, Mullins went at once to singing songs about circus animals, which I found very tiresome. I had encountered songs of this kind before, and closed my mind to them. Finally, Mullins ran out of breath and stopped singing. Then he turned to me and said: "Mister, my friend here, Creswell Tolliver, is a pure belly-binder."

This was news. I had heard of a belly-band, a length of cloth used to tie up the lower abdomen of an infant in the mistaken idea that it would prevent him from becoming pot-bellied before his time. But a belly-binder was obviously something different. Mullins explained that a belly-binder (male or female) is a person who can make magic and who — to quote Mullins — "can see things before they take shape."

Creswell Tolliver may have been a belly-binder, but he was also a singer, and although his voice was light and faint it was accurate. I had some trouble in keeping Mullins from singing with his friend Tolliver until I hit on the idea of giving him some food. That kept him engaged.

Tolliver called his song "The Lady and the Shepherd," and I can report that it was a long time coming. First, I had to listen to all the details of the ginseng business. (Tolliver said they had the promise of a job in a cultivated "sang" garden up near Whitesburg. Mullins was going to be a slat-mender.) Then, there was a long story concerning Tolliver's early life. He had been a teacher in a school of bookkeeping in Chattanooga. He had taught penmanship, and borrowed my pen to demonstrate his ability to write with great flourishes. Mullins could neither read nor write, and he took enormous pride in his friend's accomplishments.

Yes, "Tolly" had once worked in a streetshow. He had sung in a male quartet, and sometimes even in churches when he was sober and the good ladies would let him. Tolliver was a tenor. He had a slight lisp, and a pair of the bluest blue eyes I had seen in a long day's journey.

I said to Mullins, "Mister, what do you do with your time?"

"Oh," said he, "I just love comfort. I rest."

By this time, the belly-binder Creswell Tolliver had heard enough of Mullins. He had apparently heard enough of me, too, so he began singing, almost to himself.

When we had finished, they asked whether they might ride back to Whitesburg with me. They were anxious to start working on their new job. I waited a moment or two, supposing they would close up their little shack, lock the door, pull down the windows. But the door swung on one hinge. There was no lock. All they had was on their backs. They walked out of their lean-to quite gaily, leaving nothing behind but a large square box full of unopened newspapers.

# The Lady and the Shepherd
## (Niles No. 54 A)

*(Minor mode on F)*

1. There was a lady in our town,
   And none as fair as she.
   Courted she was by six men of renown
   And a shepherd most tenderly,
   *Oh fol-le-dol-le-dol-le,*
   *Fol-le-dol-le-dee,*
   And a shepherd most tenderly.

2. Oh, she washed up and she washed down,
   And she combed her black, black hair
   To please the lords of high degree
   And the shepherd who loved her sair.
   *(repeat refrain & last line of each verse)*

3. Oh, the shepherd walked in, and the shepherd
      walked out,
   Until he came to Yarrow,
   And there six men without a doubt
   Did wait to draw his marrow.

4. "Oh, I'll fight you all, by one, by two,
   And suffer myself small pain,
   For each in turn I'll do to death
   If the others will but refrain."

5. He fit them hard, he fit them sound,
   And left them where they lay.
   Upon the green beflowered ground
   With their folly he did repay.

6. Now this lady had of brothers one
   Who had no heart for fight,
   While he did steal the shepherd on
   And stab him as he might.

7. "Oh John, oh John, you might have been
   A brother unto me,
   But by this dark and backward sin
   You've foully murdered me.

8. "Go back unto your sister's side
   And speak small words of cheer,
   That she may dig a grave full wide
   And join her lover here."

# The Dreary Dream
## (Niles No. 54 B)

"THE DREARY DREAM" was sung in Jefferson County, Ky., as long ago as my earliest recollections — that is, about 1907. In my notebook I find that it was written down in June 1909, and that it was sung most often in a family of ne'er-do-wells who had once been an important, even a rich, farming family. They had owned large acreage in the south end of the county, had operated a general store, and one of the male members of the family had invented a new kind of baking powder (he called it quick-acting rising powder). But, as time passed, the men's chief boast was that they were "too lazy to come in out of a light shower of rain." The women made the wrong kind of marriages. The banks finally took the acreage.

I made friends with one female member of the family who was something of a singer. It was rumored that during the family's affluent days she had attended a finishing school for young ladies in Harrodsburg, Ky., known as Daughters' College. I was never sure of this, but there is one thing of which I was sure: she had a finely spun voice, which she used with considerable skill — with almost professional skill, as I remember.

She was a great reader of magazines and newspapers, and had a smoldering kind of temper. On one occasion, the womenfolk in the family were preparing dinner for a thrashing crew, when a lean hound-dog walked through the kitchen and, seeing a large mold of butter on a side table, seized it and ate it on the spot. My singing friend calmly took down a loaded shotgun, shot the hound point-blank, kicked the carcass onto the back porch and down the steps

# The Dreary Dream

## (Nilès No. 54 B)

*With sorrowful resignation*

For __ I __ have dreamed a drear - y dream, Oh, who is free of sor - row? Oh, my love __ was dead on a leaf - y bed Be - side the __ riv - er __ Yar - row. Oh, my love __ was dead on a leaf - y bed Be - side the __ riv - er __ Yar - row. __

*(Minor mode on A)*

into the yard, and went back to fluting the edges of a chess pie. This ne'er-do-well family was famous for its chess pies.*

Once I had written down the ballad my friend called "The Dreary Dream," I began to wonder how it might be employed. I learned to sing it, and later I took it to a well-known organist and choir director in Louisville. He was impressed by the beauty of the melodic line, and suggested that I keep it safely for some future use. Later I sang it to a music teacher who was a folklorist and a composer. She, too, was delighted with "The Dreary Dream" — and amused at my way of crowding so many words and notes onto one small page in my notebook. She said the song sounded like something that might have come from France.

## The Dreary Dream  (Niles No. 54 B)

1. For I have dreamed a dreary dream,
   Oh, who is free of sorrow?
   Oh, my love was dead on a leafy bed
   Beside the river Yarrow.
   Oh, my love was dead on a leafy bed
   Beside the river Yarrow.

2. And many men did come and go,
   And all were armed with knife.
   They've slain, they've slain my own dear swain,
   They've twined him of his life.
   They've slain, they've slain my own dear swain,
   They've twined him of his life.

3. It's I will read your dreary dream,
   It's I will tell your sorrow,
   It's I will tell you that your love
   Is dead beside the Yarrow.
   It's I will tell you that your love
   Is dead beside the Yarrow.

* I can supply their recipe.

# In the Lonely Glens of Yarrow

## (Niles No. 54 C)

*(Minor mode on E)*

# In the Lonely Glens of Yarrow

## (Niles No. 54 C)

ON OLD-TIMERS' DAY 1933 at Gatlinburg, Tenn., I made friends with many wonderful old people. Some came to look on, some came to show their handiwork, some came to join the singing, some came to enter the rifle-shooting matches, and some, I suppose, simply came along for the ride.

I worked diligently with singers from early morning till sundown. Among them was one delightful person, Sarah Jane Hadley, who admitted that she was a poet. She deplored the fact that there were no classes for poetry, so that she might enter her best works and win a prize.

Miss Hadley (she made much of the "Miss") was somewhere between 65 and 70 years of age. When I asked her what year she was born, she objected to my questioning. An old grizzled mountain man, sitting beside us, said, "She's a-pushin' seventy," and Miss Hadley retorted in a good-natured way, "I wish you'd shut your mouth!" But her age was not nearly so important as the 5 verses of a ballad she called "In the Lonely Glens of Yarrow."

In the course of our conversation I found out that Miss Hadley had been singing in church choirs from her earliest youth and that she also played the organ when the regular organist failed to appear. She knew about *The Sacred Harp* and *The Southern Harmony*, but she preferred a shape-note book called *The Christian Harmony*.

The old grizzled mountain man sitting on my right was greatly amused, and he went to whispering in my ear. Said he: "I know that female person, and I can tell you straight — if she had married herself up with a man many a year ago, she wouldn't be singin' love-ballards to this day, and she wouldn't be writin' the kind of poems she writes, either. All that business about placin' a kiss on her true-love's mouth means she's man-hankerin'. She's been teachin' school and man-hankerin' forever."

He shook his head and dropped his whisper even lower. "Sarie Jane's been a man-hankerin' too long. You know, mister, when a woman-person marries up with a man, hit cures her of an awful lot of things."

Noontime dinner that day was a memorable event. To this day I have memories of the gooseberry jam, the crusty biscuits, the chicken pie, and apple cobbler. There was a big plate of sliced cucumbers in salt and vinegar heaped six inches high. I looked for some at the end of the meal, and they were all gone.

Miss Hadley, the grizzled old philosopher, the wonderful menu — all this is noted in great detail in my notebook, and the final line indicates "Quarts of coffee."

## In the Lonely Glens of Yarrow

1. Oh, Lady Sarah she was fair,
   But she had lived with sorrow,
   For they have slain her sweetest swain
   In the lonely glens of Yarrow,
   The lonely glens of Yarrow.

2. He's ridden east, he's ridden west,
   He's ridden to his sorrow,
   And there he spied those nine young men,
   A-watering their steeds in the Yarrow.
   (*repeat last line of each verse*)

3. And they were hurt by one, two, and three,
   And then six more he slew,
   Till from behind her brother John
   Did slyly run him through.

4. Oh gentle wind, oh tender wind,
   How blow you, north or south?
   Go take this kiss to her true love
   And place it on his mouth.

5. She dreamed a very dreary dream,
   She dreamed it o'er and o'er,
   It's they have slain her sweetest swain,
   And she'll ne'er see him more.

# 55

# James Harris (The Daemon Lover)

(Child No. 243)

## The House Carpenter

(Niles No. 55)

After a study of the 65 American texts of this ballad, it seems to me that the lover in question has lost both his name and much of his daemonic quality. In this part of the world, the James Harris of the original ballad is a sailor who manages to persuade a young wife to desert her husband and child and go through an elopement, with the usual sad consequences.

In the original ballad (taking Child No. 243 A as an example), a young man and a young woman are to be married. The man is James Harris and the woman is Jane Reynolds. The young man is pressed into service at sea, and is reported to have lost his life. The young woman grieves, and when her tears are dry she marries a ship-carpenter, lives quietly and happily, and produces three children. Presently, James Harris reappears, having been out of sight for seven years,

and though the ballad makes it clear that he is a ghost, it is also established that in the eyes of Jane Reynolds he appears as a natural man. After much argument, the young wife deserts her husband and her three babes, and goes off with her first love. No one ever sees her again, and the ship-carpenter hangs himself.

In America the ballad of "James Harris (The Daemon Lover)" is very widespread. It is safe to say that it has been found almost as many times as "Barbary Ellen," but is by no means as popular with audiences as many other ballads. This is perhaps the result of the subject matter: had the woman in the ballad deserted only a husband to depart with an earlier lover, all would have been forgiven. But the fact that she deserts small children as well makes her peculiarly unappealing.

## The House Carpenter

(Niles No. 55)

It was a bright clear day in the late summer of 1933, the place was Harrogate, Tenn., and I was delighted at the chance to spend most of the

afternoon with Miss Katherine Pettit of Lexington, Ky.

Miss Pettit had retired from her position as

co-director of Pine Mountain School,* and was enjoying the latter years of her life visiting friends in the Southern mountains. At that time, I was working diligently on my dictionary, or glossary, of Southern mountain speech, and Miss Pettit was a most valuable source of information on word usages and meanings. In the midst of it all, I began singing, and this led others to singing, and presently Miss Pettit sang her wonderful version of "James Harris."

Her text is truly poetic, and although her tune is not one of the best, it has a haunting loveliness strangely suited to the text. It should be noted that only at the very end of the ballad is the lover's daemon status suggested; at the beginning, we are led to believe that he has returned from sea as a natural man to claim his first love. It is only when he declares that he has brought them both to the gates of hell that there is any suggestion of his supernatural status.

Katherine Pettit was all for fun. She enjoyed a good laugh as much as anyone I have ever observed. She was an educated and highly informed person, with a rare sense of humor. Finally, toward the end of the afternoon, as we had in Miss Pettit's own words "laughed out nearly all of today's laughs," she took to telling me the legends of Cutshine Creek, an area not far from her original base at Pine Mountain School. One of these concerned a young girl named Jane Ledford, and I believe it deserves retelling, for Jane was as beautiful as any young woman who walked in shoe leather, and she had great promise; but her life turned tragic, and after she had sold off her inherited lands she died at a greatly advanced age, alone and the object of local charity.

It seems that Jane Ledford had met and fallen in love with a young man who was not a Cutshine boy. He lived up near Hyden, Ky., some miles away, and worked in a hardware store. He wore citified clothes, and through his contact with the public had developed a certain polite manner.

The local Cutshine boys did not favor Jim Pennington, the hardware salesman from Hyden, and they told Jane all about it. Indeed, they told her in no uncertain terms that if she went on and married this citified outlander type, "hit would come to no good." But Jane had already woven the material for her wedding dress, and Jane had discovered that comfortable quarters could be rented in the village of Hyden, and the date was set, and all save the local Cutshine boys were delighted. Finally, the wedding day came. The night before there was a play-party at the Ledford home, and Jim Pennington was naturally present. He planned to spend the night with friends nearby.

Jane Ledford, age 16, arose at the earliest crack of the following dawn. Jim Pennington had left their wedding license with her. In the half-light she read the large print and the small, for she had been to school and had learned to read and write at Pine Mountain School. She was indeed radiant with happiness over her approaching marriage. Once dressed, she wandered into the loom room, a smallish room where cards, spinning wheels, and other weaving devices were kept. There was a figure slumped over her loom. The figure was half sitting, half lying on the weaver's bench. It was the body of Jim Penning-

* Pine Mountain School, founded in 1913 by Miss Katherine Pettit and Miss Ethel de Long, on land given by Uncle William and Aunt Sally Dixon Creech. The school was in one of our most isolated areas, 18 miles across a mountain from the nearest town. Miss Pettit served as co-director of Pine Mountain School until her retirement in 1930, and as a member of the Board of Trustees until her death in 1936.

William Creech (Uncle William to all those who knew him well and loved him greatly) was a tooth-puller, an herb doctor, a bone-setter, a storekeeper, a onetime Union soldier, a farmer, and a philosopher. Concerning the children of the mountains, he said: "I don't look after wealth for them. . . . I have got a heart and a craving that my people should grow better." But Aunt Sally, the wife of this bearded patriarch, is credited with an even more poignant statement concerning education: "We'uns that cain't read and write have got a heap of time to think, and that's why we know more than you-all."

These two wonderful people gave the land and the lumber, supplied the charter, the vision, and the motivating force behind the establishment of Pine Mountain School. The original cost of operating the school was $700 a month, and this was supplied entirely by free-will offerings.

# The House Carpenter
## (Niles No. 55)

*Gracefully*

"Well met, well met, well met, my own true love! Well met, my love," cried he. "I've just come back from the salt, salt sea, And all for the love of thee."

*(Major mode on E♭)*

ton. The local boys had made good their threat. Instead of a wedding there was a funeral, and Jim Pennington was buried, and with him Jane Ledford buried her hopes.

The murderer (or murderers, in some versions) was never apprehended. Jane folded her wedding dress away, and never looked at it again.

As the years passed, Jane Ledford became a legend in her own right. She fed the hungry, she clothed the ragged, and she tried to cure the sick. She became a midwife, she cooked yarb-medicines, and when her parents died she looked after a small hillside farm.

Little by little she sold off the land she had

inherited, and at a greatly advanced age, unable to move around very much, she became a silent sitter in the sun. At her death no one knew exactly how old she was, but all were intrigued by the little leather pouch she had carried all her life — a little leather pouch attached to her right wrist. When she was dead, and at last the leather pouch was opened, it contained not some jewel of great price, as her friends and neighbors were sure it would, but a folded scrap of paper. The ink was hardly legible and the entire document was in tatters from having been folded and unfolded so many times. It was the license, issued so many years ago, for the marriage of Jane Ledford and James Pennington.

The stubborn Cutshine boys had had their way, but Jane Ledford had had her quiet way, too. She remained unmarried to the end. The wedding license was buried with her body.

## The House Carpenter (Niles No. 55)

1. "Well met, well met, well met, my own true love!
   Well met, my love," cried he.
   "I've just come back from the salt, salt sea,
   And all for the love of thee.

2. "I could have married with a great lady,
   For her heart was set on me.
   But I forgave her golden crowns,
   And all for the love of thee."

3. "If you could marry with a king's daughter,
   I'm sure you are to blame,
   For I have married with a house carpenter,
   Sweet Willie is his name."

4. "Forsake, forsake, forsake your carpenter,
   And come go 'long with me,
   And I will take you where the grass grows green,
   Hard by the sweet lily."

5. "If I forsake my fine house carpenter
   And go to sea with thee,
   Oh how, oh how will you keep me then
   From shame and slavery?"

6. "I have six ships a-sail upon the sea,
   I have six ships more on the land,
   And all those bright jolly sailor-men
   Will be at your command."

7. She picked up her own, her sweet baby,
   And she gave him kisses three,
   Said, "Stay at home with your daddy, my love,
   And give him company."

8. She dressed herself in silk and satin red,
   She dressed in green and gold,
   And she walked through her rooms once more,
   The last she would e'er behold.

9. She had not sailed the sea more than two weeks,
   And I'm sure it was not three,
   When she sat down and she did weep,
   And mourn most bitterly.

10. "Alas, alas, my love, why do you weep?
    Or is it for gold and store?
    Or is it for your house carpenter
    That you will never see more?"

11. "I do not weep for silver or for gold,
    Nor do I weep for store,
    But I do weep for my darling sweet babe,
    The one I ne'er shall see more."

12. They had not been to sea but three short weeks,
    And I'm sure it was not four,
    When they did spring a longwise seam,
    And sank to rise no more.

13. "What banks, what banks of land is that, my love?
    What banks so dark and so low?"
    "It is the land of hell you see,
    Where you and I shall go."

14. "What banks, what banks of land is that, my love?
    What banks as white as snow?"
    "It is the land of the Heavenly God
    Where your sweet baby will go."

# The Suffolk Miracle

(Child No. 272)

## The Sad Courtin'
(Niles No. 56)

CHILD IS surely not impressed with the English version of "The Suffolk Miracle." He refers to it as being "in a blurred, enfeebled, and disfigured shape" compared to the impressive form in which it existed on the European continent. From the forematter on this ballad, one is almost inclined to conclude that Child was not impressed with ghost stories of any kind. Having seen many a ghost, and told many a ghost story (both in public and in private), and having made a special study of what we in Kentucky call "the restless ghost" or "the traveling ghost" or "the hitch-hiking ghost," I am obviously impressed with this form of the supernatural.

Variants of the basic motif in this ballad are found enlarged and amplified by local devices in Russian, Serbian, Croat-Slovenian, Bohemian, Wendish, Magyar, Gypsy, Bulgarian, Albanian, and High and Low German folklore. The English legend, as found in the ballad, is as follows:

A pair of young people, living in a rural setting, are in love and hope to be married. The father of the girl sends her away to live with a relative in a distant country until she has time to forget her lover. Meanwhile, the young man dies. Some time later, he appears at the relative's home with a horse belonging to the young woman's father and some traveling clothes belonging to her mother. They gallop away together. As they travel, the young man complains of a severe headache and the young woman comforts him and wraps her handkerchief around his head. They arrive at her father's door, and the young man goes to the barn to put the horse up for the night. He is never seen again. The father is alarmed to see his daughter, and declares that he had no part whatever in the night's happenings. But when they go to the barn they discover that the horse they had ridden so far and so fast is "all in a sweat," and when the young man's body is exhumed the girl's handkerchief is there, tied about his head.

If there were time and space, I would tell a story I have told countless times — a story called "The Pendennis Club," involving a girl-ghost and a topcoat, or the one called "The Frederick Road," concerning twelve ghosts, all members of an infantry company once engaged in a battle at Gettysburg. In both of these ghost stories a concrete object is left behind by the ghost or ghosts. And, after all, a handkerchief is a handkerchief, and a topcoat is a topcoat, and — ghost or no ghost — a roll of Confederate money is still a roll of Confederate money.

Today, past the middle of the 20th century, the legend of the restless ghost is more widely known than ever in the past, and the interesting part of it is that it is being rapidly made over to fit automobiles and airplanes, World War I, World War II, and the Korean conflict.

300

# The Sad Courtin'

## (Niles No. 56)

IN THE SUMMER of 1932 I encountered an elderly woman named Mrs. Nuckols, who lived somewhere north of Yerkes, Ky. She was in Hazard, Ky., with her husband on some matter involving a coal-rights claim. She was pointed out to me as a person who knew and would sing "the ghost ballad." Indeed she did know it, but alas and alack, she would not sing it. At least, what she did sing was altered so often that I finally gave up and made as clear a record of the text as I could. She was the most unwilling singer I had encountered in a long while. Perhaps I offended her. I never knew, for I never saw her again. Here are her verses:

1. Sing courtin', sing courtin',
   All courtin' is vain:
   It brings us small pleasure
   For all it brings pain.

2. As soon as her father did come for to know,
   She loved a farmer boy, said, "No, daughter, no,
   I'll send you a travelin' some miles from your home."
   'Twas then that her lover did make heavy moan.

3. The clerks and the clergy, the doctors all tried,
   But now 'tis a year this young man he died.
   And now he comes ridin' a dappled white steed,
   A-seekin' his sweetheart with horseback and speed.

4. "I've brought you a horse from your old father's barn,
   Your own mother's coat to keep you from harm."
   He said as they came to her father's own gate,
   "My dearest, my head, it is all of an ache."

5. She reached to kiss him, his lips were as clay.
   She looked at his face, and his face it was gray.
   She took a fine handkerchief off from her neck,
   And wound it around her dear lover's head.

6. "It's Father, oh Father, dear Father," cried she.
   "It's welcome, most welcome, dear daughter," cried he.
   "The one that you sent, my dear lover of old,
   Is bedding the horse, the night is so cold."

7. Now come all ye parents of daughter or son,
   Part not your true loves, once love is begun,
   For they opened the grave of her lover long dead:
   Her kerchief was wrapped round his moldering head.

# 57

# Our Goodman

(Child No. 274)

## The Good Old Man

(Niles No. 57)

*The cuckoo is a pretty bird,*
*She sings as she flies.*
*She brings us glad tidings,*
*And she never tells lies.*

And she apparently has the disturbing habit of laying her eggs in another bird's nest, thereby relieving herself of the problem of feeding fledglings. The legend of this tiresome habit on the part of the cuckoo undoubtedly provided us with the word "cuckold." There is this difference, however, in the application of the term to human beings: the odious title is bestowed not on the adulterer but on the deceived husband. (All this seemingly irrelevant information is given here because "Our Goodman" concerns the most famous cuckold in balladry.)

Female-persons who are not readers of history may conclude that deceiving a husband is a more or less modern concept. But this is far from the facts. Ever since the invention of husbands and wives, a certain amount of deception has been practiced, and the amount was sufficient to warrant the invention of a word to describe the deceived husband in his plight. It is interesting to note that while the word "cuckold" appears in the original English versions, it is never used in the American survivals, though the story line remains almost unchanged. The nearest approach to it is found in Arthur Kyle Davis's *Traditonal Ballads of Virginia:* there we have the words "whole couple," because, as Mr. Davis

points out, the word "cuckold" meant nothing to the singer. Actually, I do not recall ever hearing it used in the Southern mountains.

In "Our Goodman" (Child No. 274) we have what seems to be an elderly, or at least a middle-aged, married man arriving home to find all manner of incriminating evidence — strange horses in his stable, boots, swords, a "muckle" (very large) coat, and finally a man, or at least a head, where no head should be.

The wife tries to brazen it through with what she hopes to be conclusive, or at least evasive, answers. At the same time, she calls her husband an old cuckold, and in some instances, a blind cuckold — not behind his back but to his face. In this case, she certainly ought to know.

According to his wife, the horses turn out to be milking-cows, the boots are a pair of water pitchers, the sword becomes a stick to stir porridge, the wig is a hen, the coat is a pair of blankets, and the head is the head of a milking-maid. Furthermore, according to the wife, all these items have been sent by her mother.

The husband replies that saddles do not fit so well on cows, that though he has ridden a far piece, he has never seen silver spurs on a water pitcher, and that a long beard on a maiden is indeed a curiosity.

The ballad is known to the Flemish. There, in one example, the wife admits, after the usual routine, that the man is indeed her lover. In another, the wife says that the man in her bed is a foster child, and the husband remarks that he has never seen whiskers on a foster child.

There is an interesting German version of this ballad wherein the becuckolded husband, being unconvinced by his wife's arguments, beats her soundly, declaring that each lick is a caress her mother has sent her.

The ballad is found in the Scandinavian countries, among the Magyars, French, Italians, and Russians. Beyond the Vistula, where human life is not overly prized, the deceived husband, on being told that the head he sees in his bed is a cabbage-head, produces a dagger, removes the head from its body, hands it to his wife, and tells her to cook it for dinner.

In the American tradition, "Our Goodman" is not very widely known. Where it does appear, it is quite close, however, to the English and Scottish originals, with the omission of certain items that are less familiar to the American scene, such as swords and wigs.

# The Good Old Man

## (Niles No. 57)

SOME TIME BETWEEN July 11 and July 13, 1913, in Hazard, Ky., a onetime blacksmith named Jules Napier, an elderly fellow with a good singing voice, sang me 12 verses of a ballad much liked by men. This is a curious preference, in view of the fact that the principal character is a man deceived by a woman. Perhaps the woman's deft answers contribute to the ballad's popularity among male citizens. (Jules Napier was related to the "Red Jules" and "Black Jules" mentioned in connection with Niles No. 5 B.)

The reason for the long time involved in getting a clear copy of the text and tune of "The Good Old Man" was that my singer was employed in helping dismantle a large tent, recently used by a revivalist. The dismantling crew worked very slowly, all of them being old men. Mr. Napier would stop in between jobs and sing a little. Then he would go back to work, and I would wait around.

I tried to find him again in 1936, but was told that he had gone out west. Several of his relatives lived in Oklahoma.

Following my usual procedure, I asked Mr. Napier what he thought the ballad was all about, whether it contained a lesson, whether he thought it was based on actual happenings, whether he felt that the old man in the ballad had acted wisely, etc.

Napier said he thought the good old man was simply collecting evidence, and that in a short while the wife would find herself in the courthouse with a divorce action to defend. Yes, there was a lesson in the ballad, but he was not quite sure what it was. He felt sure that it must all have happened, though perhaps not quite in this way, and would continue to happen so long as there were hard-working, trusting old men married to young females with roving eyes. In this connection, it should be noted that the use of the term "old woman" does not indicate that the wife is old. It is common parlance in the Southern mountains, and elsewhere in rural areas; for a man to refer to his wife as "the old woman," even though she is no more than 18 years of age.

Mr. Napier thought the good old man was very wise in not "going into action" as soon as he saw three strange horses in his stable. "Just think," said Napier, "what might-a happened if this nice old feller had gone to rampin' and club-swingin' through the house. Why, a body might-a got injured!"

At the bottom of my notebook page I find these words: "Slow workers. All old."

# The Good Old Man

## (Niles No. 57)

*(Dorian mode on A)*

1. Home come the old man, buzzing like a bee,
   "Traveled four-and-forty miles, mayhap 'twas only three,
   Tell me, old woman, what might all this be,
   Horses in yon stable stand, by one, by two, by three?"

2. "You old fool, you blind fool, or can't you so well see?
   'Tis nothing but a milking-cow my mother sent to me."
   "Traveled four-and-forty miles, mayhap 'twas only three,
   Saddle on a milking-cow I never more did see."

3. In come the old man, buzzing like a bee,
   Found a man a-standing where himself ought to be.
   "Tell me, old woman, what might all this be,
   What's this man a-doing here without the leave of me?"

4. "You old fool, you blind fool, or can't you so well see?
   'Tis nothing but a milking-maid by mother sent to me."
   "Traveled four-and-forty miles, mayhap 'twas only three,
   Breeches on a milking-maid I never more did see."

5. In walked the old man, buzzing like a bee,
   Saw some boots a-leaning where his boots ought to be.
   "Tell me, old woman, what might all this be,
   Unco* boots a-leaning here without the leave of me?"

6. "You old fool, you blind fool, or can't you so well see?
   'Tis nothing but some coffee-pots my mother sent to me."
   "Traveled four-and-forty miles, mayhap 'twas only three,
   Bootstraps on a coffee-pot I never more did see."

7. In walked the old man, buzzing like a bee,
   Looking in the kitchen to see what he could see.
   "Tell me, old woman, what might all this be,
   Whose hat is that hat, where my hat ought to be?"

8. "You old fool, you blind fool, or can't you so well see?
   'Tis nothing but a butter-churn my mother sent to me."
   "Traveled four-and-forty miles, mayhap 'twas only three,
   Hatband on a butter-churn I never more did see."

9. Out walked the old man, buzzing like a bee,
   Looking in the passage to see what he could see.
   "Tell me, old woman, what might all this be,
   What's this coat a-hanging here, without the leave of me?"

10. "You old fool, you blind fool, or can't you so well see?
    'Tis nothing but a blanket my mother sent to me."
    "Traveled four-and-forty miles, mayhap 'twas only three,
    Buttons on a blanket I never more did see."

11. Up walked the old man, buzzing like a bee,
    Looking in the bedroom to see what he could see.
    "Tell me, old woman, what might all this be,
    Whose head is that head where my head ought to be?"

12. "You old fool, you blind fool, or can't you so well see?
    'Tis nothing but a cabbage-head my mother sent to me."
    "Traveled four-and-forty miles, mayhap 'twas only three,
    Whiskers on a cabbage-head I never more did see."

* Unfamiliar.

# 58

# Get Up and Bar the Door

(Child No. 275)

## The Old Man and the Door
(Niles No. 58)

"GET UP AND BAR THE DOOR," although not widely known in the United States, is known to the French, the Germans, Italians, Arabs, and Turks. In some cases it appears as a ballad; in others, it is a fable. The basic idea is almost invariably the same.

In the three examples given by Child, a goodwife is cooking puddings. The man of the house, or the goodman, demands that she give up her cooking and bar the door against the wind and cold. This she will not do. Thereupon they retire, agreeing that whoever speaks first will get up and bar the door. Two travelers arrive, enter the house, and, being unable to get a reply from either the goodman or the goodwife, proceed to eat and drink up everything in the house. One of the travelers proposes to shave the goodman, and the other proposes to kiss the goodwife. At this last suggestion, the man cries out in anger, and of course it is he who must bar the door.

I have known this ballad from my earliest childhood. From time to time the Niles family used the dramatic material in the writing of a one-act play. We were all convinced that the plot made a better play than a ballad. This may have been because the music we employed was neither interesting nor graceful. We had fun with it all the same.

# The Old Man and the Door

## (Niles No. 58)

*With humor*

With a heigh - ho for the dum - mer - ie - do, The wind blew in the win - dow. With a heigh - ho for the dum - mer - ie - do, The wind blew on the floor - o.

*(Major mode on D)*

1. With a heigh-ho for the dummerie-do,
   The wind blew in the window.
   With a heigh-ho for the dummerie-do,
   The wind blew on the floor-o.

2. The goodman to the goodwife said,
   "Old woman, shut the door-o."
   With a heigh-ho for the dummerie-do,
   "Go shut the door yourself-o."

3. They made a paction* good and strong,
   The first to speak a word-o,
   With a heigh-ho for the dummerie-do,
   Would rise and shut the door-o.

4. The travelers whooped, the travelers howled,
   The travelers drank his ale-o.
   With a heigh-ho for the dummerie-do,
   They swilled her puddins, too-o.

5. The goodman leapt from out his bed,
   "Ye scald my beard with brew-o!"
   With a heigh-ho for the dummerie-do,
   "Ye cannot kiss my Jane-o!"

6. Our goodwife skipped upon the floor,
   Our goodman he was angry-o.
   With a heigh-ho for the dummerie-do,
   'Twas he who closed the door-o.

* Agreement.

# 59

# The Wife Wrapt in Wether's Skin

(Child No. 277)

## The Unwilling Bride
### (Niles No. 59)

Aaccording to the Scottish versions of this ballad a young man by name of Robin has married a woman considerably above him in station. She, thinking herself too great a lady, will not be debased with menial housework. Robin has a solution, however. He kills a castrated lamb (a wether), wraps the unwilling wife in the wether's skin, and beats the wether's skin soundly. In this way he can say that he did not beat his wife but, rather, the wether's skin.

The reformation of the unwilling wife is complete. The beating over, we hear the young woman cry

*"It's I will wash, and I will wring,*
*And never mind my gay goud ring.*

*"It's I will bake, and I will brew,*
*And never mind my comely hue. . . .*

*"Gin ye ca for mair when that is doon,*
*I'll sit i the neuk and I'll dight your shoon."*

What man could ask for a happier ending?

Another example of this method of wife-management found its way into a ballad imprinted before 1575 at Fleet Street, London, at the sign of St. John the Evangelist, by H. Jackson, containing somewhat the same story line. Printer Jackson's title is interesting: "A merry jeste of a shrewde and curste wyfe lapped in Morrelles skin for her good behauyour." Morrell was the name of a horse whose skin was salted and wrapped around the beaten wife to cure her wounds more quickly. She, too, appears to be a better woman for the experience.

The ballad of "The Wife Wrapt in Wether's Skin" is widely sung in the United States. Twelve texts have been recovered in Virginia, 5 in West Virginia, and 9 in Kentucky, besides my own. It is popular everywhere with men. Whether this popularity stems from its humor or from its barbarousness, or from both, is any man's guess.

## The Unwilling Bride

### (Niles No. 59)

Aunt Etta Howard was quite lovely looking, middle-aged, and motherly. Her menfolk worked in a Leslie County sawmill, and she lived not far from this buzzing, teeming, beehive-like enterprise. She said, "My menfolk work in the saw-mill when the sawmill is a-workin'." She didn't say what they did the rest of the time, and I didn't ask.

Discussing "The Wife Wrapt in Wether's Skin," which she called "The Unwilling Bride," she said: "I'm against wife-beatin'." And she waited for the idea to soak in, because, after all, we had oceans of time; then, continuing: "No, havin' been a wife for more years than I like to remember, I don't recommend wife-beatin'. Hit ain't legal. Hit's a jailhouse offense, if the beaten wife would swear to it. But it seems like a beaten wife don't favor more beatin', and that's why she won't testify in a law court."

I was reasonably sure that none of this could be found in Blackstone, but it sounded like gospel to me. All during the conversation Aunt Etta was cutting up and peeling a large cushaw. I felt sure the family was heading for some wonderful pies.

"Now take a case right here in our community," Aunt Etta said. "Yes, right on Cutshine.* About seven or eight years ago there was a young couple here, married just a few months when the husband ups and almost beats the daylights out of the young wife. He used a tobacco stick. [An oak stick about 52″ long, 1″ wide, ¾″ thick.] There was a certain amount of bawlin' and carryin' on in the cabin, and then it was quiet. But the next mornin', whilst the young husband was sittin' at the breakfast table, the young wife crept up from behind and beat the tar out of her man before he could set down his coffee cup. She was a-swingin' the same tobacco stick, but where he used only one hand, she used both. There was an awful outcry. The young man was so bad off and so debased, he couldn't work that day. The young woman told some friends that if her family had lived nearby she would have gone home after being beaten, but they lived so far away she beat up her husband instead."

I could hardly wait for the final chapter in this family saga, and ultimately, I discovered that the young woman lived "out" for a few days, either in the woods or with neighbors, and then, returning, made up with her husband and all was well. Of course, there was no law involved in the case, because both of them were guilty of assault and battery.

As years passed, the young man sold the "hard-scrabble" land he had inherited, because it wouldn't raise anything but pennyrile and poke-weed, pigeonberry, and hog peanuts. With the money he bought a small wagon mine,† which produced fairly well, and the young wife went to mothering two fine young sons.

Finally, Aunt Etta was ready to sing. Having reaffirmed her opposition to wife-beating, even when it had a somewhat happy ending as it did in the ballad she called "The Unwilling Bride," she sang with gusto and spirit.

The singing and the yarn-spinning had collected quite a few folk, young and old. There was a 13-year-old whom everyone called Knoxie-boy. He was already working at the potter's wheel, and doing well with it. When Aunt Etta had finished her song, I asked him, "Lad, what do you think of this young man who beat up his wife and made her cook?"

He smiled, nodded his head and said, "That man, he done pure right."

Everyone was greatly amused, and Aunt Etta said, "Oh, Knoxie-boy, you're such a sweet feller . . ."

One very old man, who answered to the name of Uncle Cabe and whose exact relation to the family I could not determine, obviously had something to add, and as I was putting my dulcimer in its bag, he took the floor.

"Once upon a time they was many a b'ar in them hills —" and he took in all the hills with a wide sweep of his arm, "many, many a b'ar. But men cotched 'em and trapped 'em, and carted 'em off to cities to put 'em in zoos and circuses. But now they be wild hog, wild hog called boar, and they be full o' danger. 'Treckly you spy a boar, you best climb a tree, 'cause they ain't no use runnin' away. Boar can outrun

---

* A creek gaining its name from the rocks along its bottom, which caused unwary travelers to cut their shins.
† Usually a small coal mine inaccessible to railroads. The coal is carried away in wagons or motor trucks.

# The Unwilling Bride
## (Niles No. 59)

*Boastfully*

Oh, I mar - ried a wife and I tuck her to home, As the gen - tle young jen - ny, the rose - mar - y tree, But I man - y times wish - ed I'd left her a - lone, As the doe skims o - ver the green___ val - ley. ___

(Minor mode on G)

a racehoss, and boar is always lookin' fer trouble."

So, loaded with music, legend, lore, and wild-life advice, I started walking down Cutshine in the direction of a road which I hoped would take me to Wooton and finally back to the Hibbler Hotel in Hazard, Ky. I was weary and dreadfully hungry. It was late September, and the hills looked for all the world like a paisley shawl.

# The Unwilling Bride (Niles No. 59)

1. Oh, I married a wife and I tuck her to home,
   *As the gentle young jenny, the rosemary tree,*
   But I many times wishèd I'd left her alone,
   *As the doe skims over the green valley.*

2. But I, bein' young, I tuck me to wife,
   *As the gentle young jenny, the rosemary tree,*
   A woman who plagued me out of my life,
   *As the doe skims over the green valley.*

3. Oh, for fear of her spoilin' her pretty cloth shoes,
   The pots in the kitchen she never would use.

4. Oh, first day when so weary I come from my plow,
   Said, "Wife, dearest wife, can I eat a bit now?"

5. "Lays a piece of stale pone on yon highest shelf,
   If you want more for dinner, go git it yourself."

6. Next day, as before, come I in from my plow,
   Said, "Wife, dearest wife, can I eat a bit now?"

7. Oh, she grabbed a hot spider,* said, "You git away,
   'Cause they hain't no more cooked than they was yesterday."

8. Oh, I went to my woodland, aside of my barn,
   And I cut me a hickory as long as my arm.

9. And then, in a twinkle, I quickly went back,
   And whacked my woman a lackety-smack.

10. Next e'en, as before, come I in from my plow,
    Said, "Wife, dearest wife, can I eat a bit now?"

11. Oh, she flew and she fluttered, the board it was spread,
    And when I bespoke me, 'twas "Yes, sir!" she said.

* Skillet, frying pan.

# 60

# The Farmer's Curst Wife

(Child No. 278)

### The Old Woman and the Devil
(Niles No. 60 A)
### The Farmer and the Devil
(Niles No. 60 B)

THE LEGEND of a violent, repulsive old hag who can outdevil the devil himself is widely known, and it is one that never fails to be funny. The story is part of the folklore of the Orient, and in India it turns up in the *Panchatantra.*\* The Setu tribe in Estonia know it well; I have heard it told by peasants and scholars in Finland and Sweden. I remember hearing it sung by German immigrants in Louisville, Ky., and once, in the same city, a chorus of visiting Bohemian singers sang a sweetened-up version of it with great verve. This was in 1905 or thereabouts.

Wherever the ballad appears in the English, Scottish, or American tradition, the story line is about the same. The devil appears to an ancient hen-pecked farmer and demands the farmer's wife. The farmer is understandably relieved, because at first he feared that his son or daughter might be the object of the devil's devilment. But Satan comes a cropper. The old wife is hell on earth and a double dose of hell in Hades. In one case she employs a mell† to bash out the brains of several small devils. Finally, after various outrages, his satanic majesty can take no more, and we find the old wife being carried back to earth, and to her unfortunate farmer-husband, who surely does not want her. In the American text (Niles No. 60 A) the old wife sums it up in one tight couplet:

*Oh, what I will do now the devil won't tell.*
*I ain't fit for heaven and I'm too mean for hell.*

Students of balladry will find interest in the text below, one full of violence and humor. It is, by the way, quite similar to the text of Niles No. 60 A.

The version quoted below comes from a collection called *Ancient Poems, Ballads, and Songs of the Peasantry of England,* edited by James H. Dixon, and is titled "The Farmer's Old Wife." The idea of a chorus of whistlers has been carried to the United States and is employed by that wonderful family of folk singers, the Ritchies of Viper, Ky.

---

\* A Sanscrit collection of fables and stories compiled in the 6th century by an Indian scholar for the moral instruction of the sons of a king. It is no dull, pedantic volume, however, but a superb collection of folk legends and parables, and is recommended to young and old alike. It is full of talking animals, and seems to have anticipated our own talking-dog and talking-horse stories by some centuries.

† A Scottish form of the word "maul," meaning a heavy metal or wooden hammer or mallet. The word is still used in the Southern mountains, wherever shingles or roofboards are made by hand. The two tools used for this operation are a mell and a frow (or froe). This latter is a wedge-shaped device with a handle set at right angle to the blade.

*There was an old farmer in Sussex did dwell,*
    *(Chorus of whistlers)*
*There was an old farmer in Sussex did dwell,*
*And he had a bad wife, as many knew well.*
    *(Chorus of whistlers)*

*Then Satan came to the old man at the plough, —*
    *(Chorus of whistlers)*
*Then Satan came to the old man at the plough, —*
*One of your family I must have now.*
    *(Chorus of whistlers)*

*It is not your eldest son that I crave,*
*But it is your old wife, and she I will have.*

*O, welcome! good Satan, with all my heart,*
*I hope you and she will never more part.*

*Now Satan has got the old wife on his back,*
*And he lugged her along, like a pedlar's pack.*

*He trudged away till they came to his hall-gate,*
*Says he, Here! take in an old Sussex chap's mate!*

*O! then she did kick the young imps about, —*
*Says one to the other, Let's try turn her out.*

*She spied thirteen imps all dancing in chains,*
*She up with her pattens and beat out their brains.*

*She knocked the old Satan against the wall, —*
*Let's try turn her out, or she'll murder us all.*

*Now he's bundled her up on his back amain,*
*And to the old husband he took her again.*

*I have been a tormentor the whole of my life,*
*But I ne'er was tormented so as with your wife.*

# The Old Woman and the Devil

## (Niles No. 60 A)

THE MONTH WAS October, and the year was 1912, and the place was Jackson, Ky. The singer was an old granny-woman (midwife) who gave her address as "over near Chavies." She had come to Jackson to employ legal counsel in the defense of her son, who was implicated in a murder case. The singer apparently did not want to give her name; it is not in the jottings of my notebook.

An early fall rain had put a chill in the air. The old granny-woman and I sat around a pot-bellied stove in a hardware store. There were other sitters, "a-warmin' their shins," and they seemed interested in my interest in their old-timey music. A short time earlier a shooting had occurred just in front of this hardware store, but, naturally, it was not discussed. There was a rumor going around concerning a man who, when he walked " 'broad," carried a very young infant in his arms to discourage his enemies from shooting at him. I never saw the man, I never saw the infant — and I never heard a single shot all the while I was in Jackson.

There was a certain amount of mild teasing going on between the shin-warmers and the granny-woman.

"I know these fellers well," said she. "They're always a-funnin' me about my trade." She paused, then added: "Midwifin'. They're always a-askin' me what I do about a wood's colt — you know, an early harvest. I tell 'em that the mother bares it like any other baby, and that the mother seems to love it more than if it was a church-house child. And as far as namin' the father is concerned, the old folks will tell you that hit's a poor mother that can't daddy her youngun by its favor."*

* Resemblance.

# The Old Woman and the Devil

## (Niles No. 60 A)

*Very gaily*

There was an old farm-er went out for to plow, With a

nu sing nag-gle sing nu, _____ There was an old farm-er went

out for to plow, He hitched up an ox and an ass and a cow, With a

nu sing nag-gle sing nu, nu, nu, A nu sing nag-gle sing nu. _____

*(Major mode on A)*

This was greeted with rounds of laughter.
"What was all that?" cried out an ancient bearded one, who was apparently hard of hearing.

"He's got two ears, and he can't hear once," said the granny-woman.

"I can hear mighty good," said the ancient one, "if a body will give up mumblin'."

"Like a lot o' folks, you can hear what you want to hear," answered the granny-woman, "and it ought to be that you could hear only what was good for you."

And the laugh was on the ancient one with the long white whiskers.

For fear that the fun-making would lead to more fun-making, or that someone would get riled at a chance remark, I went to singing. The crowd increased. One motherly person stood straight and silent, apparently absorbed, a small boy on each side of her. The boys were obviously twins. The granny-woman said to me: "Them little fellers are as alike as a pair of fried eggs."

Finally I got my granny-woman friend to sing for me, and, of course, for the assembled company. This was a new experience for me; as a rule my informants were secretive about their talents. But the granny-woman had been dealing with the world outside her valley. The public was no surprise to her.

Little did I know, that gloomy morning in Jackson, Ky., that I was about to write down one of my most successful pieces of performance music, for "The Old Woman and the Devil" has become as popular with my audiences as "Bar-

## The Old Woman and the Devil (Niles No. 60 A)

1. There was an old farmer went out for to plow,
   *With a nu sing naggle sing nu,*
   There was an old farmer went out for to plow,
   He hitched up an ox and an ass and a cow,
   *With a nu sing naggle sing nu, nu, nu,*
   *A nu sing naggle sing nu.*

2. The devil flew by with a flickety-flack,
   *With a nu sing naggle sing nu,*
   The devil flew by with a flickety-flack,
   He carried a pitchfork wrapped up in a sack,
   *With a nu sing naggle sing nu, nu, nu,*
   *A nu sing naggle sing nu.*

3. The old farmer droppèd his lines and he run,
   "The devil's a-lookin' for my oldest son."

4. "I don't want your son nor your daughter fair,
   But your old scoldin' wife what's lost all of her hair."

5. So sayin', he harvest her up on his back,
   And he left like a peddler a-totin' his pack.

6. He toted her down to the gates of hell,
   Said, "Blow up the fire, boys, we'll roast this one well."

7. Seven small devils came rattlin' their chains,
   She handled a poker and mellered their brains.

8. The other small devil looked over the wall,
   Said, "Take her back, Daddy, she'll murder us all."

9. He harvest her up on his poor old tired back,
   And he left like a peddler a-totin' his pack.

10. Seven years goin' and six comin' back,
    She asked for the cornpone she left in the crack.

11. "Oh, what I can do now the devil won't tell,
    I ain't fit for heaven and I'm too mean for hell."

b'ry Ellen," "Little Mattie Groves," or "The Hangman."

Later I took the granny-woman out and bought her some breakfast. Some of the impromptu audience followed and demanded more music. I sang, and to my delight discovered another singer — a waitress who sang a charming version of "The Holy Family."

Later in the morning I passed one of the men I had met around the hardware-store stove. He smiled and nodded his head knowingly: "Pardner, I'll tell you a little news. If anybody could sing about the devil and know what they was a-singin' for gospel truth, that old granny-woman could do it."

We laughed a bit, and I asked him about the "troubles" the granny-woman's son was into.

"They'll never find him guilty," said my sidewalk wise man. "No, they never will . . . He's jail-hampered now for shootin' a man, but he ain't guilty of deliberate murder, because he was shootin' at the feller's brother. Hit's pure accidental . . ."

# The Farmer and the Devil

## (Niles No. 60 B)

I CAME UPON the singer of "The Farmer and the Devil" as she sat on a morning-glory-bedecked porch in Cherokee County, N. C. She was shelling out a varicolored bean known to seed catalogs as the Horticultural Pole Bean. A small boy had been sitting on the edge of the porch and was trying to slip away.

"Don't go, honey," cried the old lady. "Don't go! This man won't eat you, he'll sing to you."

The boy returned to the farthest end of the porch, and viewed me with fear in his eyes.

" 'Tis said," continued the old lady, "that when you visit this youngun's family, you might get to see the old folks, but the children will break for the hills as soon as they get the scent of you."

" 'Tain't so," said the boy, who had his head bandaged.

"What hit you?" I asked.

"Nothin' hit me," snapped the boy. "Somethin' bit me."

" 'Twer a gal-nipper,"* said the old lady.

" 'Tweren't no gal-nipper," declared the boy. "I was sarpent-bote."†

"Rattler, copperhead, black racer, cow sucker, or fishin' worm?" I inquired, hoping to be humorous.

"It were a sarpent with four legs, and each leg had fingers and fingernails on it," said the boy, who did not consider me the least bit funny.

"No doubt a scaly lizard then," said the old lady. "The little feller's head is swole a bit, but hit'll go down. I jest put a flaxseed poultice on it."

I made some remark about the beauty of the morning-glory vines which festooned the porch.

"Those blue moonvines," said the old woman, "they was a gift from some little girls belongin' to one of them do-right clubs.‡ Now if you could stay till sundown, you'd see the white ones open up. They just pop right out in your face, and they sure smell pretty."

The old lady's singing was nothing to brag

---

* In the Niles family, a gal-nipper was simply a large mosquito. I have heard others say it is a dragonfly. And I understand that in Canada it is used to describe a kind of fishbait.

† "Bote" is an ancient form of "bitten." Sarpent-bote means bitten by a snake.

‡ The 4-H or one of the other farmgirl groups.

# The Farmer and the Devil

## (Niles No. 60 B)

*Quietly*

The farm-er went to plow, Nu - nu - nu, The farm-er went to plow With an ox and a cow, Nu - nu - nu-nu-nu.

*(Major mode on F)*

1. The farmer went to plow,
   Nu-nu-nu,
   The farmer went to plow
   With an ox and a cow,
   Nu-nu-nu-nu-nu.

2. The devil, he passed by,
   Nu-nu-nu,
   The devil, he passed by,
   The farmer, he didn't know why,
   Nu-nu-nu-nu-nu.

3. "Oh, take my mean old wife,"
   Nu-nu-nu,
   "Oh, take my mean old wife,
   She bothers all my life,"
   Nu-nu-nu-nu-nu.

4. She went to hell and back,
   Nu-nu-nu,
   She went to hell and back,
   And gave her man a whack,
   Nu-nu-nu-nu-nu.

on, but her sense of humor was something to remember. She was greatly amused at the idea of the farmer in the ballad getting a good sound whack from the wife he thought he was rid of.

She wanted to make sure I got the moral: "He thought he was shed of her, but she learned 'im! Women like that are powerful old and powerful smart, and as folks do say, the eyebrow is older than the beard, and a heap smarter."

The old lady concentrated a text of nearly a dozen verses into 4 five-line stanzas, but the story is told quite adequately. The tune leaves much to be desired. The singer, however, declared that it was very good for quieting babies.

After quite a lot of singing, the little frightened boy warmed up enough to ask how the old lady had heard about me.

"My boy," said she, "a hungry eye sees a long way." I had indeed brought a small poke of the kind of household necessities the old lady could not afford.

# 61

# The Sweet Trinity
# (The Golden Vanity)

(Child No. 286)

## The Weep-Willow Tree

(Niles No. 61)

THE STORY of the ballad of "The Sweet Trinity (The Golden Vanity)," Child No. 286 A, would lead us to believe that Sir Walter Raleigh caused a ship named *The Sweet Trinity* to be built in the Netherlands and that this fine ship was captured by a galley sailing in the vicinity of the Low Country. The captain calls for a seaman to take the galley and redeem the *Sweet Trinity*. A "little ship-boy" speaks up and is offered gold and fee and the captain's eldest daughter as payment for the sinking of the galley.

The little boy employs a magic auger, sinks the galley, frees the *Sweet Trinity*, swims back, and demands his pay. But the captain, now that his ship is no longer in danger, will not pay in full. He will pay the gold and fee, but there will be no

eldest daughter for the little ship-boy. The boy swims away, saying:

*Then fare you well, you cozening lord,*
*Seeing you are not as good as your word.*

And apparently drowns.

In the text indicated as version B, the ship is called *The Goulden Vanitie*, and the little ship-boy is now the little cabin boy. He fares rather better, but only after he threatens to sink the home ship with his magic auger.

This ballad is widely distributed throughout America. However, I only encountered it once in native tradition, and that by the rarest luck, in a bus terminal in Jackson, Breathitt County, Ky.

## The Weep-Willow Tree

### (Niles No. 61)

ONE OCTOBER EVENING in 1932 I did a short performance of music for some friends in Jackson, Breathitt County, Ky. Next day about noon, as I was leaving for Lexington, I stopped at the

bus station for a bite of lunch. One of the local peace officers, having heard of my performance the previous night, asked me to unpack a dulcimer and sing him a ballad. This I did, and I have

321

# The Weep-Willow Tree

## (Niles No. 61)

*Quietly and slowly*

Oh, my fa - ther has a fine ship a -
sail - in' on the sea, And they call her by the name of the
Weep - Wil-low Tree, And she sails up and down on the lone-some low, And she
sails on the lone - some sea,_____ And she sails on the lone - some sea.

(Minor mode on A)

# The Weep-Willow Tree (Niles No. 61)

1. Oh, my father has a fine ship a-sailin' on the sea,
   And they call her by the name of the Weep-Willow Tree,
   And she sails up and down on the lonesome low,
       And she sails on the lonesome sea,
       And she sails on the lonesome sea.

2. Now they be another ship and she sails on the sea,
   And they call her by the name of the Turkish Piree,
   But I fear she will sink the Weep-Willow Tree,
       As she sails on the lonesome sea,
       As she sails on the lonesome sea.

3. 'Twas a sailor, a sailor, who quickly spoke, spake he, sayin':
   "Captain, my Captain, what will my prize be,
   If I should go sink you the Turkish Piree,
       If I sink her in the lonesome sea,
       If I sink her in the lonesome sea?"

4. "Oh, I will give you gold and I will give you fee,"
   Said the Captain to the sailor of the Weep-Willow Tree,
   "And my eldest fairest daughter your sweet bride will be,
       If you sink her in the lonesome sea,
       If you sink her in the lonesome sea."

5. Oh, the sailor-man was brave and the sailor-man was bold,
   As he augered and he augered through the Turkish Pirate's hold;
   And some did play at cards while some did play melee,
       As they sank in the lonesome sea,
       As they sank in the lonesome sea.

6. Now the sailor-man crept down and slowly back swam he,
   And he swam round the side of the Weep-Willow Tree, cryin':
   "Help me, my Captain, and come give me my fee,
       Lest I drown in the lonesome sea,
       Lest I drown in the lonesome sea."

7. Oh, he swam the tother side of the Weep-Willow Tree,
   And he cried, "Oh my messmates, pray come and succor me,
   'Cause I augered forty holes in the Turkish Piree,
       And I'm sinkin' in the lonesome sea,
       And I'm sinkin' in the lonesome sea."

8. Oh, they hauled him o'er the side of the Weep-Willow Tree,
   And he died on the deck with his messmates three,
   And they sewed him in his hammock and they sent him out to sea,
       And he sank in the lonesome sea,
       And he sank in the lonesome sea.

been forever grateful to the peace officer for asking me to sing.

Hardly had I finished my impromptu bus-terminal concert than up came a young man and a young woman who said they had once won a prize for singing an old "ballard" and would be pleasured to sing it for me. Never was folk music so willingly offered or so enthusiastically received. The bus came and left, but we went right on singing. My informants, Christopher McIntosh and his wife Margie, were going to Akron, Ohio, where they had a promise of employment. My car was handy, and I drove them to Winchester, where they had intended to transfer.

The McIntoshes were high school graduates and well-informed people. They sang accurately and willingly. Instead of "The Sweet Trinity" or "The Golden Vanity," they called their delightful version "The Weep-Willow Tree."

There is a note in the margin of my notebook to the effect that a 16-ounce steak with all the trimmings could be purchased in the Jackson bus-station restaurant for 75 cents. This was in 1932.

# 62

# The Mermaid

(Child No. 289)

### The Mermaid
(Niles No. 62 A)

### The Mermaid
(Niles No. 62 B)

CHILD TELLS us that just before the turn of the 20th century the ballad of "The Mermaid" was still in circulation as a broadside. I can remember "The Mermaid" at that time as a song sung in the grade schools of Louisville and Jefferson County, Ky.

Accounts of the appearance or capture of mermaids are continually turning up in communities bordering on the sea. Though I have searched diligently, I have not been able to discover any legendary lore concerning fresh-water mermaids. Nor have I ever encountered anyone who actually saw a mermaid: she was always seen by a friend.

According to legend, mermaids are given to making dire prophecies, and even when a mermaid prophesies good fortune it is likely to turn out badly. A mermaid may, for a short time, assume the appearance of an ordinary human being; and conversely, a human being may be changed into a mermaid (see Joyce's *Old Celtic Romances*). Seeing a mermaid is almost always an omen of bad luck, as in Niles No. 62 A and B.

The ballad of "The Mermaid" is well known in American folk tradition.

## The Mermaid

(Niles No. 62 A)

AS A GESTURE of neighborliness the Crawley brothers, Luke and Brent, came down the hill from their house to my home in Boone Creek valley, sat comfortably in my music room, warmed their shins, and sang "The Mermaid." Never had I collected folk music more easily or more pleasantly. I thought back to the mud and the heat, the rain and the cold, the endless miles

of walking and the innumerable unpalatable meals, the endless disappointments, the occasional discoveries, while I sat in a deep arm-chair, folding table before me, dulcimer and piano handy, all my notebooks spread out — and the Crawley brothers willing, even anxious, to sing.

As I recall, the original purpose of their visit

# The Mermaid

## (Niles No. 62 A)

One Sa-tur-day night, as we set sail, Not ver-y far from land, We there did spy a pret-ty mer-maid With a comb and a glass in her hand, With a comb and a glass in her pret-ty, pret-ty hand, With a comb and a glass in her hand.

(Dorian mode on D)

# The Mermaid (Niles No. 62 A)

1. One Saturday night, as we set sail,
   Not very far from land,
   We there did spy a pretty mermaid
   With a comb and a glass in her hand,
   With a comb and a glass in her pretty, pretty hand,
   With a comb and a glass in her hand.

2. This pretty mermaid sprung into the sea,
   The storm hit began to roar.
   The snow and rain come thick and fast:
   "We'll never see land any more,
   We'll never see land any more, more, more,
   We'll never see land any more."

3. The first one on deck was the captain of our ship,
   With a plumb and a line in his hand,
   He plumbed and he plumbed and he plumbed for to see
   How far it was to the sand,
   How far it was from the sea to the sand,
   How far it was to the sand.

4. The next one on deck was the mate of our ship,
   And a well-looking man was he,
   "My wife and my child are in Merry England,
   And tonight a widow she'll be,
   And tonight a widow she'll surely, surely be,
   And tonight a widow she'll be."

5. The next one on deck was our little cabin boy,
   And a very pretty boy was he,
   "Oh what, oh what will my mother say
   When she knows I'm drownded in the sea,
   When she knows I'm drownded in the salt, salt sea,
   When she knows I'm drownded in the sea?"

6. Oh three times 'round went our gallant ship,
   And three times more went she,
   And as the storm did rage and roar,
   She sank to the bottom of the sea,
   She sank to the bottom of the deep blue sea,
   She sank to the bottom of the sea.

was to talk about some flagstones they proposed to sell me. But no matter; they also sang "The Mermaid," and explained that they had learned it from their granny, who had lived as a child in Rockcastle County and as an adult in Madison County, Ky. The date was December 5, 1942.

# The Mermaid

## (Niles No. 62 B)

IN THE LATE AUTUMN of 1933 I encountered Razor Bill Barlow, who was "straw-boss" of a construction gang near Jenkins, Ky. It was Barlow's job to get a short spur of railroad track into operation.

The Bill part of his name was not an abbreviation for William, because his actual given name was James. He got the name Razor Bill because of the remarkable shape of his head and face — hook-nosed, gap-toothed, and with an extremely narrow head structure — which was definitely reminiscent of the bird known as a razorbill (a species of auk).

Razor Bill was humorous as well as odd looking. He laughed at almost everything, even at the rain, which fell incessantly, increasing the floodtide and damaging the roadbed of a nearby coal railroad.

The whistle in a coal-mine tipple nearby announced noontime. The men dropped their picks and shovels as if they were hot. Razor Bill and I retired to the warmth and protection of the company store. It was there that he recited his verses concerning the mermaid. He would not sing a single note because, he said, if his gang of work-

men found out he was a singer he would never hear the end of it.

"Hit's enough to be called Razor Bill, without being called a singing Razor Bill!" He laughed and laughed, and I laughed with him, and even the glum "honest John" type behind the counter smiled.

Said the counter man, "Bill could be a politician, what with his smilin' and laughin' and back-slappin'."

"And his baby-kissin'," added a woebegone woman with a great bag of groceries and several small children.

"I'm takin' a correspondence course on bridges and culverts," Razor Bill confided to me, "and when I finish it, I'm headin' out."

He recited his verses in a low voice, as if he were slightly ashamed of the whole process. I was sorry I could not get him to sing. Note that the rhythmic pattern in verse 1 is quite different from that in the following three verses. This is the sort of thing which happens so frequently when a ballad text is spoken rather than sung: it gradually becomes unsingable.

# The Mermaid

1. Oh, the stormy winds do blow
   With the landlubbers down below,
   And the sailor-men a-climbin' to the top
   To haul in the riggin'-o.

2. 'Twas Sunday night, our sails were set,
   We hardly cleared the land-o,
   When we spied a mermaid a-swimmin' by,
   A comb and a glass in her hand-o.

3. The captain plumbed with a lead and a line,
   He plumbed for to reach the sand-o,
   While the winds and the waves did toss and roar.
   We knew we'd never see land-o.

4. Then three times 'round went our gallant ship,
   And three times more went she,
   And the mate and the cabin boy said goodbye
   As we sank in the salt, salt sea.

# John of Hazelgreen

(Child No. 293)

## John of Hazelgreen
### (Niles No. 63)

IN THE ORIGINAL Scottish and English texts of this ballad we find that a gentleman walking along the highroad encounters an exceptionally well-favored young female who is weeping for the love of a person by name of John of Hazelgreen.

And nothing will do but John of Hazelgreen — not even fine newly purchased raiment, a belt containing silver coinage of the realm, the offer of the gentleman's eldest son as an emergency spouse, and, of course, comforting words. Nothing will do but John of Hazelgreen, and there is much weeping and hand-wringing until John himself steps out, helps the lovely distraught female dismount her horse, and promptly kisses her 120 times (40 times on the cheek, 40 times on the chin, and 40 times on the mouth). One might almost say that the Hazelgreen tribe was greatly given to kissing.

Thereupon the beautiful damsel discovers that the gentleman, who has been trying to benefit her is actually the father of her lover, John of Hazelgreen, and that the wedding will be celebrated that same day, and that there will be dancing and other delightful forms of diversion that same night.

In its North American form, which is quite close to the original, "John of Hazelgreen" is widely sung in the Southern states.

## John of Hazelgreen
### (Niles No. 63)

HAD MY INFORMANT not been dead this many a year, I would not now be telling his story. Of course, I would report his delightful version of "John of Hazelgreen," but his own saga would remain untold. Even so, I will not divulge his address, for some of his assistants might still be carrying on the manufacture of homemade whiskey. To me, he was known as Uncle Brother, and I promised him that if I ever wrote a single line about him, I would simply say that he lived in that wonderful part of the U.S. usually referred to as "south of the Mason-Dixon line."

"Hit's a big place," said Uncle Brother. "All the way from the salt sea to Tennessee."

"All the way over to the Mississippi," I said.

"Hit's a big place," continued the old man. "If the law come a-lookin' for me, it would cause 'em a power of bother." If Uncle Brother were alive today, he would be well over 100 years old, and that's a little old for blockading.

For those who are not versed in the ways of homemade whiskey, it might be well to explain that a blockader is a person, male or female, who manufactures alcoholic beverages and sells them without the benefit of the U.S. revenue stamp. The blockader exists today, but the demise of national Prohibition has robbed him both of glamour and of trade outlets.

When I knew Uncle Brother in 1932, Prohibition was still with us, and Uncle Brother enjoyed a status that would not be his today. The product of the blockader is romantically called moonshine, because it is mistakenly thought that all such liquids are made at night when the moon is out. This may have happened at one time or another, but from what I have observed I would say that most illicit liquor, if made in rural surroundings, is made in the daytime, when the workmen can see exactly what they are doing. It is also made in the temperate months of the year, because when the leaves are off the trees, "a body with an eye for snoopin' can see a lot farther." Then, too, fires burning in winter make more smoke than fires burning in summer, presumably from the greater moisture in winter wood. I have gained these and a few other facts concerning blockading from many years of observing blockaders.

One thing I have been forced to conclude is that backwoods people in my part of the world have never, and perhaps will never, accept the realities of the revenue-stamp tax law with much willingness or delight. Quite a few of these people, who could well afford to purchase drinking whiskey, will make it in small quantities because it is dangerous and fun. Furthermore, these small private operators are convinced that their product is both more palatable and more potent than anything bought in stores. And although their neighbors may not operate stills, they would

* Jailhouse.

never betray friends who are in the private "stilling" business.

At one time during the period of the "noble experiment," the smoke of fourteen private stills could be seen, from my main farm gate, faintly sifting skyward. None of these were very high-class operations. In fact, the operators were famous for stealing any wooden object they could find to help fire their boilers. Wooden fences were in dire danger, and even outdoor privies were dismantled, a board at a time, and burned to warm the fermented mash. All this took place in spite of the efforts of the officer delegated to enforce an unenforceable law. This officer finally left the community. He was shot at continually by people who apparently could not hit a bull in the behind with a double-bass fiddle. He survived the shooting, but he was defeated psychologically.

Uncle Brother, when I knew him in 1932, was not only a blockader and a singer and a running-set dancer of some note, but he was also a mine of colorful information. I asked him about his assistants, both of whom seemed to be either mutes or hopelessly moronic.

"The both of 'em are as quiet as a mouse in a sugar-sack," said Uncle Brother, "and that's the way they want to be. I once had a flibberty-gibberty young man here, workin' for me. I paid him well in wages and whiskey . . . he was learnin' the trade, and I was hopin' he'd carry on after my dyin'. But he was such a loosel — his tongue flapped like a bell-clapper tied in the middle and loose at both ends!

"He about talked me into confine,"* continued Uncle Brother, his eyes squinted and his head nodding. "But I've got friends, and I got told I was in danger of bein' jail-hampered . . . Now, mister, I don't like jail-hamperin'. Hit ain't no fun, and then, the whilst you're hampered, somebody over the hill gets all your good customers, and you don't never get 'em back. So I closed up shop, and I told my loosel that I was quittin', goin' to Florida. But I never went nowhere much.

"I dismantled my still and sold off my supplies and went fishin'. Six months later I was a-stirrin' yeast, cornmeal, and sugar.

" 'Treckly, I hired these boys. They be distant relations of mine, and they're both down-gone.* When they're drinkin' coffee, they'll hardly ask for the sugar."

Uncle Brother said that he made about 10 gallons a week for about 8 months a year, and that was enough to keep body and soul together. He yearned for a chance to do some fox hunting. He and a friend had a pack of hounds in partnership, and among them was a famous bitch named Queen Elizabeth. "Her feet hits the ground so fast when she's a-runnin'," said Uncle Brother, "sounds for all the world like cloth a-tearin'."

After the custom of this section of the country, I stirred a pot of mash, and that made me a party to the operation.

"If you had time and could stay awhile," Uncle Brother said, "I could teach you some of the secrets of the trade."

Brother, according to local legend, "could take off liquor, day or night, and tell you the very moment the bead breaks." I admit I was mystified by all this technical talk. His still was about four country miles from where he lived. They were four of the longest, hottest, hardest-climbing miles I have ever encountered. The "supplies" (that is to say, the salable whiskey) were not kept at the place of manufacture. They were still another mile away. I later discovered that during the working months of the year, Uncle Brother did not stay at his home but slept in a lean-to, just outside his supply house. This supply house was nothing more than a small cave with a boarded-up front containing a door. Against this wooden front Uncle Brother had constructed a little tin-roofed lean-to. It was directly in front of the supply-house door, and it contained the old man's cornshuck bed. Thus, access to the supplies could be gained only by stepping over Uncle Brother's body. It was the best and simplest burglar alarm ever devised.

In his early days, Uncle Brother had been a fiddler, and he had a wide reputation as a singer of "old-timey music." His "Barbary Ellen" was very interesting. He said he knew a little of "The Old Woman and the Devil" (Niles No. 60 A). "I used to know enough songs to fill your little black book," said he, "but I can't put my head to it anymore. I'm too tore-down."†

He did, however, put his head to one quite wonderful ballad. I knew it had been reported 6 times in Virginia and that Cecil Sharp had recovered several examples during his 1917–18 tour. But I had never encountered a convincing version before, as sung by a native. He even called it by its actual name, "John of Hazelgreen," which was a surprise to me.

As I was about to leave, Uncle Brother said to me sadly, "I hate to see a singin' man go away. If you could rest with us a while, we could learn you the trade, and you could learn us a power of music. I love them church songs particular . . .

"Trouble is, they ain't no money in this business anymore. In the old days, a body could pay off a few officials, and that was the end of it. They was usually God-fearin' men and nondrinkers. Nowadays, with Prohibition, the demand is greater, and the payoff is greater, and the officials has such a yen for whiskey, they drink me out of house and home. No, there's no money in this business, not anymore.

"When I was a young man, my wife and me, we was powerful dancers. Every time they was a set-runnin' we was there. But she died of a cancer twenty years ago — they ain't no cure for cancer — and hit's been lonely since then, nothin' but mash-tubs and a little fishin'. And remember, boy, don't never, never deal with upscudderers.‡ They may not always get you jail-hampered, but they could keep you bodaciously§ tore up."

We shook hands, and Uncle Brother said: "I trusted you, because you seemed to be a simple sort and interested only in old-timey music." Uncle Brother didn't know how right he was on both counts — simple-mindedness and old-timey music. I never saw him again.

---

* Silent, glum, noncommunicative.     † Weary, no-account, unwilling.     ‡ Troublemakers.     § Very much.

# John of Hazelgreen
## (Niles No. 63)

*Gaily, with assurance*

Oh ear - ly, ear - ly in sweet May, the sun had not yet shone, I

chanced up - on a maid - en fair who made a heav - y moan. "Why

make you yet this heav - y moan, and what doth all this mean?" But

all that she would ev - er say was "John of Ha - zel - green."

(*Minor mode on E*)

8 *va*

# John of Hazelgreen (Niles No. 63)

1. Oh early, early in sweet May, the sun had not yet shone,
   I chanced upon a maiden fair who made a heavy moan.
   "Why make you yet this heavy moan, and what doth all this mean?"
   But all that she would ever say was "John of Hazelgreen."

2. "You're welcome to my house and lands, and here I do confide
   That you may have my eldest son to take you for his bride."
   "I do not want your eldest son, for I am far too mean,
   And I intend to bride no one but John of Hazelgreen."

3. "What for a man is Hazelgreen, what for a man is he?"
   "He is the lord of all our kin, who live in this country.
   With arms so long and shoulders broad, as fair as e'er was seen,
   With hair that hangs like links of gold, my John of Hazelgreen."

4. He tuck her by the lily hand and led her to the town,
   He bought a sweep-tail petticoat, and hit did trail the ground.
   But silk and satin hit did pale agin her lovely sheen,
   And all the while she made a moan for John of Hazelgreen.

5. As they did ride the lengthy lane that took them from the town,
   Out stepped John of Hazelgreen and helped his lady down.
   Ah, forty times he kissed her cheek and forty times her chin,
   And forty times he kissed her lips as he did lead her in.

6. "My son, my son, go hold your tongue, let talk and mournin' be,
   For here I've brought a fair young maid who wants no one but thee.
   Today shall be your wedding day, and you shall dance this e'en.
   Here's health and happiness to all who live in Hazelgreen!"

# 64

# The Brown Girl

(Child No. 295)

## The English Lady Gay
### (Niles No. 64)

IN THE ENGLISH originals offered by Child as No. 295 A and B, we find a young man apparently very much enamored of a girl whose skin is very brown in color. In the first of these two variants, in the first verse, the girl describes herself as brown of color, with eyes black as a sloe, and she as brisk as a nightingale and wild as any doe.

In spite of these secondary charms, the color of the girl's skin is too great a handicap. The young man writes the fateful letter of rejection, and thinks his brown sweetheart is safely dismissed. Soon thereafter, however, the young man falls prey to what we would call a psychosomatic illness. At least the doctors cannot cure him, and the young man is convinced that if he can bring back his rejected brown girl, she will give him back his faith and his health. There is also some mention of golden rings, but this is not overly clear in the English texts.

The brown girl, on arriving at the bedside of her onetime lover, cannot stand for laughing; she tells him she will not forget his insulting rejection, she will not be his wife, and, furthermore, she will dance with delight on his grave.

In every American example I have observed, the situation is reversed: it is the young man who is rejected and unforgiving. The business of the rings — either one or "one, two, and three," changed from golden to diamond rings — is clearly established in 15 of the 22 American texts I have studied.

## The English Lady Gay
### (Niles No. 64)

ON A MORNING late in October 1932, I left Middlesboro, Bell County, Ky., and drove westward in the direction of Jellico, Tenn. My objective was a twenty-square-mile section of land, partly in Tennessee and partly in Kentucky, called the thermal belt. I had been told that the tempera- ture in this small area, owing to its unique altitude, was almost subtropical. Cotton was grown in this area, and certain very fine grapes. I spent the entire day studying several small communi- ties — Pruden, Anthras, Clairfield, Morley and High Cliff, all near the Tennessee-Kentucky line.

I had been told that if I could find this so-called thermal belt, I would also find a beekeeper who was an eminently fine ballad singer. He was supposed to have kept written records of the ballads he had sung over a period of 50 years, as well as of the ballads he had heard others sing. The old beekeeper was said to be over 80 years old, and to have a magnificent white beard. He was said to be quite a philosopher and endowed with clairvoyance. Altogether, there was something mysterious and almost magical about him.

I never found the thermal belt that day, but the fall coloring was so fabulous and the Indian summer sun so so wonderful that I didn't mind too much. At noon I sat at the side of a little back road and ate a lunch I had bought in Middlesboro. To this I added some watercress I had found in a nearby stream. I had found no thermal belt, no bee-man, no fifty years of documented balladry, but as I ate my lonely lunch four lines of a poem occurred to me:

*Slant the sun, October is at hand.*
*Sift the moonlight through half-shredded leaves.*
*Hear the gasp of summer-wearied land,*
*For winter's near, and even autumn grieves.*

Sundown found me back at High Cliff, Tenn., and it was dark when I pulled up beside a cozy little restaurant in Jellico.

The food was excellent, particularly the hot bread. I observed that the entire operation was carried on by one middle-aged woman. She later explained that in the summer, when there was more travel, the owner of the restaurant and several assistants were on hand. But now it was the end of October — and had I heard tell of the national depression?

Yes, I had heard tell of the depression, and as a little conversation leads to more conversation, I asked her about the philosopher bee-man. She had never heard tell of a bee-man in that section, but there was a bee-woman some miles up the road who was thought to be "quare-turned." "By robbin' many a hive she supports herself and an odd collection of no-count hog-chokers* — men and boys too lazy to swing a stick at a snake."

What did I want with the bee-man? Mayhap I was a honey collector? No, I explained, I was a ballad collector, and I went into a considerable explanation of my strange profession — ballads, music generally, composition, teaching, instrument-making. The waitress was visibly interested. She even seemed to be impressed.

Suddenly she turned around, and took a book off a shelf just behind the counter. She opened it and lay it before me. It was a tattered copy of *The Sacred Harp,* and it was my turn to be impressed.

Together we turned the thumbed pages of Benjamin Franklin White's wonderful shape-note hymnal, and when we came to "Greenfield," the singing began:

*How tedious, how tasteless the hours*
*When Jesus no longer I see.*
*Sweet prospects, sweet birds and sweet flowers*
*Have lost all their sweetness to me.*

A collection of truck drivers came in, and she went to pouring them cups of steaming coffee, and never stopped singing a moment. The waitress with the motherly manner and the white hair knew "the book" from memory.

I'm not prepared to say that two voices can sing the four-part setting of "Greenfield," but the truck drivers didn't seem to miss the other parts the slightest bit. In the middle of it all, I went outside to my car, brought in a dulcimer, unpacked it, tuned it up, put it down on the counter, and went to playing the part I knew so well — playing and singing the "old-timey" music for anyone who would listen. It was "Go 'Way from My Window," and "Black Is the Color of My True Love's Hair," and "Jimmy Randal," and "Barb'ry Ellen." Finally, after what seemed to be quite a long while, when the truck drivers had "headed out," the waitress turned to me and said that her name was Opal Prewitt. That was when I began to make notes.

Yes, her name was Opal Prewitt, and her age

* Persons who are too no-account to work in a legitimate manner, but will choke a hog to make him spit out a small coin.

# The English Lady Gay

## (Niles No. 64)

*With a promise of grief*

There was an Eng-lish la-dy gay, From high de-gree—she came.— Her beau-ty was of such re-nown, And Sar-ah was her name.— Tra-la, la, la, la, la, la, la, And Sar-ah was her name.—

*(Minor mode on G)*

was above 60, and she was a graveyard widow of many, many winters. She had lived a good life, and she had a devoted man-friend, and she was a foot-washing Baptist and a member of a shape-note singing group. For good measure, she declared that almost everyone ate too much fried food. "A body's liver can't stand it," said Opal,

"and then it stinks up the kitchen so bad."

We discussed *The Sacred Harp,* and she said that she thought "the Lord had directed the hand of Benjamin Franklin White, way back there, nigh on to a hundred years ago." Then I asked her if she knew any old-timey music (I may have used the word ballad). She said she did — and would I like her to sing one? I said yes, and presently I realized that I was listening to a ballad I could not identify. Later I was to discover that Opal Prewitt was singing "The Brown Girl," with the characters in reverse, that Cecil Sharp had recovered 11 examples of this ballad and Arthur Kyle Davis, Jr., had 10 (all from Virginia, in the Davis collection) — and that all of these embodied the peculiar reversal in roles.

But at the time, I was only aware of the loveliness of the tune and the appealing story line, and I knew that if I could approximate the wistfulness of Opal Prewitt's performance I had a very valuable piece of concert material.

The hour grew late, and I grew weary. I had 75 rather difficult miles of driving before me, if I hoped to spend the night at Boone Tavern, in Berea, Ky. Customers had come and gone. It was my turn to take my leave. We shook hands. Later, I discovered that Opal Prewitt had taken a part-time job in the cafeteria at Norris Dam. From there I lost track of her.

It was long past midnight when I arrived in Berea and disturbed a sleepy night clerk at Boone Tavern. The next morning, out of my window, I saw the tree-covered campus of Berea College.

## The English Lady Gay (Niles No. 64)

1. There was an English lady gay,
   From high degree she came.
   Her beauty was of such renown,
   And Sarah was her name.
   *Tra-la, la, la, la, la, la, la,*
   And Sarah was her name.

2. When spring bloomed out with leaves of green,
   A youth come merrily,
   And she did know, as ladies do,
   It was for courtery.
   (*repeat refrain & last line of each verse*)

3. Then he was tangled up in love,
   And knew so very well why,
   But on this far and wealthy girl
   He quickly cast his eye.

4. She spoke with spite, she spoke with scorn,
   And all without much reason,
   "Not you nor any man I'll wed,
   Not now nor any season."

5. Now days did pass, and months did go,
   I'm sure not more than six,
   When this great lady of high degree
   Did fall to be quite sick.

6. But she was tangled up in love,
   She hardly knew for why.
   She sent with speed for this young man,
   The one she did deny.

7. "Oh, doctor, doctor, cure me,
   When I shall surely die.
   I know you are the very one
   I treated so shabily."

8. "Oh, Sally, pretty Sally,
   Your love was all but scorn.
   It's I will ne'er forgive of you
   Although you're past and gone."

9. "Forget, forget, forget what's gone,
   Forget and pray forgive.
   It's cure me, that I have some time
   In this vain world to live."

10. "You laughed at me when I did court,
    You slighted me with scorn.
    It's I will sure reward of you
    When you are past and gone."

11. "I'll wear your diamond rings of three,
    And dance each night away
    Upon the grave that you will own
    When you have turned to clay."

Never had I seen such fall coloring. A mocking-bird sat in a maple tree just below my window, sat and sang his very best. The tree was orange and scarlet and pink and yellow and tan.

Breakfast that morning was gay, and the food was quite wonderful, too. I've always thought breakfast was the best meal of the day.

# 65

# Trooper and Maid

(Child No. 299)

## The Bugle Britches
### (Niles No. 65 A)
## The Soldier and His Lady
### (Niles No. 65 B)

IN CHILD NO. 299, we find that a soldier is received affectionately by his lady. She, knowing the demands of soldiering, realizes that the soldier and his horse are hungry. Both are fed bountifully. Presently we discover that the soldier and the lady have decided to spend the night together. In some cases the lady removes only her petticoat; in others, she casts off her gown of Holland-made calamanco cloth. The soldier is a little more reticent; he removes his silken beaver, his big watch-coat, a pair of pistols, and then "he lay down beside her."

It is easy to see that soldiers have been soldiers this many a year, and not even in English or Scottish ballads do they vary. For when morning dawns and the trumpet blows, our soldier departs, telling his love that they will meet again and marry when "cockle-shells grow [silver] bells" or "when fishes fly, and seas [go] dry" — neither situation containing much comfort for the lady.

Reading the Scottish, English, and American texts of this ballad, I am reminded of an army show during World War I. The situation was similar, the characters being a Red Cross girl and an American aviator. At the end of the skit, when the soldier bids the girl goodbye, a group of soldiers, à la Greek chorus, sang from stage left:

> *Oh, he loved her where he found her*
> *To the tune of a merry song,*
> *And when it was goodbye, my dear,*
> *She fain would go along.*
>
> *But he left her where he loved her,*
> *Although her eyes were blue,*
> *And what happened to her after that,*
> *He never, never knew.*

The writer of the skit was a Harvard man, and it all happened 44 years ago, but I can still see myself, pounding out a trumped-up accompaniment on the worst pianoforte ever to have disgraced the proud title. The instrument, hopeless to begin with, was made still worse by having a quart of milk punch poured into its innards. The singers were not much better than the piano, or the pianist.

"Trooper and Maid" is not widely known in the United States, but wherever it appears, it usually tells pretty much the same story, and it is received by all males, and some females, with the greatest gusto.

341

# The Bugle Britches
## (Niles No. 65 A)

*(Minor mode on A)*

1. Oh, she took him by the bridle rein,
   And she led him to the stable.
   "Here's fodder and hay for your horse, young
     man,
   And me to bed if you're able,
   And me to bed if you're able."

2. She took him by the lily-white hand,
   She led him to the table.
   "Here's drink and meat for us to eat,
   And me to bed if you're able."
   *(repeat last line of each verse)*

3. She's up the stairs, her skirts a-flounce,
   To make the soldier's bed.
   "Come up, come up, my bonny boy,
   I ween you have been fed."

4. She pulled off her lily-white gown,
   She laid it on a table.
   "Come bed me quick, my bonny boy,
   I'm sure that you are able."

5. Oh, it's meat and drink for bonny boys,
   And then to bed with lasses,
   It's oats and hay and fodder, too,
   For horses and for asses.

6. They had not been abed a-long,
   It was not hours three,
   When he did hear the bugle,
   A-blasting merrily.

7. "Don't leave, don't leave," the maiden cried.
   "The task is not half done.
   A soldier ne'er should sheathe his sword
   Until the battle's won."

8. "I'll have to sheathe my dagger,
   My codpiece is withdrawn.
   I'll don my bugle britches,
   I hear the merry horn."

9. "Oh, when shall we e'er meet again,
   And when shall we be wed?
   For surely I am all but ruined,
   And truly would be dead."

10. "When mussel-shells turn silver bells,
    Then we will up and marry.
    But now I'm bound to London town
    Nor can I ever tarry."

# The Bugle Britches

## (Niles No. 65 A)

As SUNG BY my father, John Thomas Niles. From my observation, ladies used to be more easily offended than they are today. There was a time when a ballad like "The Bugle Britches," my father's version of "Trooper and Maid," could not be sung if a female-person were within earshot. My recent observation of folksong jam sessions leads me to believe that this is no longer true. To quote one very great figure in the field of entertainment, "You can say anything so long as you sing it."

Even in my father's time, melody seemed to soften the blow of "The Bugle Britches." And Father was never one to slur his diction. There was no mumbling in his performance of the 6th, 7th, or 8th stanzas. Indeed, a country preacher once said, looking pityingly at me: "That poor little Niles boy is being brought up in the worst possible atmosphere, what with his playing the piano almost continually and his father singing those vulgar, old-timey songs in such a way as to make the worst words sound loudest and best."

Somehow I survived, even to this writing, balladry, piano playing, and musicology to the contrary notwithstanding, and if I had it to do over again, I would never change a bit of it. Else I should miss hearing my father sing "Mary Hamilton," "The Bugle Britches," and "The Shepherd's Daughter and the King."

"Trooper and Maid," presented by Child as his 299th ballad, is certainly direct, but "Bugle Britches" is even more candid, and in addition is bitterly humorous.

# The Soldier and His Lady

## (Niles No. 65 B)

*(Dorian mode on C)*

1. A soldier come from Georgia way,
   Of ridin' he was weary.
   He tingled on the side-door ring
   To hearken up his lady,
   To hearken up his lady.

2. She's took him by the bridle line,
   She's led him to the stable.
   "Here's oats, here's corn, here's hay for your
   horse,
   Let him eat what he is able."
   *(repeat last line of each verse)*

3. She's took him by the lily-white hand,
   She's led him to the table.
   "Here's cakes and wine for you, my dear,
   Come eat what you are able."

4. She's went to smooth his downy bed,
   And she smoothed it like a lady,
   And off she took her red, red dress,
   Said, "Dearie, are you ready?"

5. Off come his bugle soldier's coat,
   Off come his boots of leather,
   And quickly into bed he jumped,
   And there they lay together.

6. He held her high, he held her low,
   For hours one, two, and three,
   When the bugle she did fear so much
   Did sound forth cruelly.

7. "When shall we meet and marry, dear,
   If you cannot tarry?"
   "When cockle-shells turn silver bells,
   'Tis then that we shall marry."

# The Soldier and His Lady

## (Niles No. 65 B)

LIGE GAFFNEY, a very old Tennessean, was living temporarily in 1934 at a smallish place called Bender's Fork in North Carolina. He said that as soon as he could settle up his problems with his relatives and his sapsucking in-laws, he would buy himself a ticket back to Sevierville, Tenn., and sit in the Tennessee sun, and rest.

"Yes," said Lige rather bitterly, "my relatives and my in-laws is a triflin' lot. With them, it's come-day, go-day, God-give-Sunday. Now the Sunday part is all very well — that's Holy Writ — but a body can't dwaddle his time away forever, and have anythin' at all. I says it's too late to start savin' when your hand's at the bottom of the bag."

I was writing furiously. A pretty girl walked by and ruffled Lige's hair. "Hi," said she, "you ole sweet do-lolly! Who's your city friend?"

"He's a furriner," said Lige, "and you let him be!"

I thought there was an affectionate quality to his voice when he spoke to this particular relative or in-law. The girl ran on her way, and Lige looked after her.

"That'un is seventeen, and she's my choice of the lot. But they all keep tellin' me how old I am. I know I'm as old as the itch, but I don't like hearin' about it from others. Now take that youngun who just walked by. I made up to her a bit, because she was kind to me, and not askin' for things all the time. Givin' in this family is all on one side, somethin' like a jug handle. 'Course, I'm feedin' 'em all, and when I go back to Tennessee, I wonder what they'll do. No, I don't wonder, not really. I know: man and boy they'll go to work. I keep tellin' 'em that a fat kitchen makes a lean will, but they go right on, eatin' theirselves out of house and home!"

Lige was proud to tell me that he was a great hymn singer, though he was not familiar with either *The Sacred Harp* or *The Southern Harmony*. He demonstrated his hymn singing with several loud and lusty examples, all of which ran into many verses. When he went to singing "The Soldier and His Lady," which I quickly recognized as a version of "Trooper and Maid," I wondered just how such an enthusiastic hymn singer would get around some of the verses. But, he smiled and he sang with a twinkling eye that surely endeared him to me. His tune sounded not unlike some I had heard before, but it had a nice Dorian turn just at the end.

Lige Gaffney may have looked upon his in-laws and relations as sapsuckers, but to my casual view they were rather interesting. While I was trying to take down a clear copy of "The Soldier and His Lady," a considerable group of them and their friends started rehearsing the steps of a running-set for a dance contest to be held the following Saturday. There was quite a prize at stake. Later I was delighted to hear them sing "Little Omie Wise," "Sweet Betsy from Pike," "The Nightingale," and nearly all of "Barbary Ellen." Their melodic material was all somewhat alike, and I noticed the similarity to the tune Lige Gaffney used for "The Soldier and His Lady." I never got the names of the relatives, but they were a handsome bunch of people and a joy to watch, even if they wouldn't work.

# Postscript

So, I HAVE COME to the end of my ballad book, the end of more than 100 examples, some long, some short, some boastful, some violently tragic, and a few humorous. Once, while a student of Greek drama at the Université de Lyon in France, I was told by one of my masters that "starkest tragedy and the most bombastic, slapstick comedy are the most likely to remain in the current of human consciousness. They are quite sure to be republished as books, attended as plays, and revered as music."

Perhaps this explains why 39 surviving ballads in my collection of 65 Child titles are tragic in varying degrees. Surely in that long-ago golden age of ballad and carol creation, there must have been quite a few sweet, pleasant ditties and ballads with happy endings. But they fell by the way, while the American pioneers, who lived with tragedy so near at hand, understood and cherished ballad tragedy.

As I have said earlier in this book, ballads concerning battles seldom survived in our country, because they were no longer germane to the situations in which the pioneers lived. They fought their own battles, and for all we know, some Revolutionary veteran may have come up with a ballad concerning the Battle of King's Mountain, where those magnificent Tennessee riflemen won the Revolutionary War, and it may still be sung somewhere in Tennessee to this very hour. The fact that I did not encounter it is no sign that it does not exist. Who knows what words and music lay just out of reach in the memories of the singers who gave me so much?

Many times, after a public performance, I am besieged by young singers who want to know how to sing a ballad. This is very discouraging, principally because I have just finished 90 to 100 minutes of practical example. And then, after a demanding performance — and *every* performance is demanding — the artist is seldom ready to go into the business of teaching, the hour being late and the artist so dreadfully hungry.

I know I am on dangerous ground when I try to teach singing, or even offer a few hints to fledgling performers, but I believe that the first requirement of the ballad singer is to sing from the inside out — that is, never superficially but always from the heart of the singer to the collective heart of the audience. And always try to sing to the entire audience. The listeners on the far right and the far left, and those in the balconies and galleries have paid admission as well as those who sit in the very center of the house. And if it is your good fortune to have an SRO house and the management has sold out the stage, then a few numbers must be sung for the people sitting behind and around you. Incidentally, the folks on stage will want to shake hands with the performer before the program begins. They seem to think this is part of the show. But I recommend against it, because the artist's hand will be crushed and he will be unable to perform.

So far as the actual singing of a ballad is concerned, I would suggest that the reader take the music to the piano and play the melodic line with one hand. Play it over and over, until it sticks in the mind. Then take one verse of the text and add it to the melodic line. As soon as one verse can be sung with the help of the melodic line, allow the voice to rest and study the accompaniment. The performer might hum along with the accompaniment. And after a short while he will discover that he is actually singing the text of the ballad.

As time passes, the performer will find himself singing more freely. And that is as it should be. Ballads were never conceived in regular measures. In order to make them available to a wider public, they must be confined to the printed page. But no two performers will sing them in exactly the same way, and no two performances by the same performer will be exactly alike. And if the singer is his own accompanist, the freedom achieved will be all the greater.

It is with real reluctance that I come to the end of this book and wave goodbye to Hugh Stallcup and Uncle Brother, to Miss Telighthul, to Beth and Solomon Holcolm and to Aunt Flory French, to Pine Mountain and the Cutshine country, to the valley of the Big Sandy and to the French Broad, to the Chickamauga battlefield, to Gatlinburg and Cherokee County, North Carolina, to the purple sunset over Chunky Gal Mountain and to the fabulous Bluebird Mountains in that part of the world where western North Carolina and Tennessee join.

This I can say with all my heart: my 52 years in the field of balladry have been greatly rewarding. My informants were almost invariably wonderful people. I loved them all, and they seemed to like me well enough to sing their very best for me. Their voices still echo in my heart as part of the life of these ballads.

KEY TO GUITAR CHORDS

BIBLIOGRAPHY

INDEX OF TITLES

INDEX OF FIRST LINES

INDEX OF

EXPLANATORY

MATERIAL

# Key to the Guitar Chords Used in This Book

THIS INFORMATION is intended only for beginners of guitar playing. Accomplished players will be able to read the guitar chords indicated on the music. The others should study each position as indicated on the music and interpreted on this page, and then try for simple inversions of the same chords, in the hope that with a bit of experience easier positions may be discovered.

No two hands are alike, and no two ears are entirely satisfied with exactly the same chordings. With this in mind, the following key is offered. It is intended to represent the standard chord combinations; but as accompaniment for ballad singing, guitar playing is most beautiful and effective when it is free, when it contains inventions and innovations. One very great guitarist has said, and quite rightly, that the fewer the chords, and the fewer the strings plucked, the better. He was referring to the guitar chordings employed in accompanying Spanish folk music.

In the case of the American folk ballad, entire verses can be accompanied on the dulcimer by plucking one string, for, after all, a ballad is a song that tells a story. And if it is a song there must be singing, and, to move on to the next and final conclusion, it is the voice that matters, whether it be great or small, and the piano or the dulcimer or the guitar is merely an accompanying device and should be kept exactly at that level.

Here is a key to the finger positions:

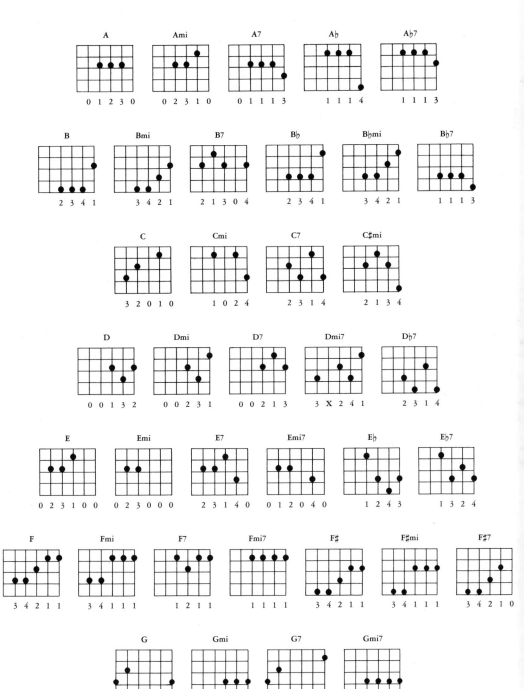

# Bibliography

## I. Books of Ballads and Related Songs

Byron Arnold, comp., Folksongs of Alabama. University, Ala.: University of Alabama Press, 1950.

Sabine Baring-Gould and H. Fleetwood Sheppard, colls., A Garland of Country Song: English Folk Songs with Their Traditional Melodies. London: Methuen, 1895.

Phillips Barry, Fannie H. Eckstorm, and Mary W. Smyth, eds., British Ballads from Maine. New Haven: Yale University Press, 1929.

Paul G. Brewster, coll. and ed., Ballads and Songs of Indiana. Bloomington, Ind.: Indiana University, 1940.

Lucy E. Broadwood and J. A. Fuller Maitland, comps. and eds., English County Songs, Words, and Music. New York: Scribner, 1893.

Arthur H. Bullen, ed., A Christmas Garland: Carols and Poems from the Fifteenth Century to the Present Time. London: Nimmo, 1885.

Richard Chase, coll. and ed., Old Songs and Singing Games. Chapel Hill, N.C.: University of North Carolina Press, 1938.

Francis James Child, ed., The English and Scottish Popular Ballads. Boston, New York: Houghton, Mifflin, 1882-97. 5 vols. (Dover reprint)

Josiah H. Combs, coll. and ed., Folk-songs from the Kentucky Highlands. With piano accompaniments by Keith Mixson. New York: Schirmer, 1939.

Frances M. M. Comper, ed., Spiritual Songs from English MSS. of Fourteenth to Sixteenth Centuries. New York: Macmillan, 1936.

John H. Cox, ed., Folk-songs of the South. Cambridge: Harvard Press, 1925. (Dover reprint)

Helen Creighton, coll. and ed., Songs and Ballads from Nova Scotia. Toronto: Dent, 1932. (Dover)

John P. Cutts, coll. and ed., Seventeenth Century Songs and Lyrics, Collected and Edited from the Original Music Manuscripts. Columbia, Mo.: University of Missouri Press, 1959.

Arthur K. Davis, Jr., ed., Traditional Ballads of Virginia. Cambridge: Harvard University Press, 1929.

Helen H. Flanders and George Brown, eds., Vermont Folk-songs and Ballads. Brattleboro, Vt.: Stephen Daye Press, 1931.

Richard L. Greene, ed., The Early English Carols. Oxford: Clarendon Press, 1935.

Elisabeth B. Greenleaf, coll. and ed., Ballads and Sea Songs of Newfoundland. Cambridge: Harvard University Press, 1933.

Francis B. Gummere, ed., Old English Ballads. Boston: Ginn, 1894.

T. F. Henderson, ed., Sir Walter Scott's Minstrelsy of the Scottish Border. New York: Scribner, 1902.

Mellinger E. Henry, ed., Beech Mountain Folksongs and Ballads. Collected, arranged, and provided with piano accompaniments by Maurice Matteson. New York: Schirmer, 1936.

——, coll. and ed., Folk-songs from the Southern Highlands. New York: Augustin, 1938.

——, comp., Songs Sung in the Southern Appalachians. London: Mitre Press, 1934.

——, coll., Still More Ballads from the Southern Highlands. New York: 1932. Reprinted from the

Journal of American Folk-lore, Vol. 45 (Jan.–Mar. 1932), No. 175.

George P. Jackson, coll. and ed., Spiritual Folk-songs of Early America. New York: Augustin, 1937. (Dover reprint)

——, White Spirituals in the Southern Uplands. Chapel Hill, N.C.: University of North Carolina Press, 1933. (Dover reprint)

Josephine McGill, comp., Folk-songs of the Kentucky Mountains. New York: Boosey, 1917.

W. Roy Mackenzie, comp., Ballads and Sea Songs from Nova Scotia. Cambridge: Harvard University Press, 1928.

Arthur K. Moore, The Secular Lyric in Middle English. Lexington, Ky.: University of Kentucky Press, 1951.

William Motherwell, Romantic Ballads. Edinburgh: Ballantyne, 1861.

Holger Olof Nygard, The Ballad of Heer Halewijn. Memphis: University of Tennessee Press, 1958.

The Oxford Book of Carols. Edited by Percy Dearmer, Ralph Vaughan Williams, and Martin Shaw. London: Oxford University Press, 1928.

Thomas Percy, ed., Reliques of Ancient English Poetry. London and New York: Dent and Dutton, 1906. 2 vols. (Dover reprint)

Edith Rickert, coll. and ed., Ancient English Christmas Carols, MCCCC to MDCC. London: Chatto & Windus, 1925.

Hÿder E. Rollins, ed., The Pepys Ballads, 1535–1702. Cambridge: Harvard University Press, 1929–32. 8 vols.

Carl Sandburg, ed., The American Songbag. New York: Harcourt, 1927.

Cecil J. Sharp, comp., English Folk Songs from the Southern Appalachians. Edited by Maud Karpeles. London: Oxford University Press, 1932. 2 vols.

——, ed., Folk-songs of England. London: Novello, 1908–12. 5 vols.

Julia S. Stevens, A Pioneer Songster: Texts from the Stevens-Douglass Manuscript of Western New York, 1841–56. Edited by H. W. Thompson, assisted by E. E. Cutting. Ithaca, N.Y.: Cornell University Press, 1958.

Edith B. Sturgis, coll. and ed., Songs from the Hills of Vermont. Tunes collected and piano accompaniments by Robert Hughes. New York: Schirmer, 1919.

John Tufts, An Introduction to the Singing of Psalm-tunes, in a Plain and Easy Method. Boston: Gerrish, 1731.

William Walker, The Southern Harmony and Musical Companion. Spartanburg, S.C., 1835.

Evelyn K. Wells, The Ballad Tree: A Study of British and American Ballads, Their Folklore, Verse, and Music. New York: Roland Press, 1950.

B. F. White, The Sacred Harp. Philadelphia, 1844.

Alfred Williams, coll. and ed., Folk-songs of the Upper Thames. London: Duckworth, 1923.

Loraine Wyman, comp. and ed., Lonesome Tunes: Folk Songs from the Kentucky Mountains. Pianoforte accompaniment by Howard Brockway. New York: Gray, 1916.

## II. Books on Balladry, Folkways, and Related Literature and Music

T. F. Barker, The Cross-Road Store. Lexington, Ky.: Privately printed, 1892.

Henry M. Belden, ed., Ballads and Songs Collected by the Missouri Folk-lore Society. University of Missouri Studies, Vol. XV (1940), No. 1.

Morrison C. Boyd, Elizabethan Music and Musical Criticism. Philadelphia: University of Pennsylvania Press, 1940.

John M. Brewer, Dog Ghosts, and Other Texas Negro Folk Tales. Austin, Tex.: University of Texas Press, 1958.

Tristram P. Coffin, The British Traditional Ballad in North America. Philadelphia: American Folklore Society, 1950.

John Jay Daly, A Song in His Heart. The Life and Times of James J. Bland. New York: Winston, 1951.

Jane E. Harrison, Ancient Art and Ritual. New York: Holt, 1913.

Sigurd B. Hustvedt, Ballad Books and Ballad Men: Raids and Rescues in Britain, America, and the Scandinavian North Since 1800. Cambridge: Harvard University Press, 1930.

The Liber Usualis. Edited by the Benedictines of Solesmes. Tournai, Belgium: Desclés, 1950.

Evelyn Martinengo-Cesaresco, Essays in the Study of Folk-songs. London and New York: Dent and Dutton, 1914.

The Oxford History of Music. 2nd ed. London: Oxford University Press, 1929–38. 7 vols.

Roderick Peattie, ed., The Great Smokies and the Blue Ridge: The Story of the Southern Appalachians. New York: Vanguard, 1943.

Vance Randolph, The Ozarks: An American Survival of Primitive Society. New York: Vanguard, 1931.

Gustave Reese, Music in the Middle Ages. New York: Norton, 1940.

Dorothy Scarborough, A Song Catcher in Southern Mountains: American Folk Songs of British Ancestry. New York: Columbia University Press, 1937.

Reed Smith, South Carolina Ballads. Cambridge: Harvard University Press, 1928.

Archer Taylor, English Riddles from Oral Tradition. Berkeley, Calif.: University of California Press, 1951.

Samuel C. Williams, Tennessee during the Revolutionary War. Nashville, Tenn.: Tennessee Historical Commission, 1944.

Edwin H. Zeydel, tr. and ed., The "Tristan and Isolde" of Gottfried von Strassburg. Princeton, N.J.: Princeton University Press for the University of Cincinnati, 1948.

## III. Periodicals and Serial Publications

The Frank C. Brown Collection of North Carolina Folklore. Edited by Newman I. White and Others. Durham, N.C.: Duke University Press, 1952–. 4 vols. to date.

Filson Club, Publications. Louisville, Ky., 1884–.

Folk-lore: Quarterly Review of the Folk-lore Society of London. 1890–.

Svend Grundtvig and Others, eds., Danmarks Gamale Folkeviser. Copenhagen: Various publishers, 1853–. 11 vols. to date.

The Journal of American Folk-lore. Publication of the American Folklore Society. 1888–.

Journal of the Folk Dance and Song Society. London, 1932–.

The Modern Language Association of America, Publications. Baltimore, Md., 1886–.

The Musical Quarterly. New York: Schirmer, 1915–.

Southern Folklore Quarterly. Jacksonville, Fla.: University of Florida and Southeastern Folklore Society, 1937–.

Texas Folk-lore Society, Publications. Austin, Tex., 1916–.

## IV. Books Which Have Been of Inestimable Value to the Author in His Work, but Which May Lure the Unwary Reader Far Afield from the Subject of Balladry

Geoffrey Chaucer, The Canterbury Tales. Works, edited by F. N. Robinson. 2nd ed. Boston: Houghton Mifflin, 1957.

Francis J. Child, A Scholar's Letters to a Young Lady. Boston: Atlantic Monthly Press, 1920.

Barrows Dunham, Man against Myth. Boston: Little, Brown, 1947.

Beulah Folmsbee, A Little History of the Horn-book. Boston: Horn Book, 1942.

Jacob Grimm, Teutonic Mythology. London: George Bell, 1883-88. 4 vols. (Dover reprint)

M. A. DeWolfe Howe and G. W. Cottrell, Jr., eds., The Scholar-Friends: Letters of Francis James Child and James Russell Lowell. Cambridge: Harvard University Press, 1952.

William Dean Howells, Literary Friends and Acquaintance. New York: Harper, 1900.

Aili K. Johnson, tr., Kalevala. Hancock, Mich.: Book Concern, 1950.

Amy R. Kelly, Eleanor of Aquitaine and the Four Kings. Cambridge: Harvard University Press, 1950.

W. F. Kirby, tr., Kalevala: The Land of Heroes. London and New York: Dent and Dutton, 1907. 2 vols.

Daniel H. Lambert, ed., Cartae Shakespeareanae, Shakespeare Documents: A Chronological Catalogue of Extant Evidence Relating to the Life and Works of William Shakespeare. London: Bell, 1904.

William Langland, The Vision of Piers the Plowman. Translated and edited by W. W. Skeat. London: Chatto and Windus, 1922.

Richard O'Connor, Hood: Cavalier General. New York: Prentice-Hall, 1949.

——, Thomas: Rock of Chickamauga. New York: Prentice-Hall, 1948.

Melrich V. Rosenberg, Eleanor of Aquitaine. Boston: Houghton Mifflin, 1937.

Denis de Rougemont, Love in the Western World. Translated by Montgomery Belgion. Garden City, N.Y.: Doubleday, 1957.

George Saintsbury, French Literature and Its Masters. New York: Knopf, 1946.

Massey H. Shepherd, Jr., The Oxford American Prayer Book Commentary. New York: Oxford University Press, 1950.

Walter W. Skeat, coll., A Glossary of Tudor and Stuart Words, Especially from the Dramatists. Edited, with additions, by A. L. Mayhew. Oxford: Clarendon Press, 1914.

Sir Roger Wilbraham, An Attempt at a Glossary of Some Words Used in Cheshire. 2nd ed. London: Privately printed, 1826.

# Index of Titles

Titles in italic are Child titles

# Index of First Lines

# Index of
# Explanatory Material